WHAT DID
YOU SAY?

WHAT DID YOU SAY?

a guide to oral and written communication

STANLEY B. FELBER

ARTHUR KOCH

Milwaukee Area Technical College
Milwaukee, Wisconsin

PRENTICE-HALL, INC., Englewood Cliffs, New Jersey

Library of Congress Cataloging in Publication Data

FELBER, STANLEY B.   1932–
    What did you say?

    1. Communication.   I. Koch, Arthur, 1931–
joint author.   II. Title.
P90.F4   808   72-10485
ISBN 0-13-951855-X

© 1973 by Prentice-Hall, Inc.
Englewood Cliffs, New Jersey

Printed in the United States of America

10   9   8   7   6   5   4   3   2   1

PRENTICE-HALL INTERNATIONAL, INC., London
PRENTICE-HALL OF AUSTRALIA, PTY. LTD., Sydney
PRENTICE-HALL OF CANADA, LTD., Toronto
PRENTICE-HALL OF INDIA PRIVATE LIMITED, New Delhi
PRENTICE-HALL OF JAPAN, INC., Tokyo

The quote from William A. Nail on p. v is taken from
"What Did You Say?" *Vital Speeches*, XXXVIII, No. 23 (September 15, 1971), 726.

prologue

The role of the broadcaster, the communicator, the
advertising copy writer, the public relations man, the
public speaker, the guy who writes the business letter,
the guy who writes the love letter, the guy who writes
the letter home—is to get ideas and information across
simply, in an easy to understand and attractive way.
Elizabeth Barrett Browning, in one of her Sonnets from the
Portuguese, "How Do I Love Thee" said more in a very few
lines about love than many of us could say in our broken
prose if we filled up as many pages as are in a Sears
Roebuck catalog.
What it all boils down to is this: Anybody who has
anything to say in words or in pictures to be transmitted
from one mind to another—regardless of all the modern
electronic paraphernalia and hard work you go through to
reach that reader, viewer or listener—has to ask himself
the question "What did you say?" before he begins to transmit.
The only way we can be sure that our ideas achieve their objective
is to be clear about what we want to say and who we are trying to
reach. That means understanding the guy on the other end. . . .

William A. Nail

contents

preface

With the multitude of textbooks already available to freshman English classes, any new manuscript must justify itself. The distinctive feature of *What Did You Say?* is that it combines both oral and written communication skills within an integrated framework. An ever-increasing number of career-oriented educational programs in our community colleges, vocational and technical institutes, and universities has occasioned the rapid growth of communication courses. These courses seek to provide occupationally-minded students with the language skills that will enable them to function with efficiency and perception in society. It is to this market that our book is aimed.

Chapter 1 lays the foundation for the units that follow. Subsequent chapters deal with the planning, preparation, and presentation stages of effective communication. Most of the fifteen chapters are fully integrated; however, because differences between writing and speaking exist, some are devoted exclusively to either writing or speaking. While there is a logical progression from the basics to the more sophisticated aspects of communication, each chapter represents a self-contained study unit; consequently, chapters may be rearranged without disrupting the over-all plan of the book.

We are indebted to our colleagues at MATC for reading portions of the manuscript and making many positive suggestions and to our students for field testing all of the exercises and speech and writing assignments. We are particularly grateful to our wives, Estelle and Betty, for their constructive criticism and, above all, their patience and understanding. Finally, we are indebted to our children for trying to understand why so many of our evenings and weekends were spent preparing this manuscript. The better world we all seek can only come about through improved communication. For our children and all children we hope these pages represent a step in that direction.

Stanley B. Felber
Arthur Koch

1

an overview

WHY STUDY COMMUNICATION?

If you are like most high school graduates, the prospect of another year or two of English far from excites you. You have formally studied our complex, at times illogical language since elementary school, and you have engaged in the process of communication all your lives. Now college. And more English!

English teachers often pride themselves on the importance of their discipline. "We are the largest department on campus and rightly so. All students, regardless of future educational and vocational objectives, need to learn to communicate more effectively. A good command of language skills can lead to a challenging, creative future. Inadequate mastery of the techniques of communication can only lessen the possibilities available to you."

In recent years, English teachers have found a powerful ally in industry. Employees are frequently sent to college at company expense in an effort to improve their communication skills. The following excerpt from an industrial publication addressed to technical students is typical of industry's concern with language skills:

To understand and be understood. A good education provides the tools for understanding. The first and most important of these tools is language for communication. It may surprise you that we've begun by putting the need to study English first rather than stressing science or mathematics. After all, our business is primarily concerned with science and the useful application of technological developments. Nevertheless, we are convinced that no matter what your career, a command of the English language is the most important skill you can acquire. Learning rules of grammar and acquiring the abilities to write effectively and to read accurately are vital. This background provides the skill to express yourself in speaking and writing and to extract maximum meaning from the spoken and written words of others.

This process is called communications. In today's world, and even more so in tomorrow's, the person who cannot communicate clearly labors under a tremendous handicap.

The young engineer, for example, might have his most brilliant idea rejected if he is unable to explain its significance to others. In addition, he will be unable to keep up with advances in his own field if he cannot get the facts from the flood of technical information available to him.

Think of any career you like: teacher, naval engineer, actor, salesman, auditor, lawyer, physician, news reporter. Is there one in which you won't have to communicate effectively with others in order to perform successfully?

A time to prepare. The best foundation for whatever career you eventually choose is a broad-based education that increases your understanding and appreciation of everything in life.

It is essential that you start "building in" this kind of background now, for there is no way that you can predict the exact requirements of life or what your interests will be in the future. In short, now is the time to prepare for an education rather than a job.

Obviously, most successful careers today call for special training—often long and intensive. Does this mean that you must commit yourself now to a specific plan of action? Not necessarily. How can you plan for a career that may not even exist today?

The answer is stay flexible. Don't cut yourself off from the future. Keep to the march of knowledge in general. Top careers will more and more demand people with specialized skills in combination with diversified backgrounds.

If there is one rule you can apply that will keep the door open to almost any future career, it is this: when you have a choice of courses, pick those which will help broaden your background—mathematics, language, physical sciences, literature, the social studies.

There's always the chance you'll want to switch your field of study in midstream. Why not? That's one and only one of the advantages of starting with a sound basic education and staying flexible.

Reprinted with the permission of General Electric Company.

You probably agree that the arguments of education and industry have validity, but somehow a continuance of the day-to-day struggle with "nouns and verbs and stupid things like that," as one student put it, leaves you a bit cold. Perhaps you feel that English cannot be as stimulating as a course in your area of specialization, but we don't want you to think of your communication study as just another English course.

The pages that follow will involve you in the practical aspects of written and oral communication. You will discover that in the performance of one of life's most important functions—communicating effectively with your fellow human beings—language can be one of the most exciting and demanding of studies.

A PHILOSOPHY OF COMMUNICATION

Traditionally, language study has been fragmented and compartmentalized, involving separate courses in grammar, composition, and literature. Reading and listening have recently emerged as highly specialized fields within the study of language. Most high schools and colleges offer reading workshops, reading and study skills programs, and courses in speed reading. The last named has become a lucrative enterprise for private educational concerns that capitalize on our inability to assimilate ever-increasing amounts of printed material with speed and comprehension. According to the *Harvard Business Review*, "The busy executive spends 80% of his time . . . listening to people . . . and still doesn't hear half of what is said." *Nation's Business* reports that most of us "really absorb only a scant 30%" of what we hear. Our increasing awareness of the importance of effective listening has resulted in some highly specialized listening courses, most of them programmed. The subject matter of this book—language and communication—has been subdivided into numerous highly specialized fields which are usually studied separately. For practical and philosophical reasons, we propose to treat the study of language as a single subject.

Our treatment of communication is primarily intended for you, the college student. Because most of your course work is directly related to your chosen field of specialization, the amount of time set aside for general education courses in your curriculum is necessarily limited. It is usually impractical to schedule separate courses in speech, composition, literature, grammar, reading, and listening. Although this book does not attempt to combine all these skills, it does effect a workable, realistic compromise by integrating written and oral communication.

Furthermore, and more important, we believe an integrated approach to be philosophically sound. The communication skills, despite various conflicts among them, have much in common. We propose to indicate both their similarities and differences throughout our study.

THE SKILLS OF COMMUNICATION

Expressive Skills

Speaking and writing are generally referred to as expressive skills; they provide the means whereby we express ourselves to others. Both skills are usually discussed under the same heading, because effective speaking and writing involve many similar problems, such as selecting a subject, communicating purposefully, relating material to a single, dominant idea, and organizing logically.

Obviously, there are also important differences. Writing is a relatively private affair between you and your reader, allowing ample time for revision and correction. When you are speaking publicly, however, all eyes are focused on you. A mistake cannot be readily erased. Speaking and writing employ different means to achieve emphasis and variety, but the primary purpose of both skills is the same: to get the message to your audience in an interesting way.

Receptive Skills

When we listen or read, we receive information through the spoken word or printed page. However, frequently we *hear*, but do not really *listen*. An entry in the American College Dictionary clarifies the distinction between these two terms:

Hear, Listen apply to the perception of sound. To hear is to have such perception by means of the auditory sense: *to hear distant bells*. To listen is to give attention in order to hear and understand the meaning of a sound or sounds: *to listen to what is being said, to listen for a well-known footstep.*

Similarly, sometimes we read words without understanding their meaning. Have you ever spent an hour or so reading an assigned chapter without having more than a vague notion of its contents? Perhaps you were distracted by interruptions or your own thoughts. Concentration is essential to both listening and reading, with the basic difference that if you cannot concentrate on what you are reading, you can always return to it at another time. You cannot, however, expect your instructor to repeat his lecture after class because your thoughts drifted during his presentation. Both skills involve breaking down a communication into main ideas and supporting details. Listening to your instructor's lecture is more demanding than listening to a friend relate a personal experience; reading Spenser's *The Fairie Queene* requires more concentration than reading a popular novel like *The Godfather.* However, all effective reading and listening share a common purpose: to receive messages clearly.

THE COMMUNICATIVE ACT

Communication results when a response occurs to a stimulus. For example:

Stimulus	*Response*
1. Strong winds and heavy rain	Baby cries
2. Strong winds and heavy rain	Man closes window

Our stimuli for the above examples, strong winds and heavy rain, are non-verbal. The baby is frightened by the nonverbal stimuli, and his response is an automatic one based on fear. In the second example, the man's response is motivated by other considerations, perhaps his desire to block out outside noise, or to protect his family and his belongings. Because he must decide among alternatives, the man's response involves reasoning. Thus, we see that a response to a nonverbal stimulus may or may not be automatic.

Let us consider another stimulus-response situation:

Stimulus	*Response*
3. Dog barks	Baby cries
4. Dog barks	Man feeds dog

Although once again our stimulus is the same, this time it is verbal. The baby's response to the stimulus is automatic, again based on fear. The fourth example illustrates a nonautomatic response—feeding—to a verbal stimulus. Thus far we have differentiated between two types of stimuli, nonverbal and verbal, either of which can result in automatic or nonautomatic responses.

The stimulus in a communicative act includes a sender and a message. Study the following analyses of stimuli previously referred to:

Stimulus	=	Sender + Message
1. Strong winds and heavy rain		Depending upon your philosophical and theological convictions, you may conclude that "nature" or a supreme being is the *sender*; the *message*, strong winds and heavy rain, is then transmitted to a receiver.
2. Barking dog		The dog is the *sender*, his bark is the *message*.

Before one can respond to a stimulus (sender and message), he must first receive the message. Therefore, the response in an act of communication implies a receiver. Initially we defined communication as a response to a stimulus, but our modified definition now includes a sender, a message, a receiver, and a response.

Sender	Message	Receiver	Response
1. "Nature"	Strong winds and heavy rain	Baby	Crying
2. "Nature"	Strong winds and heavy rain	Man	Closing window
3. Dog	Bark	Baby	Crying
4. Dog	Bark	Man	Feeding dog

When a breakdown in communication occurs, one or more of the four basic requirements have not been fulfilled. If you tell a friend you will meet him outside a building after your class, and he waits patiently in front while you wait near the side entrance, the message you sent to him was either incomplete or misunderstood. If your instructor must ask you to repeat your answer to his question in an audible voice, you, as a sender, have failed to establish meaningful contact. If you jump the gun at a traffic light because you were thinking of tomorrow night's date instead of concentrating on the signal, a traffic citation may be your reward. If you fail to hear your instructor announce a quiz for the next class meeting because you were talking to a classmate, you cannot respond with study to a message you never received. Life is filled with communicative acts. If we are to function effectively, breakdowns must be kept to a minimum.

EXERCISES

1. Analyze the following cartoons as examples of communication, indicating the sender, message, receiver, and response. Where breakdowns in communication occur, indicate why.

"Hey! *This* isn't the best cup of coffee in town!"

Drawing by Lorenz; © 1971 The New Yorker Magazine, Inc.

Drawing by Chas. Addams; Copr. © 1931 The New Yorker Magazine, Inc.

"Phone for you, Al."

Drawing by Stevenson; © 1963 The New Yorker Magazine, Inc.

Drawing by W. Miller; © 1970 The New Yorker Magazine, Inc.

II. From your own experience, cite two examples of breakdowns, one involving speech, one involving writing.

1. Identify the causes of the breakdowns.
2. State what could have been done to improve the communication.

III. Study the following photographs and respond to the questions asked.

1. What is the message you receive from this photograph?
2. Suggest an appropriate caption.
3. How can we safeguard our environment from the effects of industrial pollution without endangering our economy? Cite an example of a specific industry in your response.
4. Investigate a company in or near your community alleged to be guilty of excessive pollution. Propose a solution that would safeguard the citizenry without driving the company out of business.

Reprinted with permission of the Milwaukee Journal.

Reprinted by permission of the photographer, Samuel Gansheroff.

1. Does the boy in the photograph have the same opportunities you had when you were his age? Discuss.
2. Suggest an appropriate caption.
3. Can we provide equality of opportunity for minority groups without infringing on the rights of the majority? Discuss.

Reprinted with permission of the photographer, Samuel Gansheroff.

1. How has our society handled the problems of its aged citizens? Discuss.
2. How have the chess players in the photograph adjusted to old age?
3. Suggest an appropriate caption.

Reprinted with permission of United Press International.

1. What is your reaction to this photograph? Shock? Dismay? Indifference? Gladness? Explain.
2. Is such a marriage legal in your state? Should it be?
3. Discuss your feelings about the individuals involved: the two bridegrooms, their families, and the minister who officiated.

SPEECHES AND COMPOSITIONS

I. DIRECTIONS: Develop a presentation, written (200–400 words) or oral (2–4 minutes), in which you: (1) introduce yourself to the audience; or (2) explain an area of interest, e.g., a sport, hobby, or pastime.

II. DIRECTIONS: Experience any two of the following sensitivity modules. Prepare a written report of one of the two experiences. Be prepared to relate the other to the class orally.

SENSITIVITY MODULES

1. Wear old clothes and sit in the waiting room of the Welfare Office. Listen, observe, read the announcements on the bulletin board, and talk to some of the other people there.

2. Attend a church service in a storefront church.

3. Go to an inner city elementary school and read a story to a child in kindergarten or first grade. The child must be held on your lap.

4. Go to magistrate's court and keep a list of the kinds of cases brought before the magistrate. Who are the "customers" being tried? How are they dealt with?

5. Sit in the waiting room of the maternity ward of a city hospital whose patients are mostly charity cases. Strike up a conversation with any other person in the waiting room.

6. Live for three days on the amount of money received by a typical welfare mother to feed a son or daughter close to your own age.

7. Read at least two issues, cover to cover, of a newspaper primarily aimed at a minority group.

8. Go to the community health center and take a place in line. Watch the attitude of the personnel who work there. Talk to some of the other patients coming for help.

9. Turn off the heat in your own house some night in January or February and spend the night in a cold house.

10. Read The Autobiography of Malcolm X, Manchild in the Promised Land, **or** some other book which tells what it is like to grow up black in America.

11. Attend a meeting of a civic group, such as the Human Relations Committee, the Welfare Rights Organization, or the Neighborhood Association.

12. Find a neighbor whose landlord has not given him heat, or has not repaired a roof leak or a toilet. Offer to help him get it fixed by calling City Hall and registering a complaint.

2

purposeful communication

CLASSIFYING THE PURPOSE

The purpose of this course is not to teach you how to communicate, but rather to help you communicate more effectively. This distinction is not merely one of semantics, since we have all engaged in the process of communication with varying degrees of success from the day we were born.

When we were hungry, we cried, and our message was answered. When we experienced pain or discomfort we made our feelings known long before we learned to talk, and our parents responded. We sent and received messages of sorrow, despair, frustration, joy, and ecstasy. As we learned our native language, our messages and responses became more sophisticated, and consequently our communication grew more complex. As we matured we learned how to manipulate symbols, starting with pictures, progressing to letters, and finally to words, word groups, and sentences. Because the process of communication parallels the life cycle, we have experienced and will continue to experience hundreds of thousands of communicative acts. Our purpose, therefore, is not to learn new skills, but to refine and polish those we already possess.

Have you ever listened to a speaker ramble on without a sense of direction? Have you ever, merely to get the job over with, written a paper about a subject of no particular interest to you? When we try to communicate about a subject without sufficient organization, without relating each point to a controlling dominant idea, our speech or paper will lack a *sense of purpose.*

The effective speaker or writer has his purpose in mind during the planning stages of his communication. The overall purposes of a communicative act may be divided into the following categories:

1. *To inform*, to add to the knowledge of the reader or listener. News stories, weather reports, wedding invitations, stock market closings, traffic reports, baseball scores, and simple descriptions are examples of informative communication.

2. *To entertain*, to provide pleasant diversion, to amuse, to hold a passive audience's attention. All forms of comedy, television, games and quiz shows, music, sports events, and escape literature have entertainment as their primary purpose. Humor, while frequently employed, is not necessarily a prerequisite of entertainment.

3. *To persuade*, to convince, to actuate, or to reinforce. Because persuasion is more complex than information or entertainment, we shall deal with the three types of persuasion separately.

    a. *To convince*, to change a reader or listener's mind, or to commit him to our point of view on a subject upon which he is still undecided. A politician addressing an audience previously committed to another candidate or as yet uncommitted to any candidate must first convince them that he is the best man for the job. For example, Republicans have seldom received strong labor support in recent national elections. While a Republican may realistically write off the support of the organized labor movement, he will, nevertheless, attempt to *convince* working men to support his candidacy. In urban areas, Republican candidates must *convince* growing numbers of traditionally Democratic voters to support them if they are to win elections, while the converse is frequently the situation in rural areas. The politician must analyze his constituency in order to decide whom he must convince and how best to accomplish that task.

b. *To actuate,* to put into action. In our previous example, the politician's task was to convince his constituents to vote for him. Having accomplished this purpose to the best of his ability and resources, convincing large blocks of voters—Blacks, Jews, businessmen, white collar workers, blue collar workers, professionals—his purpose then shifts to one of *actuation.* If voters committed to his candidacy do not actually get to the polls in sufficient numbers, he will not benefit. Many a politician has lost an election because prospective voters committed to him never exercised their ballots. A change in the weather may keep the farmer on his farm and lose the election for his candidate. In 1948 pollsters and political analysts agreed that Thomas E. Dewey would easily defeat Harry Truman for the Presidency, yet the ballots returned President Truman to office in the major political upset of our century. The post-election analysis was that Dewey supporters suffered from complacency, staying away from the polls in the conviction that their candidate could not lose. The Republicans failed to actuate sufficient qualified voters committed to the Dewey candidacy.

c. *To reinforce,* to strengthen and invigorate those previously committed to the point of view of the communicator. Note the basic distinction between persuasion to convince and persuasion to reinforce. In the former, the sender attempts to change his receiver's point of view; in the latter, the sender and receiver are already in agreement.

Why would a communicator attempt to persuade a receiver with whom he is already in agreement? Consider a coach who talks to his men before an important game. He need not convince his team of the importance of winning. But he does want to prepare them psychologically and emotionally for the big game. The late coach Vince Lombardi was a master at persuasion to reinforce.

In another example of reinforcement, it has become customary for both major political parties to designate a keynote speaker to address their national conventions. His fellow party members are generally committed to the same candidates and political philosophy, so his primary purpose is to emphasize party unity and deemphasize minor differences, thus enabling the party to emerge from the convention on a positive, unified note.

The football coach and political keynoter in our two previous examples are both addressing members of their respective teams. Because they seek to strengthen those previously committed to their points of view, their primary purpose is to reinforce.

EXERCISES

DIRECTIONS: What is the primary purpose in each of the following situations— (a) to inform, (b) to entertain, (c) to convince, (d) to actuate, or (e) to reinforce? Be prepared to explain and defend your answer in class discussion.

1. A defense lawyer pleading for the acquittal of his client during his final summation to the jury
2. Cheerleaders "doing their thing" as their team drives down field toward the goal line
3. A short speech entitled, "How to Peel a Grape"
4. A meeting agenda
5. A course in beginner's bridge
6. An instruction booklet for your new camera
7. An episode of your favorite situation comedy show
8. A door-to-door salesman who would like to demonstrate his company's latest vacuum cleaner for you
9. A solicitation for a contribution to charity
10. A carnival barker in action

SELECTING AND RESTRICTING A SUBJECT

Once you understand clearly the purpose of a speaking or writing assignment, you are ready to think about a specific choice of subject. Your decision should be based on a number of considerations:

1. Is my subject in keeping with the general purpose of the assignment?
2. Is my subject interesting to me?
3. Is my subject one about which I am sufficiently knowledgeable?
4. Will my subject be of interest to my audience or reader?
5. Is my subject sufficiently restricted?

Let us consider each of these questions in some detail.

1. *Is my subject in keeping with the general purpose of the assignment?*

Assume that you are asked to prepare a composition or speech whose primary purpose is to inform. If you select as your tentative subject, "Why I Believe United States Involvement in Vietnam Was in Error," your communication will be primarily persuasive, not informative. However, the war in

Vietnam could be a proper subject for an informative or even an entertaining communication. If you concentrate on *how* we became involved in the war, your communication will be in keeping with the informational purpose of the assignment. On the other hand, when a comic such as Bob Hope visits our troops overseas and makes topical and humorous references to the difficulties they encounter, his primary purpose is to entertain.

2. *Is my subject interesting to me?*

Students rightfully complain when they are assigned such chestnuts as "How I Spent My Summer Vacation." When you have the opportunity of selecting your own subject, choose one in which you are genuinely interested. Your communication will thus be easier to prepare, because interest leads to enthusiasm, and enthusiasm is contagious.

3. *Is my subject one about which I am sufficiently knowledgeable?*

Interest and knowledge are not necessarily synonymous. You may be interested in finding out about a given subject, but if your interest is relatively recent, you may not have had sufficient time to acquire enough information to prepare a well-developed communication. When selecting a subject for an impromptu, adequate knowledge is especially important; the wrong choice will invariably result in superficial communication.

Even when you have the time to plan and prepare at a more leisurely pace, it is usually a good idea to select a subject with which you are already familiar. An introductory course in communication skills is not primarily a course in research. Your instructor is interested in purposeful, well-organized, and well-developed communication. Selecting subjects close to your own experiences will help you to achieve positive results.

4. *Will my subject be of interest to my audience or reader?*

At this point our emphasis shifts from the communicator and his message to the receiver and his response. Let us assume that your assignment is to prepare a demonstration speech for classroom presentation. You tentatively decide to explain how to score a bowling match and to accompany your explanation with an enlarged score sheet. This subject is in keeping with the purpose of the assignment, and you are interested in and knowledgeable about it. Is it, however, a subject which will engender the response you desire from your audience? For those who bowl regularly, your explanation would be repetitious, while those who do not bowl may have no reason for learning how.

Perhaps your part-time job involves skills that are particularly interesting and valuable to you, but ask yourself whether a speech about them would be of interest and value to your audience. You must adapt your communication to your audience. Of course, it is impossible to interest different individuals with varying backgrounds in everything you say or write about. The point is simply to consider your receiver and prepare your communications accordingly.

5. *Is my subject sufficiently restricted?*

The secret of a well-developed communication is to begin with a subject which is sufficiently restricted and then to develop that restricted subject in detail.

A former student recently told us about his experience in an undergraduate course in modern poetry. His assignment was to select an appropriate subject, restrict it, submit it to his instructor for approval, and then write a term paper. Remembering what he had learned about the importance of beginning with a properly restricted subject, he decided to write about a single poem, T.S. Eliot's "The Waste Land." He further restricted his discussion to the symbolism in the poem and submitted to his instructor the following tentative subject: "An Interpretation of the Symbolism in T.S. Eliot's 'The Waste Land.' "

After the student received his instructor's approval and began his research, he decided to write a line-by-line, symbol-by-symbol interpretation of the lengthy, four-part poem. However, he found that his discussion of Part One alone occupied about twenty pages of manuscript. Continuing with his original plan would have resulted in a manuscript of approximately 80 pages, well beyond the scope of the assignment. Should he change his subject to one less ambitious and involved? But what about all the time and effort already expended on research? He resolved the problem satisfactorily by changing his title to "An Interpretation of the Symbolism in Part One of T.S. Eliot's 'The Waste Land.' "

When we are involved in research, we cannot always know beforehand whether a tentative subject is sufficiently restricted. The problem of adequate restriction is not as difficult when we prepare a communication based on our own experiences, because the subject is thoroughly familiar to us before we begin.

Sometimes a subject which appears to be sufficiently restricted at first glance really isn't. A recent trip may provide you with a good subject for a speech or composition, but any trip, even a short one, is a combination of many experiences. Listing some of these should help you to further restrict your tentative subject.

MY TRIP TO WASHINGTON, D.C.

    I.   The Plane Ride to Washington
    II.   Visiting John Kennedy's Grave at Arlington
    III.   A Visit with Senator Jones
    IV.   The Lincoln Memorial at Night
    V.   Our Nation's Capitol
    VI.   The Smithsonian Institution—A Magnificent Complex

If you attempt to deal with all of these experiences, your communication will read like a shopping list. A "first we did this, then that" approach, with a sentence or two devoted to each experience, would result in an uninteresting and superficial communication. Let us continue to analyze our tentative choice of subject, a trip to Washington, D.C.

Restricted Subject	*Analysis*
I. The Plane Ride to Washington	The airline hostess spilled some coffee on my suit when the plane hit an air pocket. Perhaps I should describe this experience in detail?
II. Visiting John Kennedy's Grave at Arlington	I was deeply moved. Could I recreate in words the feelings I experienced as I watched the eternal flame?
III. A Visit with Senator Jones	Meeting the Senator gave me the opportunity to chat with him about his proposal to recycle glass, metal, and paper products. I could share these thoughts with the class.
IV. The Lincoln Memorial at Night	The photographs I took would help me to recall the specific details of this scene and to recreate them for the class.
V. Our Nation's Capitol	Much too broad. Perhaps I could restrict this subject to my visit to the Senate Gallery.
VI. The Smithsonian Institution— A Magnificent Complex	Again, much too broad. There are nine different Smithsonian buildings, each containing a multitude of exhibits.

EXERCISES

DIRECTIONS: Determine which of the following subjects are sufficiently restricted for a three minute speech or a four hundred word composition. Further restrict those subjects that are too broad to be developed adequately.

1. Electrical Technology
2. My Most Unusual New Year's Eve Celebration
3. How to Bathe a Poodle
4. Grocery Shopping on a Shoestring
5. The Drug Problem
6. Acid Rock
7. Is There Really Love at First Sight?
8. How to Study
9. My Visit to a Bohemian Night Club

10. Men's Fashions in the '70's
11. Is Religion Relevant?
12. Is There a Pollution Solution?
13. Hitchhiking to Mexico
14. Political Protest
15. Recycle Your Scrap!
16. Stamp Out VD
17. Single Lens Reflex Photography
18. How to Build a Good Hi-Fi Speaker for $15.00
19. The Hunger Hike, 1972
20. Registration—A Twentieth Century Horror

STATING THE INTENT

Once the purpose of an assignment is clear to you and your subject is carefully selected and sufficiently restricted, you are ready to formulate a statement of specific intent. We have classified purposeful communication under three main headings: to inform, to entertain, or to persuade. Our next task is to relate this purpose to the specific content of our communication. Note the following examples:

1. *To Inform*
   a. to explain how to take pictures with a Polaroid camera
   b. to describe the view from my bedroom window
   c. to define "love"
   d. to summarize the mayor's five point approach for eliminating substandard housing from our town
   e. to relate the difficulties I encountered when registering for classes
2. *To Entertain*
   a. to poke fun at television situation comedies
   b. to prepare a program of folk music for our talent show
   c. to tell my favorite mother-in-law story to a recently married friend
3. *To Persuade*
   a. to convince you to support my candidacy for the presidency of the student body
   b. to explain why the President's wage and price freeze is unfair to labor
   c. to convince members of the Council to support a new sports arena for our town

All of these statements of specific intent are infinitive phrases beginning with the infinitive form of the verb: to explain, to describe, to define, and so on. When the intent of your communication is to develop a main idea, and this is generally true of persuasion, stating that main idea in a complete sentence will help you plan your communication.

Statement of Specific Intent: to convince you to support my candidacy for the presidency of the student body

Main Idea: My election to the presidency of the student body will insure organized student resistance to a raise in tuition.

Statement of Specific Intent: to explain why the President's wage and price freeze is unfair to labor

Main Idea: The President's wage and price freeze is unfair to labor because profits, insurance rates, and dividends are not included.

Statement of Specific Intent: to convince members of the Council to support a new sports arena for our town

Main Idea: Building a new sports arena will attract professional hockey to our town.

The main idea statement should fulfill four specific characteristics:

1. It should state a point of view, not a fact.
2. It should be restricted to that which can be adequately developed in a subsequent communication.
3. It should deal either with a single idea or two closely related ideas.
4. It should contain specific language.

Main Idea: The unemployment rate in our community is 6.2 per cent.

Analysis: Since this is a statement of fact, not a point of view, it requires no further development.

Revision: The unemployment rate in our community will continue to increase unless new jobs are created more rapidly.

Main Idea: There are many reasons why the Yankees will repeat as American League Champions.

Analysis: "Many reasons" is too broad. It is better to restrict your main idea to one or two specific reasons and develop them in detail.

Revision: The Yankees will repeat as American League Champions because their pitching depth and long ball hitting are superior to those of the other contenders.

Main Idea: Raising tropical fish and collecting stamps are interesting hobbies.

Analysis: This main idea statement contains two flaws:
1. Raising tropical fish and collecting stamps are two entirely unrelated activities.
2. The word "interesting" is vague.

Revision: Stamp collecting is a painless way to learn world geography.

EXERCISES

Analyze the following main idea statements. Revise any that are not satisfactory.

1. The New York Knickerbockers are the most interesting team in professional basketball.
2. Stock car racing is an exciting sport.
3. My sewing machine enables me to keep up with the latest fashions and still stay within my budget.
4. Speeders lose their licenses in New Jersey.
5. Jogging is a great way to stay physically fit, and physical fitness is necessary for a full life.
6. Draft dodging is fun.
7. Richard Nixon was a better President than was Lyndon Johnson.
8. Marijuana should be legalized.
9. Marijuana and LSD should be legalized.
10. Our welfare system is obsolete.

PERSUASION TO ACTUATE

DIRECTIONS: Write a 200–400 word appeal or deliver a 2–4 minute speech to persuade your audience to do something specific as a result of your communication. Make clear to your audience exactly what action you wish them to take. Your purpose is to get a physical response. You are asking your audience to act: to buy, to join, to vote, to help, to donate, to march, to sign, or to participate.

SUGGESTIONS

1. Be realistic. Make sure you know exactly what action you wish your audience to take, and be certain that it is reasonable. You can't expect an audience to do something which they are incapable of doing; e.g., most students could not afford to sponsor a child for $15 a month. Nor could you expect an audience to do something they are opposed to doing, i.e., you could not expect your fellow students to join the Communist Party.
2. Insure understanding. Make clear to your audience exactly what they must do. Be specific. You must point out such things as when they should act, what the exact cost will be, and who they should contact.
3. Be sincere. Before you can get others to act, you must be sold on the sug-

gested course of action. Be sure you believe that what you propose is in the best interest of your audience.

4. Be accurate. Make sure that what you are saying is absolutely true. Use only information that you have checked thoroughly.

SAMPLE TOPICS

1. Give a life-saving pint of blood.
2. Donate generously to the United Fund.
3. Join the March to cure Sickle Cell Anemia.
4. Buy a raffle ticket. (Help St. John's School for the Deaf and perhaps win a boat.)
5. Sign a petition to bring prayer back into the schools.
6. Safety—check your home for fire hazards, today.
7. Give a dollar to Save the Children Fund.
8. Elect a representative to Student Government.

ASSIGNMENT

Plan and execute a composition, a speech, or both (as your instructor indicates), according to the following procedure:

1. Indicate the primary purpose of your communication:
    a. to inform,
    b. to entertain,
    c. to convince,
    d. to actuate,
    e. to reinforce.
2. Does your subject fulfill the following criteria?
    a. Is it in keeping with the primary purpose indicated above?
    b. Is it interesting to you?
    c. Is it one about which you have sufficient knowledge?
    d. Will it be of interest to your audience or reader?
    e. Is it sufficiently restricted?
3. Formulate a statement of specific intent and a main idea statement, if needed.
4. Write your composition and/or deliver your speech.

3

the forms of
discourse

Once the purpose of your communication has been clearly established, you are ready to begin developing your subject. Which form of discourse will be best to help you accomplish your purpose? Should you tell a story? Explain a process? Describe a person, place, or event? One of these forms of discourse should suffice for brief communications, while longer communications may require combinations of the different forms.

NARRATION

Can you imagine one of your ancestors attempting to relate a personal experience to a friend? Perhaps he was stung by a bee as he walked through the forest seeking food or shelter. Later, when the pain subsided, he recreated this experience for his companion by imitating the buzzing of the bee, gesturing to depict its flight, and uttering a sound that articulated the pain he suffered when he was stung. A baby's early attempts to communicate follow a similar pattern. The baby frequently imitates the sound associated with a particular animal or object, and this sound becomes a word in his limited vocabulary. The cat is a "meow," the dog a "bow-wow," and the train a "choo-choo." An exclamation of joy—"Ah!"—or pain—"Ow!"—accompanied by an occasional gesture help him to tell his story. Narration or storytelling is our oldest form of communicating experiences.

Classifying Narration According to Purpose

We have stressed purposeful communication as one of the primary objectives of the planning stage. A narrative may be employed in a communication whose purpose is to inform, to entertain, or to persuade.

If you simply relate to a friend the events that occupied your day, the purpose of your narrative is to inform. You might, however, attempt to communicate a humorous experience. Perhaps when you opened the front door to get your morning newspaper one cold, January morning, the wind blew the door shut, leaving you stranded outside in your T-shirt and jockey shorts. You ultimately saw the humor of the situation, although it may not have been evident to you when the door first blew shut. In relating this experience, you would want to provide your friend with an understanding of the events themselves, but your primary purpose would be to entertain.

Frequently an experience is incidental to its message. Anecdotes, fables, parables, and some personal experiences are examples of narration whose primary purpose is to persuade. Consider the following example of persuasive narration:

> I am forty-four years old now and have a wife and two small children.
> By 1963 I had reached a comfortable salary level with an insurance firm
> and the future seemed bright for us all. In May of that year I developed

a slight difficulty in swallowing. Our family physician said that if it persisted for another week he would arrange an appointment for me with a throat specialist. It did persist. The specialist diagnosed it simply as "a case of nerves," a diagnosis he was to reaffirm in October of 1963. Finally, in January of 1964, convinced that it was more than a case of nerves, I entered a hospital, where I learned that I had cancer of the throat.

The writer goes on to describe in detail the horrors he experienced in the cancer ward of a well-known hospital. He employs a narrative technique to accomplish the primarily persuasive purpose of his article. This purpose is clearly indicated in the two concluding paragraphs:

If anyone tells me it hasn't been proven that smoking causes cancer, I won't argue with him. The chances are his mind is made up anyway.

If, on the other hand, what I've written here can save even one man, woman or child from the horrors I've known, I'll be content.

EXPOSITION

Do you want to build a shortwave receiver? Bake a cake? Design your own dune buggy? Add some electrical outlets to your home? Operate a sewing machine? Tile your basement floor? Make a fortune in the stock market? Ferment your own wine? Tune your car's engine? Just go to your library or local book store, borrow or buy the appropriate do-it-yourself book, and follow the "simplified, illustrated instructions."

We define exposition as communication which explains how to perform a function. In the examples above we act as receivers of expository prose. The writer is the sender; his book, pamphlet, or instruction sheet contains the message to which we respond. Some manufacturers take pains to enclose a clear set of instructions with their product. They have learned that clear expository communication is in their own best interest. On Christmas day, for example, thousands of fathers sit on living room floors attempting to assemble their children's newly acquired toys. After an hour or so of frustrating trial and error, Dad may mutter some angry words, return the parts to their original container, and decide to replace the item with something easier to assemble. The child is disappointed, the parents frustrated, and the manufacturer has lost a sale because of unclear exposition.

The following example is typical of expository material which accompanies products that must be assembled by the consumer. Notice how the various steps in the assembly process are clearly and concisely described. Key words are underlined, and repeated references are made to the accompanying drawings.

ASSEMBLY INSTRUCTIONS

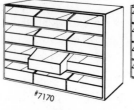

#7170

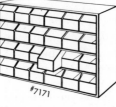

#7171

UTILITY BIN CABINET

MODEL NUMBERS
7170 & 7171

PARTS DESCRIPTION

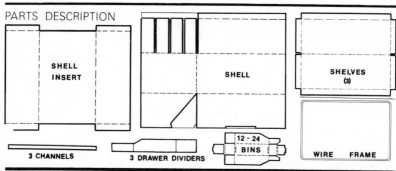

SHELL INSERT

SHELL

SHELVES (3)

3 CHANNELS

3 DRAWER DIVIDERS

12 - 24 BINS

WIRE FRAME

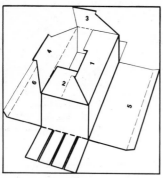

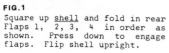

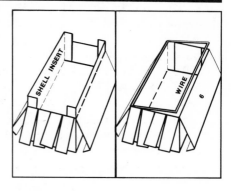

FIG.1

Square up <u>shell</u> and fold in rear Flaps 1, 2, 3, 4 in order as shown. Press down to engage flaps. Flip shell upright.

FIG.2

Slide <u>shell insert</u> into position as shown. Position <u>wire frame</u> on top of shell insert.

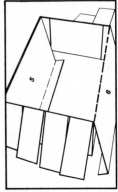

FIG. 3
Fold flaps 5 & 6 up and over wire and tuck down inside shell.

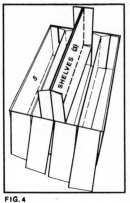

FIG. 4
Fold shelves with white side out, insert into shell, seeing to it that the narrow flaps of the shelves butt up against other shelf flaps and rest beneath wire frame as shown.

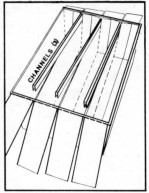

FIG. 5
Firmly press shelf channels over shelf.

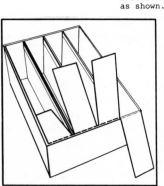

FIG. 6
Fold in remaining flaps and tuck securely against inner wall.

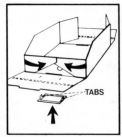

FIG. I BINS
Insert card holder tabs into the slots provided. Fold tabs over. Fold sides up, fold attached end flaps (front & back) over as shown.

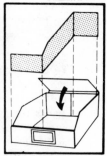

FIG. 2
Fold end panels up and over at double crease. Engage tab in slots on bottom Repeat operation opposite end. Add drawer divider as shown above.

Fidelity Products Company *A Division of Fidelity File Box, Inc*
705 PENNSYLVANIA AVENUE SOUTH, MINNEAPOLIS, MINN. 55426 • TELEPHONE (612) 544-6644

33

Classifying Exposition According to Purpose

Exposition is sometimes referred to as utilitarian prose because its effectiveness is measured by its usefulness and clarity. By definition, pure exposition is informational; however, it may also be employed in persuasive and entertaining communication.

Tom decides to try to convince his friend Bill to meet him at the stadium for a big football weekend. Sensing Bill's reluctance, Tom decides on a positive, enthusiastic approach:

Tom: I've got a couple of great seats for the State game. After the game Joe's throwing a big beer bash, and we're invited. Meet me at the Stadium Saturday at two, and we'll have a gas of a weekend.

Bill: Thanks for asking, Tom. But you know my sense of direction; I'd never find the place. Besides, I've got some studying to do for Monday's history exam.

Tom: Nothing to it, Bill. Take I-93 to the Iroquois Road Exit, about fifty miles North. When you exit, drive due East for four miles and you'll run right into the Stadium. We'll all be leaving Sunday, right after breakfast, so you'll get home in plenty of time to study.

Bill's tentative refusal is based on two reasons: He doubts his ability to find the stadium, and he needs time to study for Monday's examination. While Tom's primary purpose is persuasive (to convince), he utilizes exposition to answer Bill's first argument. Second, by arranging for an early Sunday departure so that Bill has ample time to study, Tom's chances of convincing Bill to join him have been enhanced.

Surely you have seen performers who employ varying degrees of audience participation in their acts. The singer who asks his audience to join him in the refrain or the MC explaining the rules of a TV game to contestants is involved with exposition. Explanations should be clear and brief when the purpose of a communication is primarily persuasive or entertaining. Exposition is merely a means to an end.

Definition: A Special Type of Exposition

Look around you. Regardless of where you may be at the moment, you see numerous objects whose names are familiar to you. The names we assign to are concrete words, relatively easy to define specifically. The literal defini-objects like *door, window, book, desk, floor, ceiling, grass, tree,* and *shrub* tion of a word is its *denotative* meaning. If we tentatively define a desk as a piece of furniture, our definition is too general, because there are many pieces of furniture that are not desks. The *American Heritage Dictionary* definition—"a piece of furniture typically having a flat top for writing and accessory drawers or compartments"—is more specific, and consequently more satisfactory. Notice that this definition is still sufficiently flexible to include unusual desks. The dictionary's use of the word "typically" indicates that some desks may be atypical, thereby deviating from the usual pattern.

The words indicated all refer to objects, which are easy for us to visualize. Sometimes, however, words refer to concepts, ideas, or emotions, and mean different things to different people; consequently, they are more difficult to define satisfactorily. Words like *Communism, hate, love, sorrow,* and *idealism* are abstract words referring to no specific objects. They are *connotative* in that different people have favorable or unfavorable attitudes about them, depending upon individual associations and experiences. The dedicated Communist's definition of his political ideology would be very different from that of a Wall Street banker. Defining an abstract word is a more demanding task than defining a concrete word, because the communicator must go beyond the literal meaning.

If you are asked to define an abstract word, a good starting point would be a reliable, up-to-date dictionary. The more information you discover about your word, the more complete your definition. Therefore, you might wish to consult an unabridged dictionary.

You should also pay particular attention to synonyms for the word you select. (Synonyms are words that have meanings similar to other words in the language.) However, since no two words have exactly the same meaning, distinguishing differences among similar abstract words will help you to make your definition clear and complete, and aid you in selecting precisely the right word for each situation. How, for example, does Communism differ from socialism? How does hate differ from loathing, animosity, or dislike? How does love differ from affection, fondness, or infatuation? If your general language dictionary does not contain lists of synonyms, consult a specialized dictionary of synonyms and antonyms, or a thesaurus.

Denotative and Connotative Meaning

Our main concern thus far has been with the literal or denotative meaning of a given word. Once you have established a working definition with the help of a good dictionary, you continue the process of definition through reference to your own attitudes, values, and experiences. Your definition of "love" is probably different from your neighbor's. One of your primary objectives in defining an abstract word is to make your connotative meaning clear to your reader or listener. You might view love between the sexes as primarily a physical attraction, while another might see it as a meeting of the minds on such issues as raising children, and sharing similar moral and religious convictions. Someone else might think of love as synonymous with companionship. Each of you has an obligation to supply specific examples that will enable the receiver to understand your connotative definition.

The process of definition of abstract words can be summarized as follows:

1. Consult a good dictionary, preferably unabridged, to establish a complete denotative definition.
2. Distinguish the denotative meaning of your word from that of similar abstract words with the help of a good general dictionary, a specialized dictionary of synonyms and antonyms, or both.
3. Supply your own connotative definition, supporting your judgments with specific examples.

Define an abstract word in an extemporaneous speech or short composition, as your instructor directs. Follow the three step process summarized above.

SAMPLE WORDS

1. love
2. sorrow
3. idealism
4. faith
5. success
6. despair
7. solitude
8. individualism
9. tenacity
10. hope

EXERCISES

DIRECTIONS: Indicate whether the lightface terms in the following sentences are denotative or connotative. If the term is connotative, determine whether the connotation is favorable or unfavorable.

1. I think John is thrifty; Mary thinks he is a tightwad.

2. Jim always addresses the policeman on the beat as "officer" but calls him a pig behind his back.
3. Sally, the hairdresser at Antoine's, refers to herself as a beautician or cosmetologist.
4. My boss is a slave driver if there ever was one.
5. Sam Farber is a real American, but all the do-gooders will vote for his egghead opponent.
6. I waited more than two hours for the doctor to see me; boy, those pill pushers don't care how long a patient is inconvenienced.
7. Fred thinks he is honest and straightforward, but he is really rather simple.
8. Two members of the history faculty collaborated on a book about Nazi collaboration during World War II.
9. For a lawyer who has been out of school for only a year, he certainly has been a busy ambulance chaser.
10. How's a soul brother going to make it if Whitey runs the establishment?

DESCRIPTION

Simple descriptions of people, places, and events are part of our everyday communication. A friend requests a description of your date's roommate before agreeing to a blind date. A classmate stops you at registration to ask whether you know the teacher of the history section he plans to enroll in. You make a mental note to write home to the folks, describing your new college campus. You tentatively select your senior high school trip as the subject of your next composition.

Your response to each of the above messages is primarily descriptive. Description, like exposition, is basically informational. Our primary purpose with both forms of discourse is to add to the knowledge of our audience. Expository communication, at its best, is generally simple, clear, direct, and detached. Description is more personal, more subjective. Its effectiveness depends upon how specific our details are.

Sensory Appeals

One method for achieving specific detail in description is to employ effective combinations of sensory appeals (the five senses being sight, sound, taste, touch, and smell). Although it isn't necessary to employ all five in a single description, appeals to different senses will enable you to communicate a more complete description. Which combination is most effective will depend, of course, on your choice of subject.

Let us assume that your assignment is to describe a place on campus. The overall purpose of the assignment is to inform, but the specific choice of subject is left to you. After considering your English classroom, the library, the testing center, and the automotive shop as possibilities, you tentatively decide on the student center, a place with which you are thoroughly familiar. Checking your tentative choice against the criteria detailed in Chapter 2, you conclude that your subject is in keeping with the general purpose of the assignment (to inform), is interesting to both you and your prospective audience, and is one that you are sufficiently knowledgeable about. But can it be further restricted?

Perhaps the most obvious way of restricting your subject is to describe only one part of the student center, such as the snack bar. It might also be helpful to further restrict your subject to a place in time. The snack bar during the hectic rush of lunch hour is very different from its relatively deserted atmosphere of late afternoon. Eventually you decide on "The Snack Bar at Noon" as the revised subject of your descriptive communication.

Regardless of how familiar you think you are with the snack bar, it would be a mistake to attempt to prepare your communication from memory. Go there again, notebook in hand, to find specific details that will eventually be incorporated into your finished work. Recording these details as separate sensory appeals will provide you with the raw materials needed for successful description.

Sight:	long lines of students patiently awaiting their hamburgers and fries, long-haired, jeans-clad students rapidly munching their food at crowded tables, the blue and white tiled floor covered with litter carelessly dropped by students oblivious of the perils of pollution, one unhurried couple, holding hands, having eyes only for each other in the ever-changing crowd.
Sound:	endless clanging of plastic trays making contact with the steel food rails, the din of happy, carefree voices, the raucous sound of rock music blaring over the intercom, the voice of the order-taker barking out the jargon of his trade—"BLT. down"—to the busy short order man.
Taste and Smell:	spicy chili, frothy malts and shakes, freshly baked cakes and pies, the aroma of freshly brewed coffee, the smell of stale tobacco throughout the eating area.
Touch:	bodies brushing against one another as students enter and leave the crowded area, the constant blast of warm air from the powerful, wall-mounted heater, the intermittent blast of cold air as entering students bring the winter chill with them.

THE SNACK BAR AT NOON

The relative calm of coffee break time at the snack bar changes to chaos as the noon hour approaches. At exactly 11:50 a.m. the bell tolls; fifth hour class has ended, and hundreds of students converge on the northwest side of the student center, where the snack bar is housed.

Bodies brush against one another as students hurriedly enter the crowded area, bringing a bit of winter's chill with them. The freshly scrubbed blue and white tile floor is soon covered by litter carelessly dropped by those oblivious of the perils of pollution. Jeans-clad students noisily await their hamburgers and fries. The constant clanging of plastic trays making contact with the steel food railings competes with the raucous sound of rock music blaring over the intercom. Smells of spicy chili, freshly baked cakes and pies, and richly brewed coffee fill the air.

The voice of the order-taker barks out the jargon of his trade—"BLT. down," "One burger, with"—to the busy short order man. The customers dig down into their pockets for change, pay for their selections, and scramble for the few vacant butcher block tables.

Students rapidly munch their food amidst the din of happy, carefree voices. One unhurried couple holds hands, having eyes only for each other in the ever-changing crowd.

Gradually the food line begins to subside. Students empty their trays into the huge, gray rubbish containers, then bundle themselves for departure. When the bell signals the end of the lunch hour, bodies converge on the exits, some leaving their debris behind on the tables. Soon the maintenance crew will tackle the seemingly endless job of preparing for the next stampede.

You may have noticed that not all of the sensory appeals in the notes were incorporated into the composition, and a few appeals that were in the composition are not found in the notes. Since effective communication involves repeated modification and revision, it is not necessary for you to follow your record of sensory appeals to the letter. Remember, you have merely made a random listing of initial impressions; additions, deletions, and modifications are expected and desirable.

The composition that you have just read represents one student's attempt to write an informative description. How successful is it? Is it sufficiently specific? Is it well organized? Purposeful? Interesting? Perhaps you can make suggestions for improvement.

Specific Language

A closely related technique for making details vivid is to use specific language. Try walking into your local market and asking the clerk for three pounds of fruit. He knows the meaning of the word "fruit" as well as you do, but he cannot fill your order without more specific information. What *kind* of fruit do you want? "Three pounds of apples, please," is better, but still not specific enough. As the clerk visualizes his stock of Delicious apples, Winesap apples, and Macintosh apples, he might become impatient with

your lack of specificity. A critical reader or listener becomes equally disen-
chanted with vague description.

EXERCISES

*DIRECTIONS: Write a descriptive sentence about each of the following, employ-
ing appropriate sensory appeals and specific details. A sample sentence is provided for the first phrase.*

1. A pair of shoes—My two-tone, black and rust sueded ties with wing-tip styl-
ing and decorative perforations are perfect back-to-school shoes.
2. Something good to eat
3. A rock singer or group
4. Your room
5. A teacher
6. A musical instrument
7. A soft drink
8. A game-winning touchdown
9. A treasured possession
10. An article of clothing

Classifying Description According to Purpose

The primary purpose of most simple descriptions of people, places, and
events is to inform. But sometimes the information is subordinate to another purpose: to entertain or to persuade. Notice how the effective use of
sensory detail and specific language enables the reader to experience vicari-
ously in the following example of entertaining, descriptive poetry:

THE ONCE-OVER

The tanned blonde
　　　　　in the green print sack
in the center of the subway car
　　　　　　　　standing
　　　　though there are seats
　　　　　　has had it from

1 teen-age hood
1 lesbian
1 envious housewife
4 men over fifty
(& myself), in short
the contents of this half of the car

Our notations are:
long legs, long waist, high breasts (no bra), long
neck, the model slump

the handbag drape and how the skirt
cuts in under a very handsome
set of cheeks
'stirring dull roots with spring rain' sayeth the preacher

Only a stolid young man
with a blue business suit and the New York
Times
does not know he is being assaulted

So.
She has us and we her
all the way to downtown Brooklyn
Over the tunnel and through the bridge
to Dekalb Avenue we go

all very chummy

She stares at the number over the door
and gives no sign
yet the sign is on her

Paul Blackburn
From The New American Poetry, *edited by Donald M. Allen*
© *Grove Press, New York, 1960.*

Has your mouth ever watered over an advertising brochure's description of a new car, a four-track stereo receiver, or a vacation in some far-off exotic place? In advertising description, the information given is subordinate to the persuasive purpose of selling the product or service. After studying the following example of persuasive description, answer the questions provided:

Fly away to Nassau's most fabulous world of complete resort activities . . . Nassau Beach Hotel. Just steps from your room are 660 yards of sunny, soft sandy beach washed by waters as clear, blue and warm as the breeze-swept Bahamian sky. Start your day with a suntan a la chaise, punctuated by periodic plunges into our ocean or sparkling pool. Explore the under-water world off-shore with snorkel mask and fins. Skim the waves on water skis or sail a salty catamaran. Charter a sporty cruiser for deep-sea fishing. Go scuba diving around a coral reef. Dry off with a spot of volleyball, a shot of shuffleboard, a set of tennis. Cool off with a Tropical Temptation from our beachside bar. Then, head off on a jaunty golf cart for an after-noon round of 18 challenging championship holes at the Nassau Country Club right next door. If you prefer spectator sports, don't miss the crab or goat races down by the beach . . . with the added excitement of pari-mutuel betting! Go sightseeing in Old Nassau town by scooter, bike . . .

or hire a clip-clop carriage to squire you around (your horse may be wearing a straw hat). See the Old World pomp of Rawson Square. Climb the Queen's Staircase for a panoramic view of Nassau. Visit the native Straw Market. Buy free-port booty along bustling Bay Street. But don't linger too long downtown . . . Nassau's most exciting nightlife begins right here at the Nassau Beach Hotel. Stop in at the Out Island Bar or the romantic Rum Keg for an exotic cocktail (and try the hot conch fritters appetizers). Then there's the gleaming candlelight atmosphere and gourmet dining on native and Continental cuisine in the elegant Lamplighter Room. Spend a lively hour or two in the colorful Rum Keg dancing to native rhythms, disco, steel band or Calypso. And come to the glittering sophistication of the Colony Room for the greatest nightclub shows. Wrap up your evening with a walk through our tropical garden under the stars and watch the moon turn the waves to silver along our beautiful beach. You'll understand the magic that makes one resort the most successful vacation spot on the Island . . . Nassau Beach Hotel.

With permission of Needham & Grohmann, Inc., and the Nassau Beach Hotel.

ANALYSIS OF NASSAU BEACH HOTEL DESCRIPTION

1. Formulate a statement of specific intent for the foregoing advertising copy.
2. Which of the five sensory appeals (sight, sound, taste, touch, smell) are represented? Give examples.
3. Which of the five sensory appeals predominates? Why?
4. Which sensory appeals are particularly effective? Are any of them trite, or otherwise ineffective?
5. Briefly comment on the effectiveness of this advertising copy as persuasive description.

USING NARRATION TO PERSUADE

DIRECTIONS: Deliver a 2–4 minute speech or write a short essay of 200–400 words in which you tell a story to persuade. Describe the material in enough detail to create a mental picture for the reader or listener. Develop your material informally, with emphasis on details of action. An interesting story is an excellent means of reinforcing or clarifying your ideas.

DELIVERY: If you present this assignment orally, it should be delivered extemporaneously. An audience will expect you to have almost total eye contact when talking about your own experience. The more spontaneous and relaxed you are, the more your audience will enjoy your presentation.

SAMPLE TOPICS

1. Why I always wear a seat belt.
2. Drinking and driving don't mix.
3. It always pays to be courteous.
4. Never buy anything sight unseen.
5. Never judge a person on the basis of your first meeting.
6. Keep dangerous products out of the reach of small children.

4

audience analysis

George Johnson is a marketing student at a large midwestern junior college. One Monday his speech assignment in his communication skills course was to tell a story that makes a point. Even before he finished reading the assignment sheet, he remembered a story he had heard a few weeks earlier at a party for members of the school orchestra. It was a funny story at which the audience had been hysterical with laughter, and it made a clear point. He practiced it a few times to get the timing down pat.

On the day the speeches were due, George was the first to volunteer. He walked confidently to the speaker's platform, smiled at his audience, and began. In his introduction he reminded his audience that people often waste time because they become enthusiastic about something and follow through with action before carefully considering the situation. "Let me tell you a story that I think demonstrates the danger of this," he said.

A man who lived in Chicago noticed in the paper that Jascha Heifetz was appearing the next night in Minneapolis. That evening he packed a few things, and the next day gathered his family in the car and headed north. After traveling a few hours, he ran into a violent snowstorm. The further north he traveled, the worse it got. Finally, he hit a slick spot, lost control of his car, and skidded into a ditch. An ambulance came and rushed his injured children and wife to the hospital, but he was determined to go on. He rented a dogsled and continued his journey. About 25 miles out of Minneapolis he lost his sled, but still he staggered on. Finally, he reached the concert hall. Looking at his watch, he saw that in five minutes the concert would begin. He quickly bought a ticket, rushed into the hall, and collapsed exhausted into his seat. As he looked around, he noticed that, except for three other people, the hall was empty. Just then, Mr. Heifetz strode out onto the stage, and announced that since the four people in his audience had shown so much courage in coming out on such a horrible night, he wanted them to be his guests at dinner in his hotel across the street. The other three responded enthusiastically, but the fellow from Chicago said, "Mr. Heifetz, I started out from Chicago this morning with my wife and three children to hear your concert. Halfway here I ran into a ditch and my family was taken to the hospital. But I didn't give up. I hired a dogsled and pushed on. About 25 miles out of town my lead dog took a wrong turn and the sled and dogs plunged over a cliff. I managed to jump clear and came the rest of the way on foot. I haven't eaten a thing since yesterday, and I'd love to be your guest for dinner. But before we go, could you please sing just *one* song?"

George paused for laughter, but only a few in the audience responded. Obviously shaken, he hastily concluded his speech by restating his central idea that a lot of people waste time by not channeling their energies in the right direction, and returned to his seat.

Why did George's speech fail to arouse as much laughter as he anticipated? At the Christmas party it broke everybody up, but when he told it in class it was a flop. Was it his timing? His personality? What went wrong?

The answer is simple. George was the victim of a lack of audience consciousness. Many of those in George's communication skills class didn't know something vital to the humor of the story, that Jascha Heifetz is a world renowned *violinist*, not a singer. The musicians knew who Heifetz was and laughed; many of George's audience did not know and were confused.

One crucial step in the preparation of both writing and speech is audience consciousness, an aspect too often neglected by writers and speakers. Audience consciousness means that you prepare your message and manner of presentation with your audience in mind. George didn't think of his audience when he chose his story. Chapter 1 states that the audience is a necessary part of communication. If there is no audience, or if the audience fails to understand the message, communication does not take place. To prepare an audience-centered communication, ask yourself the following questions.

WHY HAVE I CHOSEN THIS SUBJECT?

You should choose a subject that you find interesting, because the more interested *you* are in a topic, the better are your chances of maintaining the attention of your audience, and the more knowledge you are likely to have of your subject. Knowledge of your subject is imperative; a good job on a paper or speech requires that you know what you are talking about.

Choosing the right subject can make the rest of your preparation much easier. A good technique for identifying topics related to your own interests and knowledge is called *brainstorming*. List on a piece of paper as many potential subjects as you can. In searching for topics ask yourself: "What work experience do I have? What are my skills? My hobbies? What are my favorite pastimes? What do I like to read about? What do I talk about with my friends?" Write down the answers, and after you have filled the page, place a check next to the topics you find particularly interesting, about which you are knowledgeable, or which might inspire you to do research. Choose the one which interests you most.

WHAT ARE MY QUALIFICATIONS
FOR CHOOSING THIS SUBJECT?

It is important that you examine your qualifications for dealing with a particular subject. Are you qualified because of background or skill? Do you speak from personal experience? Can you offer your audience any credentials to show that what you have to say is reliable? A speech by a member of the school hockey team on buying the best ice skates for your money will probably be well received by his classmates. Similarly, an essay on the perils of combat by a decorated former serviceman carries the weight of experience. If you write or speak as a nonexpert, you will have to prove the reliability of your information. If you have special knowledge or experience, indicate this to your audience.

WHAT IS THE SPECIFIC
PURPOSE OF MY COMMUNICATION?

After you have decided on your subject, you must develop a statement of specific purpose. Write your purpose as an infinitive phrase. Your statement should clearly identify your general purpose as being to inform, to entertain, to convince, to actuate, or to reinforce.

Formulate your purpose statement by considering exactly what you wish to accomplish. You must know your goal before you can plan the best way to achieve it. Most subjects can be developed in different ways in accord with various general purposes. For example, suppose that, because of both interest and knowledge, you choose pollution as your topic. You could write a statement of specific purpose for each of the general ends:

To inform:	To explain to my audience the different types of pollution.
To entertain:	To entertain my audience by playing and singing Tom Lehrer's song "Pollution."
To convince:	To convince my audience that this nation must reorder its priorities to deal with pollution.
To actuate:	To persuade my audience to begin collecting their cans and bottles for our local recycling project.
To reinforce:	To make my audience vividly aware of the specter of a world killed by pollution.

WHAT RESPONSE CAN I
REASONABLY EXPECT FROM MY AUDIENCE?

The success or failure of any communication must be measured in terms of audience response. The TV series that fails to entertain is soon cancelled, the unsuccessful salesman will be out of a job, the textbook that is difficult to understand is seldom reordered, and the uninspiring preacher speaks to an empty church. You will communicate more effectively if you plan your message with a specific, realistic audience response in mind.

Some responses are particularly difficult to achieve. A lack of time might prevent you from teaching your audience a complicated technique, such as giving a permanent or using the slide rule. Your audience might not have the background or experience that will enable you to teach them how to replace the bearings in an alternator or sew a collar on a dress. In addition, the attitude of your audience might be so opposed to your subject that they become impossible to approach; an example would be trying to promote George Wallace for President at a black student rally. In such cases the communicator must choose another, more realistic purpose.

The case of Ralph Smith provides an example of how consideration of audience response can help a communicator determine purpose. Ralph, assigned a demonstration speech in his communications class, chose to demonstrate how to fillet a fish, something he enjoyed doing and did well. He jotted down his specific purpose: To teach my audience how to fillet a fish. Then he considered the specific response of his audience to this purpose. In order for his speech to succeed, his audience would have to know how to fillet a fish when he was through. Ralph had learned to fillet fish from his Uncle George, who had first shown him how to do it and then guided him step by step through the procedure. If he wanted to use the same approach with his audience, he would have to give them each a fish and a filleting knife, which seemed impractical. He decided instead to show his audience how to prepare fish for frying, with an emphasis on how filleting the fish made them much more pleasant to both cook and eat. The result, he decided, would be to stimulate his audience's interest in learning how to fillet fish. Ralph rewrote his specific purpose and continued preparing his speech.

WHO EXACTLY IS MY AUDIENCE?

A surprising number of communications fail because the author is not entirely clear as to the exact composition of his audience. Take Fred Johnson, for many years personnel director of a small manufacturing plant. Fred came home one night greatly disappointed because he had been passed over for promotion, and not for the first time. He called his brother-in-law, a golf partner of the company president, and asked him to find out why.

As part of his job, Fred sent out directives to plant employees. Since these were going to ordinary workmen, he was not overly concerned with style or correctness. What Fred failed to realize was that every directive sent to the workers also went to the plant manager, who read it and put it in the files. Whenever an opportunity for advancement occurred that involved Fred, those directives would be examined, followed by the comment, "How can we promote someone who communicates so poorly?" Fred paid a high price for not knowing his audience.

Before you begin to prepare your communication, consider who is included in your audience. Your classmates? Your teacher? Yourself? In this course, you will probably be speaking primarily to your classmates, so you should learn all you can about them. Listen to them carefully, make note of their interests, consider their attitudes, wants, and needs, and then develop your message accordingly.

Most students, unless specifically instructed otherwise, direct their class-room writing assignments to the instructor who gives them their grade. As long as you are not prevented from writing about subjects which you find stimulating and which are within your experience, writing to your instructor offers two distinct advantages. First, you are writing to a trained reader who can evaluate your work critically and accurately. Second, you can develop a clear picture of this reader. Your instructor will give you specific guidelines as to the standards he expects in style and grammar. Furthermore, his lectures and comments will reveal which characteristics of writing he feels are particularly important.

Regardless of whether you are writing or speaking to your classmates, your instructor, or others, strive for a correct and appropriate style. You insult both your audience and yourself when you attempt to communicate material that has not been carefully prepared.

WILL MY AUDIENCE FIND
THIS SUBJECT INTERESTING?

All too often communication fails because it has not been developed to interest the reader or listener to whom it is directed. You know how hard it is to pay attention to a speech on a subject of no particular interest to you, or to an essay that you find dull or boring. The harder you have to work to pay attention, the less chance you have of getting something out of the material. Your job as a writer or speaker is to develop your material so that your audience will find it interesting. You do this naturally when communicating with someone you know quite well.

Suppose that the college you are attending is out of town and you want to write a letter home telling what you have been doing for the last few months. What you write will vary considerably, depending on your reader. You might write about the difference between college and high school or about the pains and pleasures of being on your own to a brother or sister who will soon be entering college. The letter you send to an ex-classmate might deal exclusively with your love life or other extracurricular activities. Your parents might get a letter telling about your health, your grades, and your finances. In each case, you wrote what you felt your reader, a person you knew well, would find interesting. But how can you tell what would be of interest to strangers?

If you are familiar with the subject you have chosen, you should be able to make an educated guess. Suppose that you choose to write or speak about one of your two hobbies, coin collecting or antique cars. Your experience tells you which of these topics would be most interesting to a general audience. The majority of your friends have shown more interest in your antique cars than they have in your coins. Some of them have even changed the subject when you asked if they had seen your coin collection. Obviously, a general audience would have greater initial interest in your cars.

This does not mean that you couldn't choose to speak about coin collecting. But if you do, you must build your audience's interest to gain and maintain their attention. You might begin by telling of the time you put a quarter in a coke machine and received as change a dime worth eight hundred dollars. The thought that your knowledge as a coin collector brought you that much profit from a dime that had probably been handled by hundreds of others would be quite an attention-getter.

HOW MUCH DOES THE AUDIENCE ALREADY KNOW ABOUT MY SUBJECT?

Too technical an approach could leave your audience thoroughly confused; merely repeating what they already know will bore them. If you know that your audience has some knowledge in the subject area you have chosen, you must plan your communication accordingly. Perhaps you will deal in depth with a specific area of the subject, or you might select interesting details that are not generally known.

If your audience has little or no knowledge of your subject, you must explain unfamiliar concepts and terminology. When you are uncertain of the extent of their knowledge, treat your audience as intelligent readers or listeners with the same information as the general public has of your subject.

Mary Evans had been assigned a three to five minute visual aid speech for her communications class. Because she was an enthusiastic and skillful bowler, Mary decided to give a speech on bowling. She considered teaching her audience how to keep score, but rejected this idea after estimating that approximately one fourth of a typical audience would already know how to keep score. Even if the percentage were less, she reasoned, those who did know would find her speech dull and uninteresting. She decided instead to deliver a speech on the benefits of bowling, involving details designed to interest both the bowlers and nonbowlers in her audience.

WHAT CHARACTERISTICS OF THE AUDIENCE SHOULD I CONSIDER IN PREPARING MY SUBJECT?

Education

The educational level of your audience should determine your word choice. The word "communication" comes from the Latin *communicare*, meaning to share what is common. When you communicate to others, you share ideas with them through a common vocabulary. You must write or speak to an audience in familiar words that they can understand. For example, you probably wouldn't explain the process of circulation to your ten year old brother with the same words that you would use with your zoology instructor, because of the limitations of the former's vocabulary.

Consider the vocabulary of your reader or listener when developing your material. Omit words or phrases which might be unfamiliar. If you have the choice of two words with the same meaning, choose the more common one. Your purpose is to communicate, not to impress.

No matter what the composition of your audience, stick to your own vocabulary. Do not inject idiomatic expressions that you would not ordinarily use into your speech or paper to gain effect. Your audience might interpret this as condescension or insincerity, and react unfavorably.

Always treat your classmates as intelligent people with good vocabularies. Unless you are dealing with an unfamiliar subject, present information to them on the level you would want them to present it to you.

"LIKE YOUR KIDNEY WANTS TO SPLIT THE SCENE, AND YOUR LIVER WON'T DO ITS THING."

Courtesy of Medical World News.

Age

Knowledge of the age of your audience can often help you in determining how to handle your subject. As a rule (although not exclusively), young people tend to be more liberal than older people, more willing to try change or to take a chance. They are also usually more physically active, inclined toward being participators rather than spectators. Your approach to selling people on the idea of investing in the stock market would take these factors into consideration. You would probably be wise to appeal to older people with a list of dependable blue chip stocks which offer little risk, while for a younger audience you might choose the more glamorous speculative stocks which could double or triple overnight. Similarly, when talking about a particular sport, you might treat it as a participation sport for the younger, more active audience, and as a spectator sport for an older group. When the age of your audience is varied, you must deal with the topic in more general terms.

Special Interests

Members of an audience frequently have a common interest. They might belong to the same organization or club, be in a similar business or profession, or have gathered together out of mutual concern for a particular problem. You should attempt to determine what these interests are and relate your ideas and supporting material to them.

Consider the common interests of your communications class. As college students, everyone in the class is probably interested in such social problems as poverty, pollution, drugs, and the arms race. In preparing your communication you must be sensitive to the attitudes and needs of your audience regarding these problems; you must want to communicate your ideas about finding solutions.

As a college student yourself, you are aware of other interests shared by your classmates. Perhaps the basketball team is enjoying a winning season, or an important social event is coming up. Keep these interests in mind as you prepare your communication.

IS MY AUDIENCE'S ATTITUDE TOWARD
MY SUBJECT FAVORABLE, INDIFFERENT, OR OPPOSED?

An Audience That Is Favorable

People tend to be less critical when they agree with the position of the communicator. Consequently, a favorable audience is likely to be more tolerant of weaknesses in your writing or speech and be willing to accept your evidence. After all, you don't have to prove anything to someone who agrees with you.

This does not mean that writing or speaking to a favorable audience does not offer challenge. The chief goal of communicating to a favorable audience is to reinforce their positive attitudes. If they enjoy guitar playing, the more effectively you entertain them with your guitar, the more successful you will be. If they are looking forward to receiving information from you, their satisfaction will be measured by how clearly you can write out your explanation or directions. The more effectively you can stimulate and intensify their positive attitudes, the more likely you will be to move them to action. One of the world's foremost satirists, Art Buchwald, writes a syndicated column for over 250 American newspapers. He writes out of Washington, D.C., and although his subjects range from space to college graduation, much of his humor is focused on American politics. His readers would be considered a favorable audience whose positive attitudes are reinforced by their responses to the column. A typical Buchwald column lampoons the image-concept in politics:

GHETTO INC.

A friend of mine has just thought of a way to raise a large sum of money for poverty-stricken areas without one cent's cost to the taxpayer. He calls his program Ghetto Inc., and this is his explanation of how it works.

"From now until the Presidential elections in 1968," my friend said, "ghettos are going to be the big thing, and every politician running for public office is going to have to visit one. But most politicians don't know where to begin when it comes to touring the slums, and so Ghetto Inc. will make all the arrangements for them, for a fee, of course."

"What will you do?"

"Well, let us suppose the person wishing to tour a ghetto area is one of the many thousands of Presidential candidates who feel obligated to walk through a depressed area. Ghetto Inc. would make out an itinerary for him. First, we'd have him visit a rat-infested tenement, where he could be visibly shocked.

"Then we'd take him over to meet the parish priest who has just coached a Little League team of deprived youngsters to a city championship. After that we'd have him talk to an ex-convict who has gone straight and become a Good Humor man.

"Finally, we would arrange an interview with an unwed mother who has just lost her welfare payments. The candidate could or could not promise the woman he'd do something about it, depending on how he thinks the country feels at the time about unwed mothers."

"It sounds like a great service," I said. "How much does it cost?"

"Well, that's just a simple tour, and with transportation and including the ex-convict and Good Humor truck, we charge fifteen hundred dollars."

"That's not expensive," I said.

"Of course, Ghetto Inc. has more luxurious tours. We can arrange for a candidate to walk through a garbage dump, have him photographed with a group of striking schoolteachers, let him cut the ribbon for a new playground, and then lay the cornerstone for a low-cost housing development. The charge for this would be ten thousand dollars, and we'd supply the striking schoolteachers."

"You must be swamped with business," I said.

"Well, it's picking up nicely," my friend said. "Of course, the beauty of Ghetto Inc. is that we can service all candidates whether they're for or against the poverty program."

"How's that?"

"Suppose you have a candidate who is against welfare, opposed to coddling the poor and feels everyone should lift himself up by his own bootstraps."

"I know one," I said.

"Well, for twenty-five thousand dollars we'll arrange a tour for him which will include having rotten vegetables and eggs thrown at him, having paint spilled on his car, and, if he requests it, having the press roughed up. This will get him the sympathy of the backlash crowd, which he is appealing to in the first place."

"I could see a candidate asking for this kind of treatment, but where do you find the people to throw the rotten eggs and vegetables?"

"Oh, they're around; they're around."

"Well, I think it's a very noble experiment, and I can't see how Ghetto Inc. can miss," I said.

"It can't. As a matter of fact, with so many people running for office in 1968, our only fear is that we may run out of ghettos—or, even worse, unwed mothers—before the campaign is over."

From Art Buchwald, Have I Ever Lied to You?
(New York: G. P. Putnam's Sons, 1968). Copyright © 1966, 1967, 1968 by Art Buchwald.
Reprinted by permission of the publisher.

Most persuasion to actuate is directed at audiences favorable to the course of action proposed. The clergyman who urges his congregation to demonstrate a positive witness in their actions during the week, the football coach who fires up his team during the half, and the letter asking for a donation to a destitute Indian village are all addressing audiences likely to be predisposed to act in the manner requested. The persuaders don't need to use logical proof to support their appeals because the favorable audience has already intellectually agreed to the desirability of the course of action. This audience is likely to respond to appeals to those motives and attitudes which relate to the motives of approval. Note how the following letter directs itself at this motive, even promising to put the donor's name on an "Honor Roll" if he contributes.

224 Illini Union · Urbana, Illinois

UNIVERSITY OF ILLINOIS FOUNDATION

November 1970

Who cares?

   You might think that with over 150,000 alumni of the University of Illinois we wouldn't care that you aren't among the supporters of the Foundation's Annual Fund for 1970.

   But we do!

   We wonder why you have felt your help isn't needed. And I guess the fault lies with us. Somewhere along the line we haven't emphasized enough just how important your gift can be. No matter what the size.

   Take, for example, $1. If you, and every other alumnus, would slip a single dollar bill into the enclosed reply envelope the result would be overwhelming. Over 20 important University projects that directly benefit students and faculty would progress at the rate of $150,000! A small fortune by any standard.

   So, you see, it's not always the size of your gift that matters. It's your decision to do something now that counts. Your positive action, combined with a similar action by other alumni, will make possible scholarships and research. Student loans. Library collections. Rehabilitation of physically handicapped students. And many other alumni supported activities.

   A dime a day. For just ten days. Please care that much.

   Mark the University project you personally want to see accomplished and mail your contribution in the same envelope. Today, if you can.

      Sincerely yours,

      Joseph W. Skehen
      Executive Director

JWS:llv

P. S. We'll show others that you want to help make a great university even greater by publishing your name in the 1970 "Honor Roll" of contributors to the University of Illinois Foundation. You'll receive your copy early next year.

Used with the permission of the University of Illinois Foundation.

During the month of November of each year since 1968 the University of Illinois Foundation has mailed a similar fund-raising letter to alumni who have not responded to earlier direct mail appeals during the current or previous calendar year. A special letter is mailed to those who made a contribution the previous year but not during the current year. The results have been:

1968	$17,757 received from 3,738 alumni.	Average gift: $4.75
1969	$10,575 received from 2,684 alumni.	Average gift: $3.94
1970	$16,005 received from 3,012 alumni.	Average gift: $5.31
°1971	$ 9,303 received from 1,725 alumni.	Average gift: $5.39
1971	$13,184 received from 2,767 alumni.	Average gift: $4.76

°A simulated carbon copy of the November, 1970, "Who cares?" letter was mailed in February, 1971, to those who did not respond to the "original" letter mailed in November, 1970.

The number of letters mailed in each instance was approximately 100,000.

1. The letter copy is changed each year only as to the date and the number of Illinois graduates to which reference is made.
2. The contribution mentioned in the letter is only $1.00—the gifts received have ranged from $1.00 to $500.00, with the average gift over the five mailing efforts being $4.83.
3. Along with contributions, between 75 and 100 personal notes and letters expressing words of encouragement are received from donors with each "Who cares?" mailing. This can be compared with an average of 5 to 10 letters of the same nature received as a result of other Foundation fund-raising mailings.
4. A donor responding to the November, 1971, "Who cares?" letter probably received the same letter in 1968, 1969, 1970, and the "carbon copy" in February, 1971.
5. This one copywriting effort has produced a total of $66,874 from 13,926 contributors in three years.

Ibid.

An Audience That Is Indifferent

If you believe that your audience is indifferent to your subject, your job is to stimulate their interest. You may do this either by getting and holding their attention with a fresh imaginative approach, or by demonstrating the importance of the subject to them, or by a combination of both. This action should be taken immediately, in your introduction. Use the various attention-getting devices (explained in Chapter 5); explain how your audience is affected by your subject, or if they have something to gain by paying attention to it. As you can see, attention is of prime concern with an indifferent audience.

Brian Murphy, a staff writer for *Diablo Valley College Enquirer*, writes about what he feels is a significant issue, the fact that parents in the community are concerned about the drug problem, but no one does anything worthwhile about the cause—the lack of activities for young people. In order to awaken his readers (both the young people and their parents) to the seriousness of this inaction, he paints a shocking word picture of the variety of things young people can do at a "party."

DRUG CULTURE ALIVE, BUT SICK

What's it like trying to grow in a society that takes Excedrin for headaches, Geritol for tired blood, Doan's Pills for those nagging backaches, Alka Selzer for indigestion, Sleep-Eze for insomnia, and Haley's M.O. for occasional irregularity.

Then you are arrested for smoking grass instead of drinking Hamm's beer, for dropping bennies and sniffing cocaine instead of taking No Doz or Vivarine, for dropping reds instead of taking Sleep-Eze or Sominex, and for escaping reality for dropping acid, and mescaline instead of drinking too many cocktails.

Parents complain about the terrible drug problem in the community, but nobody wonders why the problem exists.

Let's face it, just what exciting and interesting things are there for young people to do in the community?

Well there are about 18 different movie theatres in the area. Going to the movies every Friday and Saturday night gets to be a drag and expensive. Concord has a teen center, but that's only open till 10 p.m. Pleasant Hill, Lafayette, and Walnut Creek have virtually nothing for young people to do on weekends.

Danville has finally started a teen center. You can listen to folk music on Friday and Saturday nights till midnight. YOU CAN ALSO PLAY POOL AND PING PONG.

I have discussed things that you can do, and things that some people do. The following is what a large number of people do on Friday and Saturday nights because of nonexistent alternatives.

"Parties" have the most variety of things that young people can do. You can go to a "party" and:
A) Drink beer, wine, or hard liquor.
B) Smoke grass, or hash.
C) Drink beer, wine, and drop "Reds."
D) Drop "Bennies," or sniff cocaine.
E) Drop "acid" or mescaline.
F) All mentioned above. (and it happens)
Parties these days sure seem to have a great deal to offer providing that you're NOT WILLING to suffer the consequences, not interested in rational thinking, and not interested in using your imagination. So if none of this appeals to you, there you are sitting at home watching TV.

From all of this you can guess how CONCERNED the community is about its young people. Apparently parents and the community at large don't care about people under 21. By doing virtually nothing, they are advocating, and promoting the use of alcohol, and drugs. (What else is there to do?)

What Would Happen If

What would happen if a community decided that it's not really a good thing to promote the use of drugs by their young people because of nothing better to do on weekends. And then decided to find out what young people would like to do. And then decided that those things were better to do than to use drugs.

But all that takes a great deal of time, energy, and money. I'm sure that the community has better things to do, they must, otherwise they would have done something about it a long time ago.

The community and law enforcement agencies are very reluctant to set up drug rehabilitation centers, could you imagine the opposition to setting up programs that would serve as alternatives to drug abuse?

With permission of Brian Murphy and the Diablo Valley College Enquirer.

In this article, the writer is appealing to two separate audiences: (1) the establishment which doesn't address itself to the prevention and treatment of drug abuse, and (2) the students who unwisely choose drugs as an alternative to boredom.

An Audience That Is Opposed

In most cases, the hardest audience to deal with is one that disagrees with your point of view or dislikes your subject. Who hasn't spent hours arguing about politics or religion only to find himself even more convinced that he was right and the other fellow wrong?

It is difficult to convince a person to change a point of view or an attitude that may have taken him years to form. Studies indicate that there is little change in viewpoint among those who listen to or read things with which they strongly disagree. By the time a person reaches adulthood, many of his attitudes are pretty well fixed.

Fortunately, occasions are rare when a speaker or writer must address an entire audience opposed to his viewpoint or subject. It is difficult, for example, to picture George Wallace addressing a group of militant blacks on what America has to offer them, or to imagine an article in the *Catholic Herald Citizen* on the newest techniques in abortion. Perhaps the best example of successfully changing the viewpoint of a hostile audience is found in *Julius Caesar*, by William Shakespeare. Mark Anthony faces an audience which has been convinced by Brutus that Caesar was an ambitious tyrant who was justifiably killed for the good of Rome. He takes on the seemingly impossible job of persuading the Roman citizens that Brutus, whom they hold in high regard, is actually a despicable assassin.

Anthony begins by establishing a common ground with his audience. They are his "friends," his "fellow Romans," his "countrymen." He has not come to praise Caesar, whom the crowd hates, but to bury him as any friend would do. (His audience can understand this kind of friendship.) He shows respect for the audience's friendship toward Brutus by speaking of the "noble" Brutus. At this point, Anthony raises the first question he wishes his audience to consider. "Brutus hath told you that Caesar was ambitious. If it were so, it was a grievous fault. And grievously hath Caesar answered it." The issue is, *was* Caesar ambitious? At this point, the crowd is convinced he was.

Anthony acknowledges that Brutus permitted him to speak. He calls Brutus an "honorable" man. All those who were involved in the assassination were "honorable" men. Anthony's tone of voice when he says "honorable" should suggest that he might mean just the opposite. Have you ever said one thing and meant another? Have you ever asked someone for a favor and received the response, "I don't mind," when you could tell by the tone of voice that the person really did mind? The *way* you say something can communicate a great deal to others.

Anthony begins questioning whether Caesar actually was ambitious. Brutus said he was, but what are the facts? If Caesar filled the treasury with money, where is the personal gain? If Caesar refused a kingly crown, where is the ambition? Note the reference to the personal experience of the listeners in the words, "You all did see. . . ." "*Brutus* tells you that Caesar was ambitious," says Anthony, "but you all have seen that he wasn't."

Notice that Anthony is still careful not to say anything against Brutus. Even though the audience can see the weakness in Brutus' argument, Anthony still avoids attacking him. After all, Brutus was held in high regard by the

Anthony: *Friends,   Romans, Countrymen, lend me your ears; I come to bury Caesar, not to praise him. The evil that men do lives after them; The good is oft interred with their bones. So let it be with Caesar. The noble Brutus hath told you Caesar was ambitious. If it were so, it was a grievous fault, And grievously hath Caesar answered it. Here under leave of Brutus and the rest (for Brutus is an honorable man; So are they all, all honorable men), Come I to speak in Caesar's funeral.*

He was my friend, faithful and just to me; but Brutus says he was ambitious, and Brutus is an honorable man. He hath brought many captives home to Rome, whose ransoms did the general coffers fill. Did this in Caesar seem ambitious? When that the poor have cried, Caesar hath wept; Ambition should be made of sterner stuff. Yet Brutus says he was ambitious; and Brutus is an honorable man. You all did see that on the Lupercal I thrice presented him a kingly crown, crowd for his patriotism and self-sacrifice, and there still may be respect in the minds of some.

The response of the audience onstage should indicate that Anthony has changed their point of view. Although Brutus convinced them that Caesar was murdered to protect them from his ambition to become a dictator and make them his slaves, the fact that Caesar never profited from his position and three times refused the crown proves that he wasn't ambitious. Anthony clearly establishes his image as a faithful friend by what he says and by what he does. He even weeps for Caesar. The crowd responds, "There's not a nobler man in Rome than Anthony." From this point on, Mark Anthony is speaking to friendly citizens who have been won over to his point of view.

which he did thrice refuse. Was this ambition? Yet Brutus says he was ambitious and sure he is an honorable man. I speak not to disprove what Brutus spoke, but here I am to speak what I know. You all did love him once, not without cause. What cause withholds you then to mourn for him? O judgment, thou art fled to brutish beasts, and men have lost their reason! Bear with me. My heart is in the coffin there with Caesar, and I must pause till it come back to me.

This speech exemplifies two useful suggestions for dealing with audiences opposed to your subject or viewpoint: (1) establish a common ground with the audience, and (2) clear up any lack of understanding or misinformation your audience may have about your point of view or subject.

Mary Smith, a junior college freshman, used a common ground approach in preparing a speech to inform on one of her favorite subjects, opera. She had found that most of her classmates were apathetic or even hostile about her subject. One fellow named Ron intended to cut class on the day of her speech because opera, especially Wagnerian opera, Mary's favorite, really "turned him off."

On the day she delivered her speech Mary identified with many in her audience by beginning:

> **You know, like many of you I was really turned off by opera until two years ago, when I found out an interesting fact. I didn't like opera because I didn't know anything about it. Well, ever since then the more I got to know about it, the more I got to like it. I'm sure when you get to know enough about it, you'll like it too.**

Mary realized that she needed a fresh, imaginative approach to hold the attention of her audience. She prepared carefully and thoughtfully, and delivered to the class a humorous plot summary of Wagner's opera, *Tannhauser*, which ended to even Ron's delight with the heroine getting stabbed right between the two big trees.

Mary took what many in her audience thought was a dull, boring topic and made it exciting and interesting. She used humor, novelty, conflict, and suspense to hold their attention, and the result was a successful speech.

The second suggestion for dealing with an adverse audience is to clear up any lack of understanding or misinformation they may have about your subject or viewpoint. When using this approach, the first thing you must consider is why your audience is opposed to your subject. Sometimes people form incorrect attitudes or stereotypes on the basis of inaccurate or insufficient evidence. In such cases, your job is to do what the reader or listener has not done for himself—give him the facts.

In the article below, Capt. Paul Gray, U.S. Navy, explains the reasoning behind the bombing of Cambodia in order to give those opposed to this move a better understanding of the problem.

CRISIS IN CAMBODIA

In view of the emotional, almost pathological response to the President's recent action in Cambodia, I would like to evaluate the consequences to his decision for you as I see it. I hope this brief analysis will give you a better understanding of the problem.

Putting all the glory aside, you must realize that in the end it is logistics that wins or loses wars. The South lost in the Civil War because of logistic failures. Germany lost World War I and World War II for the same reason. Any army or navy which is cut off from its supply base rapidly loses its ability to fight. A soldier on the front line is soon ineffective if he has no food or bullets. A warship without black oil and ammunition is no longer an aggressive fighting element.

Beans and bullets—you have to have them or you can't win. It's as simple as that. Ask any of our combat Marines or sailors who have been to Vietnam.

Now for Cambodia. Since about 1965 the Viet Cong and North Vietnamese have received their military supplies from two sources. Communist bloc ships were unloaded in Cambodia at Sihanoukville and the food and ammunition was trucked about 200 miles to storage points along the border of South Vietnam. Other bloc ships were unloaded in Haiphong and the supplies were trucked as far south as possible and then carried by men to other storage areas in Cambodia. The Viet Cong and NVA then used these supplies to arm themselves, infiltrate across the entire border, attack, and then quickly retreat back into Cambodia to rearm and regroup. They have done this for more than five years with complete immunity.

As a result of the President's action, these supply sanctuaries are either destroyed or being destroyed. Sihanoukville can no longer be used by the Communist bloc ships. To supply their troops, the North Vietnamese now face the stupendous problem of transporting tons of supplies about 300 miles from Haiphong to South Vietnam over unpassable roads and trails. The instant the supply lines enter Laos or Cambodia, they are vulnerable to attack from the air or ground.

Congressional Record, July 9, 1970,
with permission of the author, Capt Paul N. Gray, USN (ret.).

The writer goes on to explain how this affects the war in South Vietnam. As he indicates in his opening sentence, he sees the adverse reaction to the

President's decision to bomb Cambodia as being emotional. In this article he gives his readers the "facts" in order that they might see the "real picture."

In order to communicate successfully, it is necessary that you understand your audience. The car salesman who can size up a husband and wife who

---

AUDIENCE ANALYSIS FORM

Name_____ Date_____

Title of Speech or Essay_____

(Answer each question completely)

THE COMMUNICATOR   THE AUDIENCE

1. Why have I chosen this subject?   5. Who is my audience?

                                       6. Will my audience find this subject
                                          interesting?

2. What qualifies me to deal with
   this subject?

                                       7. What is the audience's probable
                                          knowledge of my subject?

THE MESSAGE

3. What is my specific purpose?   8. What characteristics of my audience
                                          should I consider in preparing my
                                          subject?

4. What response can I reasonably
   expect?

                                       9. Is my audience's attitude toward
                                          this subject favorable, indifferent,
                                          or opposed?

```
                        AUDIENCE ANALYSIS EVALUATION

      Name_____

      1.  What was the communicator's subject?



      2.  How interesting was this subject to you?
          |___|___|___|___|___|
          low              high

      3.  How useful was this subject to you?
          |___|___|___|___|___|
          low              high

      4.  How effectively did the communicator get attention during introduction?
          |___|___|___|___|___|
          low          high

      5.  How much preparation was put into this communication?
          |___|___|___|___|___|
          low              high

      6.  What was the communicator's specific purpose?  (One simple, declarative sentence)



      7.  How effective was the conclusion to the communication?
          |___|___|___|___|___|
          low              high

      8.  How well did the communicator accomplish his purpose?
          |___|___|___|___|___|
          low              high

      COMMENTS:
```

have come to buy a new car, and determine which of them makes the decisions in that family, knows which sales pitch to use; the politician who can tell the voter what he wants to hear and still maintains his credibility will stand the best chance of getting elected; the charitable organization that can prick the conscience of the person to whom its appeal is made will get the best response.

Remember, before you begin writing or speaking, consider your audience. Put yourself in their shoes. Try to understand them. If you don't, you are liable to wind up writing to or talking to yourself.

The samples of the audience analysis form and audience analysis evaluation form found above are designed to help you become more aware of your audience. When preparing your speech or paper, fill out a copy of the audience analysis form. Have your listeners or readers fill out copies of the evaluation form to give you feedback as to how successful you were in judging and adapting to your audience.

EXERCISES

1. Prepare a list of specific topics which should be of particular interest to your classmates.
2. Prepare a list of specific topics which should be particularly useful to your audience.
3. Select five different magazines. Analyze these to determine the characteristics of the audience to which they appeal.
4. Analyze a speech or written communication that you have recently heard or read. To what audience was it directed? How carefully were they considered? Was it effective?
5. Prepare an analysis of your class as an audience. In what ways are they similar? In what ways do they differ?
6. Choose a general topic you are qualified to deal with. Write out a specific purpose statement for a communication to inform, entertain, convince, actuate, and reinforce.
7. List five well-known participation sports. Then guess as to how many in your class have engaged in them. Survey the class to check your answer.
8. Pick a highly controversial statement. Estimate how many in your class would agree with the statement, be indifferent to it, or opposed to it. Survey the class to check your answer.

5
attention

An old Arkansas farmer once bought a mule that was supposed to be the fastest in the whole state of Arkansas. When paying for it, he was told that if he wanted the best possible results from the mule, he should treat it with kindness. So he took the animal home, fed it a hearty supper and bedded it down on fresh straw in a clean stall. The next morning he walked the mule to the field and hitched it to a plow. "Let's go, friend," he said in his most pleasant tone. But the mule didn't budge. Well, the farmer was prepared, and he reached into his overalls and pulled out an apple—and some sugar—and a turnip—but the only thing that moved on the mule was its mouth. This so infuriated the farmer that he stalked back to the house to call the "S.O.B." who had swindled him. Before the telephone wires had cooled off, the fellow who had sold him the mule arrived and headed for the field with the farmer at his heels. On the way, he picked up a big stick and when he reached the mule he let him have it right between the ears. Then he whispered, "come on, pal; let's plow the field," and the mule took off like a race horse. The farmer stood shaking his head in disbelief. "That's gotta be the fastest mule in the world," he said, "but you told me he had to be treated with kindness." "He does," said the other fellow, "but you have to get his attention first."

This anecdote points out a fundamental principle in communication—to communicate effectively you must have the attention of your audience. Without attention, communication does not exist. However, don't be misled by the way in which attention was achieved in the story. People, unlike mules, are usually unenthusiastic in their response when they are forced to pay attention.

Consider your own experience. Have you ever watched an unimaginative, poorly directed educational film because you were told there would be an exam on it? Have you listened to an uninteresting lecture because you knew the contents had an effect on your grade? How much did you learn in that course? How much do you remember? In both cases you were, in effect, forced to pay attention. Did it pay off?

These are some of the questions with which people in education are becoming increasingly concerned. They have come to realize that "hitting the student over the head" results in short-term learning which is soon forgotten. They have found that attention given on the basis of interest, rather than on the basis of reward or punishment, produces more lasting results.

MAKING YOUR MATERIAL INTERESTING

As speakers and writers you can help hold your audience's attention by making your material clear, vivid, and, above all, interesting. Two rhetorical devices which will help you to achieve these goals in your communication are *variety* and *emphasis*. Mass communicators make use of variety and emphasis to sell their products. The increase in volume when a TV commercial comes on, the vivid contrasting colors of billboards and magazine advertising, the searchlights and fluttering pennants heralding the opening of a new service station, and the sound truck blaring out the qualifications of a political candidate are all directed at capturing attention.

Variety

If you want to be a more interesting speaker or writer, use a variety of sentence patterns (simple, compound, complex, compound-complex), rather than an endless string of simple sentences. Unless your communication contains a combination of effective sentence types, it will be monotonous. In Chapter 7 we discuss a number of ways to achieve variety in expressing your ideas. Become familiar with them.

Like any skill, effective communication takes hard work. If you wanted to become a good golfer, you would learn the fundamentals, do a lot of practicing, and take every opportunity to watch professionals in action. The same procedure holds true for writing and speaking. If you become aware of how professional writers and speakers organize their ideas in meaningful, animated, interesting ways, you will be able to apply these standards to improve your own writing and speaking.

A speaker can achieve variety in his delivery as well as in the language he uses. You have had occasion to listen to a great many lectures by instructors of varying quality. Discounting the subject matter, most of us prefer to listen to the instructor who speaks in a pleasant, conversational style, who talks with you rather than to you. The key to conversational style is speaking in a natural manner. In everyday conversation a person speaks with various inflections to express his true feelings. His voice rises when he says "What a doll!" and falls as he says "What a drag." Our vocal patterns vary to suit the exact meaning we intend to convey. We give little thought to the way in which we say something when we talk to our friends, but in a public speaking situation we get up tight. We are suddenly aware that people are forming opinions about what we say and how we say it. We become conscious of our voices, our physical appearance, and of the words we are using. The result is that we take the variety out of our voices. Unless we can maintain the vocal patterns which are natural to our conversation, we convey words (instead of meaning) in a flat and colorless way.

One of the easiest ways to achieve variety in speech is to vary the speed at which you speak. The average public speaker talks at the rate of about 120 words a minute, but you shouldn't maintain a constant rate throughout the speech. Sometimes you might speak 80 words a minute, and at other times 160 a minute. An important idea might be spoken slowly, an exciting story told with enthusiastic speed. A good rule is to speak more slowly at the beginning of your speech, so that the audience can become accustomed to your style of speaking. Then, as you warm up to the occasion, you can quicken your pace.

Emphasis

Emphasis is achieved in both writing and speaking by stressing important words and ideas. In speech, we emphasize ideas not only with the words we choose, but also with facial expression, tone of voice, and use of pause, volume, intensity, and gesture. Have you ever had a parent or friend tell you that he didn't mind your going somewhere when his facial expression or tone of voice told you otherwise? You can tell when a person is really concerned by the intensity with which he says something, his increase in volume, or the way he gestures. Therefore, if you want to highlight a particular point for your audience, you must emphasize it through voice and gesture.

Remember that a great many things are conveyed by a shrug of the shoulders, a nod of the head, a look of annoyance, or a pleasant smile. The next time you are engaged in enthusiastic conversation with your friends, make note of their gestures and facial expressions. If you can transfer your animation and physical expression in informal conversation to your public speaking, you will be more interesting and enjoyable to listen to and to watch.

The use of pause is a particularly effective way of gaining emphasis. Used before an important idea, it says to the audience, "Pay close attention to what is coming next." A pause after an important idea gives the audience a chance to reflect on what was said. Its effectiveness as an attention-getting device can be judged from your own experience. Why do some of us interlace our comments with "ah" or "er" when searching for what to say next? Because we feel that an unfilled pause will call attention to our lack of fluency. However, that solution is more troublesome than the original problem, because the "ah" and "er" become part of our speech pattern and inhibit us from using pause at all. Be aware that pause *does* call attention to itself, and use it to emphasize your important ideas.

Attaining emphasis in writing is more of a problem. The inexperienced writer often attempts to indicate emphasis with frequent use of intensifiers, exclamation points, underlining, and capitalizing. Perhaps you have written or read a letter that attempts to reproduce the accents of speech by the following mechanical means:

Dearest Emma,

I had a perfectly marvelous time at your party! I *mean* it was *positively* something else. And the groovy, fantastic music was utterly devastating! I *mean* it! I wouldn't have missed that party for *anything*!

While this technique has its place in informal, personal correspondence, it is inappropriate when there is not a close personal relationship between writer and reader.

Although skillful writers use some of these devices to achieve emphasis, they do so sparingly. They most often achieve emphasis by repeating words and phrases intentionally, choosing forceful words, and changing the word order within sentences (both first and last positions in a sentence are more emphatic). Martin Luther King's speech, *I Have a Dream*, demonstrates how emphasis can be achieved by these means:

> There are those who are asking the devotees of civil rights, "When will you be satisfied?" We can never be satisfied as long as the Negro is the victim of the unspeakable horrors of police brutality. We can never be satisfied as long as our bodies, heavy with the fatigue of travel, cannot gain lodging in the motels of the highways and the hotels of the cities. We cannot be satisfied as long as the Negro's basic mobility is from a smaller ghetto to a larger one. We can never be satisfied as long as our children are stripped of their selfhood and robbed of their dignity by signs stating "for whites only." We cannot be satisfied as long as a Negro in Mississippi cannot vote and a Negro in New York believes he has nothing for which to vote. No, we are not satisfied, and we will not be satisfied until justice rolls down like waters and righteousness like a mighty stream.
>
> *Reprinted from* Rhetoric of Racial Revolt
> *(Denver, Colorado: Golden Bell Press, 1964), by permission of the publisher.*

The phrase "we can never be satisfied" is repeated by Dr. King to emphasize the idea that the Negro will keep working until he attains complete justice and equality. The contrast between what is and what should be is heightened by King's intentional use of repetition. Be warned, however, that overuse of this device will result in monotony, not emphasis.

Dr. King also gains emphasis by his use of forceful words (e.g., "unspeakable horrors of police brutality"), thus stressing the magnitude of the Negro's plight. Finally, he builds a climax by putting the answer to the question "When will you be satisfied?" in the most emphatic position, the end of the paragraph—when ". . . justice rolls down like waters and righteousness like a mighty stream."

REASONS FOR PAYING ATTENTION

As we indicated earlier, people willingly pay attention to a communication because (1) they will gain something useful from paying attention, or (2) paying attention satisfies a previous interest.

Thus, you would pay attention to the directions for filling out your income tax because you have something to gain or lose. On the other hand, you might sit up and watch the late show because it satisfies your desire to be entertained. You might listen attentively to a dull story told by your boss or prospective father-in-law (utility), or spend all evening listening to an acid rock group because you really like it (interest). More effort is required to pay attention to what is useful than to what is interesting.

Let's go back to those dull, educational films. You watched them because you had something to gain if you did or lose if you didn't. The purpose of the films was to teach something, to give information that you could use, but many films of this type fail to teach effectively because they don't arouse curiosity or hold interest. Compare this type of film to the educational TV program, *Sesame Street*. It is estimated that *Sesame Street* has a viewing audience of five million. Many of the children who watch it have learned, in a limited way, to count, read, and write before beginning school. The people who write and produce the program handle their material in such an interesting manner that learning is no longer a chore—it is fun. Suggestions for making your material more interesting follow in our discussion of attention factors.

ATTENTION FACTORS

The Startling

A minister once opened his sermon with the statement, "This is a god-damned miserable Sunday!" Needless to say, his audience snapped to attention. After a brief pause to allow them to recover, he explained that he had been just as shocked as they when he overheard the comment on his way to church that morning, and he followed with a blistering attack on profanity. Used sparingly, the startling can be an effective attention-getting device. Consider how this writer uses the startling to hold her readers' attention:

> **Dear Mother and Dad:**
> Since I left for college I have been remiss in writing and I am sorry for my thoughtlessness in not having written before. I will bring you up-to-date now, but before you read on, please sit down. You are not to read any further unless you are sitting down. Okay?
> Well, then, I am getting along pretty well now. The skull fracture and the concussion I got when I jumped out of the window of my dormitory when it caught on fire shortly after my arrival here is pretty well healed now. I only spent two weeks in the hospital and now I can see almost normally and only get those sick headaches once a day. Fortunately, the fire in the dormitory, and my jump, was witnessed by an attendant at the

gas station near the dorm, and he was the one who called the Fire Department and the ambulance. He also visited me in the hospital and since I had nowhere to live because of the burnt out dormitory, he was kind enough to invite me to share his apartment with him. It's really a basement room, but it's kind of cute. He is a very fine boy and we have fallen deeply in love and are planning to get married. We haven't got the exact date yet, but it will be before my pregnancy begins to show.

Yes, Mother and Dad, I am pregnant. I know how much you are looking forward to being grandparents and I know you will welcome the baby and give it the same love and devotion and tender care you gave me when I was a child. The reason for the delay in our marriage is that my boyfriend has a minor infection which prevents us from passing our pre-marital blood tests and I carelessly caught it from him. I know you will welcome him into our family with open arms. He is kind, and although not well educated he is ambitious. Although he is of a different race and religion than ours, I know your often-expressed tolerance will not permit you to be bothered by that.

Now that I have brought you up-to-date, I want to tell you that there was no dormitory fire, I did not have a concussion or skull fracture, I was not in the hospital, I am not pregnant, I am not engaged, I am not infected, and there is no boyfriend in my life. However, I am getting a D in History and F in Science and I want you to see those marks in their proper perspective.

Your loving daughter,
Susie

Reprinted with permission of Forbes Magazine. *Writer unknown.*

Humor

Humor can be an effective tool for the communicator. However, listeners and readers will not be amused by hackneyed, clumsy, or "unfunny" attempts at humor, so you as a speaker or writer should observe the following rules.

First, make sure your humor is relevant. Audiences are not impressed with stories which are dragged in by the heels. Your humor should be used to develop the theme of the composition. If you select the main points of your composition merely to permit the use of stock anecdotes or jokes, your humor is likely to appear irrelevant.

Second, make sure your humor is appropriate. There are some situations in which humor is in bad taste and therefore out of place. If the humor is too sarcastic or personal the audience will be offended instead of entertained; if it violates standards of good taste the audience may be embarrassed. A composition whose subject is one of dignity or solemnity will not be aided by humor.

Finally, use humor that is brief and pointed. Humor should not take up more time than it is worth, its purpose being to provide relaxation, enjoyment, and entertainment.

If humor is relevant and well-handled, it is an impressive attention-getter. One particularly effective form of humor, satire, pokes fun at a subject by reducing it to ridicule. Note how effectively Tom Lehrer satirizes what he feels is an American hypocrisy.

NATIONAL BROTHERHOOD WEEK

Oh, the white folks hate the black folks
And the black folks hate the white folks—
To hate all but the right folks
Is an old established rule.

But during National Brotherhood Week,
National Brotherhood Week,
Lena Horne and Sheriff Clark are dancing cheek to cheek.
It's fun to eulogize the people you despise.
As long as you don't let them in your school.

Oh, the poor folks hate the rich folks
And the rich folks hate the poor folks—
All of my folks hate all of your folks,
It's American as apple pie.

But during National Brotherhood Week,
National Brotherhood Week,
New Yorkers love the Puerto Ricans 'cause it's very chic.
Step up and take the hand of someone you can't stand;
You can tolerate him if you try.

Oh, the Protestants hate the Catholics
And the Catholics hate the Protestants
And the Hindus hate the Muslims
And everybody hates the Jews.

But during National Brotherhood Week
National Brotherhood Week,
It's National Smile at Oneanotherhood Week.
Be nice to people who are inferior to you;
It's only for a week, so have no fear—
Be grateful that it doesn't last all year!

Suspense

Everyone knows the value of suspense as an attention factor. We follow avidly the serial on TV or the comic strip of our local newspaper. We eagerly seek out the details of a local or national crime or scandal. We

The Case of the Shocking Carpet.

"There was something strange about that house. The thermostat registered normal, but everyone felt chilly. Furniture creaked. House plants drooped. A thin film of dust covered everything, even with daily dusting. Rufus, the family dog, was nervous and whiney. And crackling jolts of static electricity leaped from door knobs and light switches to shock unsuspecting victims."

If you've noticed some of these tell-tale signs around your house, the culprit is probably low humidity. Other clues are: family complaints about dried out skin and nasal passages; wooden furniture coming unglued; wall paper cracking and peeling; wood trim pulling away from walls; piano getting out of tune; paintings cracking.

So if your evidence points to low humidity, investigate getting a West Bend portable humidifier for your home. It will keep the humidity level just right throughout an average 8-room house. A West Bend humidifier looks like an at-tractive cabinet. But inside, West Bend's famous waterwheel action is working quietly, dependably to circulate fresh, moist air.

Want more clues on how to rid your house of low humidity? Send for our FREE 12-page booklet, "The Shocking Facts About Low Humidity." Use the handy coupon below.

Used with the permission of The West Bend Company.

watch a football or baseball game, sweating it out with our favorite team.

When using suspense as an attention factor, remember not to tip your hand too soon. For instance, don't give away the outcome of the story in your title. Titling an essay *The Game We Lost by Inches* would reveal the conclusion before the reader even begins. A composition can be organized so that the reader or listener is uncertain of the outcome of events. If you can excite the curiosity of your audience by developing your material in the form of a mystery or problem that they can solve with you, their attention will be aroused by their desire to find out the answer.

Questions also present incomplete situations. Sometimes a question or a series of questions will create suspense, as in the following example from a student theme:

> Now, he opens his mouth to speak. His answer is awaited eagerly. Will he reveal the truth? Will he rat on his friend? The courtroom is hushed. The jury and spectators lean forward on their seats. He begins hesitatingly, almost in a whisper. "The defendant and I. . . ."

The Familiar

Use of the familiar is particularly effective in speaking situations. For years comedians have used the "local" joke, a reference to people, places, or events which are distinctly familiar to the audience. Johnny Carson uses this technique in his opening monologue on the *Tonight Show*. He makes jokes about *Consolidated Edison* (the New York electric power company), Mayor Lindsay, or the New York streetwalkers, and the audience roars.

You can add local color to your material by using names and places that the audience will recognize. For instance, in describing a night on the town, a reference to a popular hangout would be appropriate to a student audience. Refer to the interests and experiences of your audience whenever practical. It is also effective to refer to something said by a previous speaker. The audience can relate to it easily, so it will help hold their attention. Whenever appropriate, make references to events or instances that are fresh in the listeners' minds. One University of Wisconsin lecturer began with an effective use of the familiar some years ago: "Today we're going to study the giant sequoia redwoods—a tree you'll be seeing when you go to California to see Wisconsin win the Rose Bowl Game!"

The Vital

The vital can be the most forceful attention factor of all, especially when it relates to a strong motive inherent in the audience. People attend to what affects them directly—their health, their security, their survival. Slogans like

"Fight Cancer with a Checkup and a Check" are directed at these motives. The student speaker who began, "Within the next ten years three people in this audience will be dead from the effects of DDT in our environment," had his classmates eager to hear what followed. In his book, *The Population Bomb*, Dr. Paul Ehrlich begins with a prologue designed to secure the interest of his potential readers by combining the startling and the vital.

> The battle to feed all of humanity is over. In the 1970's the world will undergo famines—hundreds of millions of people are going to starve to death in spite of any crash programs embarked upon now. At this late date nothing can prevent a substantial increase in the world death rate, although many lives could be saved through dramatic programs to "stretch" the carrying capacity of the earth by increasing food production. But these programs will only provide a stay of execution unless they are accompanied by determined and successful efforts at population control. Population control is the conscious regulation of the numbers of human beings to meet the needs, not just of individual families, but of society as a whole.
>
> Nothing could be more misleading to our children than our present affluent society. They will inherit a totally different world, a world in which the standards, politics, and economics of the 1960's are dead. As the most powerful nation in the world today, *and its largest consumer*, the United States cannot stand isolated. We are today involved in the events leading to famine; tomorrow we may be destroyed by its consequences.
>
> From Dr. Paul R. Ehrlich, The Population Bomb. © 1968 by Paul R. Ehrlich.
> Reprinted by permission of Ballantine Books, Inc.

The Real

Have you ever been caught up in a story in which the characters and plot were described with such vividness and clarity that you actually became part of the narrative? Writers and speakers able to create this response use the attention-getting technique called the "real"—descriptive language to present a clear and definite picture of what is taking place. The person who describes a scene for his audience is, in effect, placing a mental picture before them. It is his job to select those details that the audience needs to know in order to get a clear picture of the situation. This might involve appropriate modifiers. Note the following two statements: (1) I sat next to a girl eating fruit. (2) I sat next to a voluptuous blond in a tight green micro-mini who was munching a crisp, red apple. Which statement is more likely to hold attention and establish the picture clearly in the mind?

Sometimes effective description calls for the use of specific rather than general terms. The word "car" offers only a vague picture; the word "Ford" is more clear, and to say Thunderbird, Maverick, or Pinto helps in establishing a precise mental image. Don't say a man "walked" into the room when he "ambled," "edged," "strutted," or "staggered." Use the precise word.

Since using the "real" involves talking about actual people and places, it is wise to give names to the characters you describe, especially if they are important to the story. For example, it is easier to see you sitting next to "Marvin" or "Lolita" than next to your "friend." It is easier to picture "Miss Stonebreaker" than "the math teacher" you had.

Finally, the use of the "real" involves a combination of both abstract and concrete language. The storyteller has the advantage of being able to include his impressions of the things he is describing. In this instance, the old adage that "a picture is worth a thousand words" is not true. For example, a snapshot can show you what kind of clothes a person is wearing or the shape of his head, and from these you might draw some conclusions about his life style or intellectual ability, but it cannot show you that he is a loud-mouth, an introvert, or an agnostic. That is up to the storyteller. If the fact that your companion is superstitious has a bearing on your story, make sure that your audience knows this.

The Novel

Most of us are attracted by the unusual. Some people spend hours looking through a hole in the fence of a construction site at workers erecting a building, while others spend hours in line waiting to see the latest innovation on stage or in the movies.

Unusual personal experiences arouse interest on the part of the audience. A deep sea diver or parachutist would undoubtedly have a list of surefire experiences for holding the attention of an audience.

As a speaker or writer, you should be constantly on the lookout for new ways of saying things. Use your imagination; avoid the hackneyed and trite. Which of the following is a more interesting use of description: "The virgin forest," or "the unaxed woods"? While both say the same thing, the latter says it in a newer, more imaginative way.

Finally, consider combining the novel with the familiar. An old story with a new twist is a certain attention-getter. Obviously, not all the problems of communication are solved simply by getting and holding the reader or listener's attention.

A writer or speaker might get attention and yet fail to obtain a desired response. However, you can be sure that the better you control the audience's attention, the better are your chances of accomplishing your purpose. The ad quoted uses a technique called "scratch 'n sniff," to add the extra dimension of scent. The tape is odorless until scratched with the fingernail. Once scratched, the tape actually demonstrates the product by putting its aroma right under the reader's nose.

The sniff that launched a million sips.

Scratch the tape then sniff the tape for the world's driest martini

Back in 1870, Fleischmann developed the world's first dry gin. And today we still make the driest.

To tempt you to try it, we've even taped the scent of a Fleischmann's martini right on this page. Merely scratch the piece of tape below and then sniff it.

We hope that once you have taken a whiff of our martini, you won't be satisfied until you have a taste. Then you'll be extremely satisfied.

Fleischmann's. World's driest gin.

DISTILLED FROM AMERICAN GRAIN • 90 PROOF • THE FLEISCHMANN DISTILLING CORP. N.Y.C.

Used with the permission of the Fleischmann's Distilling Corp.

A DEMONSTRATION SPEECH

***DIRECTIONS:** Deliver a 2–5 minute speech in which you demonstrate a technique or procedure. Accompany your delivery with an appropriate visual aid. Pick something that you enjoy doing and do well. Consider whether the audience* *will see the usefulness of your information. Topics which offer little utility to the audience must be made interesting in order to hold attention.*

DELIVERY: This speech should be delivered extemporaneously. Demonstrating something requires freedom of movement. You might have to use your hands, arms, legs, or body to explain something to your listeners. Therefore, the less dependent on notes you are, the better.

SAMPLE TOPICS

1. How to take an effective snapshot
2. How to fillet a fish
3. How to set a broken leg
4. How to mix a strawberry daiquiri
5. How to dance the "Big Apple"

EXERCISES

1. Select an instructor and analyze his effectiveness in holding the attention of his audience of students. Write a three to four hundred word report in which you refer specifically to his use or lack of use of the attention factors above. Do not name the instructor.
2. Select five of your favorite short stories or TV programs. List the attention factors in each.
3. Write an introductory paragraph to an essay or the introduction to a speech using one or more of the attention factors. Write an alternate using different factors. Hand both in to your instructor indicating which is better and why.
4. Analyze an essay or speech by a classmate and indicate how they could have made it more interesting by using specific attention factors.
5. Analyze a particular ad or TV commercial that uses one or more attention factors to sell its product. Comment on its effectiveness.
6. Choose a novel by a significant writer. List the number of simple, compound, complex, and compound-complex sentences found on any two pages.
7. Make a list of names and places that your audience will recognize and relate to.
8. Make a list of issues with which your classmates are strongly concerned.

6

supporting
your ideas

The fact that you say something in a positive way is seldom enough to insure that your reader or listener will either understand or agree with you. In most cases, you must use supporting detail to make your ideas clear or persuasive to others. For example, in a communication to inform intended to give your audience an understanding of George Washington's performance as a general, you might choose from a variety of supporting techniques. You might relate a few of his experiences on the battlefield (examples). You might describe the hardships he and his men faced or analyze his battlefield strategy (explanation). You might quote significant military experts or historians who have commented on his competency as a general (testimony). You might liken him to other generals (comparison). Finally, you might cite the number of his successes and failures on the battlefield and the odds he faced (statistics).

These same five techniques can also be used in communication to persuade. In persuasion they usually appear as evidence, supporting a positive statement or assertion. Suppose, for example, that a mother wants to convince her young son to stop climbing trees. "Carl," she says, "you shouldn't climb trees." She might use any of the five supporting devices to support her assertion:

Example: "Climbing trees is dangerous, Carl. When I was your age, I had a friend named Timmy who was always climbing trees, even though his parents warned him not to. Then, one day Timmy slipped on a wet branch and fell out of a tree. He fell twenty feet to the ground and broke his neck. Two days later, Timmy died."

Statistics: "You know, Carl, last year in our state over one hundred boys and girls were killed or crippled falling out of trees."

Testimony: "Your Uncle George often climbs trees as part of his job and he says he wouldn't do it if he didn't have to. They're too dangerous."

Comparison: "Falling twenty feet out of a tree is like someone hitting you as hard as they could with a sledgehammer."

Explanation: "Sometimes a branch that looks safe can be rotten inside, eaten up by insects or disease. You might step on it, crack it, and come tumbling to the ground." (This explanation could be made even more impressive if the mother could find such a branch and show Carl how easy it is to break.)

As you have seen, supporting material may be divided into five classes:

1. Examples
2. Statistics
3. Testimony
4. Comparison/Contrast
5. Explanation

EXAMPLES

An example can be thought of as a "specific instance," a sample chosen to show the nature or character of the rest. Examples can be either abbreviated or detailed. One might cite the maxi-skirt as an example of a fad; *Jesus Christ, Superstar* as an example of rock opera; the late Vince Lombardi as an example of the power of positive thinking; or the high unemployment rate as an example of the government's inability to cope with domestic problems.

When preparing for a particular speech or essay, look for appropriate and interesting examples that fit the subject, arouse curiosity or concern, avoid wordiness, and make a point.

The amount of detail included in the example is often dependent upon your audience. If the example you choose is familiar to your readers or listeners, you need only cite it briefly. If it is unfamiliar to your audience, you must develop it in enough detail so that its point is made clear to them.

Sometimes a speaker or writer will keep his examples brief so that he can present them in groups. Note how the frequency of the examples in the article below seems to strengthen the writer's point that many hospital emergency rooms are "overcrowded, incompetently staffed, and inadequately equipped."

AMERICANS TAKE BIG CHANCE IN HOSPITAL EMERGENCY ROOMS

The oft-repeated myth by the American Medical Association that while costs are the highest, Americans receive the best health care in the world, took another solid blow to the chin last week as a result of a most revealing article in the Wall St. Journal entitled "Grim Diagnosis." After citing incredible cases of medical bungling, the article says: "This kind of horror story is being told with increasing frequency these days. As the shortage of doctors becomes acute, more and more Americans are turning to hospital emergency rooms for injuries or illnesses of all types. And often, authorities say, the emergency rooms they turn to are overcrowded, incompetently staffed, and inadequately equipped.

Studies Are Quoted

"Two studies in Baltimore bear out that contention. Research published last year by two specialists at the Johns Hopkins University School of Hygiene and Public Health found that less then one-third of a group of patients showing up at a big-city hospital emergency room with non-emergency complaints were treated adequately.

"Shortly after that, another medical team at the school reported that more than half of a group of auto accident victims who died from abdominal injuries 'should have had a reasonable chance for survival' had not hospital errors in diagnosis and treatment occurred."

Here are some typical examples cited in the article:

George McGraw considered himself a lucky man.

Patient Sent Home

To all appearances, he had emerged from a serious automobile accident near Baltimore recently with only a scraped elbow and a cut on one ear. Or at least, that's what he was told by the hospital emergency room physician who examined him and sent him home.

But for some reason the physician didn't have any X-rays made, and George McGraw walked out of the hospital door with a fractured neck and skull.

On the ride home from the hospital, bone fragments sliced into Mr. McGraw's brain and spinal cord. Today, the 58-year-old construction worker from New Freedom, Pa., is paralyzed for life.

Example Is Given

In New York, a 35-year-old unemployed man went to a hospital emergency room and complained of stomach pains. He was given a painkiller and sent home. He died 24 hours later, in another hospital, from massive hemorrhaging of stomach ulcers.

A Dallas nurse is still haunted by memories of an episode in a local hospital one night. An accident victim brought to the hospital was admitted as dead on arrival, on the word of the ambulance attendants. The emergency room was so crowded that night, according to the nurse on duty, that no one bothered to examine the man.

Several hours later, the supposed corpse coughed. The victim survived, but with serious brain damage apparently caused by the delay in treatment.

In a shocking number of cases, blatant incompetence by medical people is indicated. In Tennessee a few years ago, for instance, a teenage boy died of a ruptured liver after interns in a crowded emergency room diagnosed him as drunk and sent him away.

Nurses in Mississippi ignored a man who was bleeding to death. Near Chicago, a college football player broke his leg during a game.

The general practitioner on duty at the hospital emergency room put the cast on so tightly that the boy's leg later had to be amputated above the knee.

Hence, it's not surprising that recent studies suggest a significant portion of the 700,000 medical and surgical emergencies that occur in the United States every year are mishandled in some way that often result in preventable death or permanent injury.

Amputation Follows

In the emergency room of one Chicago private hospital, a 12-year-old boy with an open fracture of the right arm had to wait so long for treatment that gas gangrene developed in the wound and his arm had to be amputated.

The Milwaukee Labor Press, Oct. 21, 1971. Reprinted by permission.

At other times it may be more effective to communicate one example in detail. Detailed examples usually take the form of stories, which are easy to organize, since they are developed in chronological order. These stories may take the form of personal experiences, allegories, anecdotes, parables, or fables. They are excellent devices for clarifying and reinforcing ideas, and can often give the reader or listener a clear mental picture of the characters, setting, and action. For this reason, they are sometimes called word pictures or *illustrations*. These detailed examples may be real or hypothetical, humorous or serious. They should be completely relevant to the point or moral principle being illustrated. One good example of a story that illustrates a moral principle is the Parable of the Good Samaritan, found in the tenth chapter of Luke in the Holy Bible. In response to the question, "Who is my neighbor?" Jesus replies:

A certain man was going down from Jerusalem to Jericho when robbers attacked him, stripped him and beat him up, leaving him half dead. It so happened that a priest was going down the road; when he saw the man he walked on by, on the other side. In the same way a Levite also came there, went over and looked at the man, and then walked on by, but a certain Samaritan who was traveling that way came upon him, and when he saw the man his heart was filled with pity. He went over to him, poured oil and wine on his wounds and bandaged them; then he put the man on his own animal and took him to an inn where he took care of him. The next day he took out two silver coins and gave them to the inn keeper. "Take care of him," he told the inn keeper, "and when I come back this way I will pay you back whatever you spend on him." And Jesus concluded, which one of these three seems to you to have been a neighbor to the man attacked by the robbers?

From Good News for Modern Man
(New York: American Bible Society, 1966), pp. 164–65.

STATISTICS

When used properly, statistics provide an excellent means of clarification or support. However, when handled clumsily, they confuse and discourage understanding. Few readers or listeners would struggle to pay attention to an uninteresting and complicated set of statistics. Therefore, if you want to be effective, make them interesting and meaningful. Here are some suggestions you should consider in using statistics.

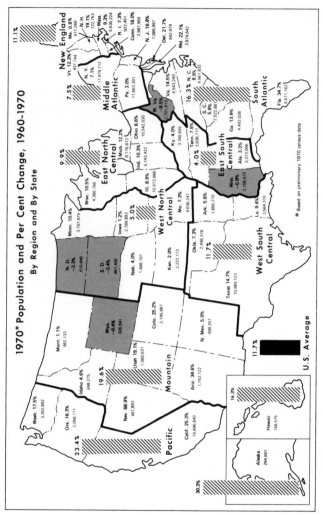

1970* Population and Per Cent Change, 1960-1970
By Region and By State

On a statewide and regional basis, the preliminary 1970 census date reflect the preference of Americans for those "less matured" areas where employment opportunities are many and environmental and social problems are less acute. For example, the Pacific states led in population growth over the decade (+23%) with the mountain states not far behind (+20%). At the same time, the heart of the eastern megalopolis, the Middle Atlantic states, gained only 7.5% in population. The impressive rise of the Pacific Region is highlighted by California's replacement of New York as the most populous state—19.7 million versus 18.0 million. Nevada (+69%), Florida (+35%), Arizona (+35%), Alaska (+30%), California (+25%), and Colorado (+25%) registered the largest percentage gains over the last decade, while only five states lost population—Wyoming (-0.4%), Mississippi (-0.9%), North Dakota (-3.3%), South Dakota (-3.4%), and West Virginia (-8.5%). Final census data may remove Wyoming and Mississippi from this grouping.

* Based on preliminary 1970 census data

Used with the permission of the Conference Board, Inc., from Road Maps of Industry.

Keep Statistics Clear and Graphic

You may use charts, tables, graphs, or pictures to help your audience grasp what is being presented. Note how the writer makes use of the combination map-bar graph to show more clearly the increase in population in those "less matured" areas where the opportunity for employment is greater and social and environmental problems are less acute.

If you wanted to make use of this map in a speech, you would either have to enlarge it so it could be seen easily or make enough copies for each listener. Use of a chart too small to be seen by everyone in your audience would be ineffective, and passing one around through the audience would be distracting.

Dramatize Your Statistics

Whenever possible, your statistics should be stated in terms which relate to the interest and experience of your listener or reader. If you can form a mental picture for your audience by presenting your statistic in some dramatic form, they are more likely to understand and remember it. In a speech on December 3, 1971, to 3,000 students at Wisconsin State University—Stevens Point, Senator George McGovern of South Dakota spelled out the enormous cost of the Vietnam war by showing what the money we spend in the war would buy in terms of humanistic needs:

> ... the price of 7 machine guns would pay the salary of an elementary school teacher. The cost of an aircraft carrier could pay for 67,000 housing units, and a B-51 bomber's cost could pay for 15 hospitals of 50 beds each and for free care for the poor at those hospitals.

> *Speech by Senator George McGovern at Wisconsin State University-Stevens Point, Dec. 3, 1971. Reprinted by permission.*

Round Off Your Statistics

Whether you are writing or speaking, when dealing with large numbers it is a good idea to round them off. Instead of saying that the 1970 census lists the population of New York City as 7,792,892, round it off to approximately 7.8 million. The shorter figure is easier for the reader or listener to understand and remember. Dr. Theodore E. Matson, president of the L.C.A. Wisconsin-Upper Michigan Synod, rounds off all the statistics he uses in this brief bulletin insert on the war in Vietnam:

FOCUS ON WAR IN VIETNAM

The total tonnage of bombs dropped during the war is now just under six million tons. The U.S. dropped just over two million tons of bombs during the whole of World War II on Europe and Japan.

We have dropped almost 20 tons of explosives for every square mile in Vietnam.

A report released last December by the American Association for Advancement of Science claims that in Vietnam, some 600,000 people have been deprived of their normal food supply by defoliation. The report claims that chemical agents sprayed by the U.S. have been responsible for killing over $500 million worth of prime hardwood, covering an area the size of Massachusetts.

Over 12% of South Vietnam's territory, including crop lands and grazing lands, has been damaged or destroyed. Sen. Gaylord A. Nelson of Wisconsin reports that "The U.S. has sprayed in South Vietnam enough chemicals to amount to 6 pounds for every man, woman, and child in that country."

There are some 400,000 prostitutes in Saigon, nearly one for each G.I. Most of them have no other means of income.

The above are just a few of the gruesome facts connected with the war in Vietnam. No matter how bad the situation ever became in our country, would you want some other country to try to save us in the same way in which we flauntingly say that we are trying to save South Vietnam?

Theodore E. Matson

Reprinted by permission of the writer.

Document Your Statistics

Avoid using such vague phrases as "recent studies indicate" or "the last surveys show." Instead, indicate clearly when and by whom the statistics you are quoting were compiled. Chances are that some in your audience have been deceived in the past by statistics. Set their minds at ease by indicating exactly where the statistics came from.

This does not mean that you must document every statistic that you use. To do so would be both uninteresting and overly complicated. When the statistics you present are consistent with the general knowledge and experience of your audience, there is probably no need to indicate their exact source.

Note that Dr. Matson documents the statistics given in regard to defoliation in Vietnam, but does not document his statistics on the bombing or prostitution. That is because there has been little publicity given to America's policy of defoliation, but the extent of the bombing and prostitution is widely known.

TESTIMONY

It is often wise for a speaker or writer to support his own ideas with the testimony of others. We live in a complex and technical age; ours is increasingly a society of specialists. The statement of an expert on a particular subject carries the weight of his education and experience. Most of us would not quarrel with a doctor who recommended an emergency appendectomy or with a TV repairman who told us that our set needed a new vertical output transformer. Unless we doubted their competency or honesty, we would have little reason to question their judgment. If you want your audience to give credence to the authorities you cite, choose people they will consider well-qualified and objective. If the experts are unknown to your audience, give facts about them to establish their qualifications. William A. Nail, Public Relations Director of the Zenith Radio Corporation, uses this method of introducing Dr. Charles Keller.

> Dr. Charles Keller, retired director of the John Hay Fellows program and retired professor of history at Williams College, goes around the country talking with teachers and young people in high schools. He has devoted the last years of his career in education to listening and sharing experiences with others—try to demonstrate what you learn, when you listen to others.
>
> Dr. Keller listens continually to young people and their ideas. In a talk that he made to a meeting of librarians last year, he used a poem by a high school student that he had met in Portland, Oregon. I would like to share with you a part of this poem, which illustrates in a way the answer to the question—"What did you say?"

> *I found beer cans floating under dead fish,*
> *and a forest converted to a chemical factory—*
> *an image on the boob-tube*
> *informed me of "100 per cent chance precipitation"*
> *and spoiled the surprise.*
> *I looked for the moon and found Apollo 8, Telstar,*
> *Halley's Comet and a Boeing 707.*
> *Beauty is neither electronic nor man-made.*
> *Stars are more silver than aluminum, and*
> *wax fruit are blasphemous. Beauty is*
> *that which is natural, original, and unexpected.*
> *I am waiting for the day when computers*
> *program themselves,*
> *and leave us to ourselves, and*
> *I am watching for the day that*
> *the last blade of grass is removed*
> *to make room for a missile factory.*
> *I am waiting for a machine that can*
> *fall in love, and*
> *I am watching for an IBM card for God.*

> Vital Speeches, XXXVII:23 (September 15, 1971), 726.

The poem above is also a form of testimony. If someone else has said something in poetry or prose that you feel is particularly well related to your subject quote him. Besides clarifying or reinforcing what you have said, this technique will add interestingness and variety to your writing or speaking.

Testimony is usually less effective as a support when you are dealing with a controversial subject. Experts tend to disagree on controversial issues. While one economist may believe in rigid price controls, another believes in none at all; one group of scientists advocates the use of unmanned rockets to explore space, another group defends our present use of manned rockets. Thus, experts who disagree may, in effect, cancel each other out.

When using the testimony of another, you can either quote him verbatim or paraphrase what he has said. However, in most cases the testimony will be made stronger by direct quotation. When you quote an authority directly, your reader or listener can decide the authority's meaning for himself. He doesn't have to depend on the accuracy of your interpretation. In his letter to the president, reprinted in full on pp. 273–41, Capt. Aubrey Daniels twice quotes President Nixon's exact words to underline what he contends was a contradiction between what the President said about Mylai and what he eventually did.

On Nov. 16, 1969, you issued the following statement through your press secretary, Mr. Ronald Ziegler, in referring to the Mylai incident:

"An incident such as that alleged in this case is in direct violation not only of United States military policy, but is also abhorrent to the conscience of all the American people.

"The Secretary of the Army is continuing his investigation. Appropriate action is and will be taken to assure that illegal and immoral conduct as alleged be dealt with in accordance with the strict rules of military justice.

"This incident should not be allowed to reflect on the some million and a quarter young Americans who have now returned to the United States after having served in Vietnam with great courage and distinction."

At the time you issued this statement, a general court-martial had been directed for a resolution of the charges which have been brought against Lieut. William L. Calley Jr. for his involvement at Mylai.

On Dec. 8, 1970, you were personally asked to comment on the Mylai incident at a press conference. At that time you made the following statement:

"What appears was certainly a massacre, and under no circumstances was it justified.

"One of the goals we are fighting for in Vietnam is to keep the people from South Vietnam from having imposed upon them a government which has atrocity against civilians as one of its policies.

"We cannot ever condone or use atrocities against civilians in order to accomplish that goal."

These expressions of what I believed to be your sentiment were truly reflective of my own feelings when I was given the assignment of prosecuting the charges which had been preferred against Lieutenant Calley.

Reprinted by permission of the writer, former Captain, United States Army, Aubrey M. Daniels, III and © 1971 by The New York Times Company.

Had Capt. Daniels paraphrased President Nixon, the reader would have to rely on the Captain's interpretation of what the president meant. By using the direct quotation, Capt. Daniels allows the reader to make that judgment himself.

Direct quotations can also be used if a person has said something so clearly or succinctly that you could not possibly say it as well, or if you want to project an image of a person by what he has said. Suppose that Professor Smith has a particularly clear explanation of deviant behavior in his sociology textbook. Instead of using your own words you may choose to quote the professor verbatim. There are also times when someone has said something so well that you reinforce your ideas by simple quotation. Here are a few examples of memorable phrasemaking.

The only thing necessary for the triumph of evil is for good men to do nothing.

Edmund Burke

Ask not what your country can do for you, but what you can do for your country.

John F. Kennedy

This above all,—to thine ownself be true; And it must follow, as the night the day, Thou canst not then be false to any man.

William Shakespeare

In Chapter 11 we indicate that a person projects his image to others in part by what he says to them. In the speech, *A Tribute to His Brother,* on pp. 181–84, Edward Kennedy devotes almost his entire content to quoting what his brother wrote about their father and what he said in a speech to the young people in South Africa. The intention was to enable the audience to perceive an image of Robert Kennedy through what he had written and spoken.

Note how President Richard M. Nixon uses quotation in this October 7, 1971, radio and television address to project what he described as the typical response of Americans to his wage-price freeze:

Thousands of letters have come to this desk since I made the announcement of the wage-price freeze seven weeks ago. Listen to what people all across America from all walks of life have written to me, the President, about this program.

Here's a letter from a schoolteacher in New Jersey. "I'm a widow raising two sons on my teacher's salary. I will lose about $300 because of that freeze. Yet I sincerely feel that we must all support your efforts to bring the economy into balance."

And here's a letter from a wage earner in Wantagh, N.Y. "As one who is expecting an increase in income this December, let me say that I will gladly go without it if that will curtail inflation."

The wife of a Government employe in Texas writes, "We are willing as a family to forego our pay raises in order to see stability in prices."

Let us all hope that Americans will once again realize that we must be willing to sacrifice for a long-term goal and once again have pride in our country.

And then from a man in Klamath Falls, Ore. "Your Administration's recent freeze on wages and prices means that I will not receive the 4 per cent raise that was written into my contract this year. Nevertheless, I support your efforts to halt inflation, including the wage freeze. The fight against inflation is everybody's fight."

I want to express my appreciation to the thousands of others of you who have written me letters like this. And I want you to know how much it has meant to me to hear that most Americans will put their country's interest above their personal interest in fighting this battle.

Vital Speeches, XXXVIII:I (October 15, 1971), 2.

The question of ethics in testimony arises in advertising, where well-known personalities endorse some product or idea. One wonders about the individual's competency to evaluate the product being endorsed. Does athletic ability give authoritative knowledge about the nutritional value of a breakfast cereal? Does being a movie hero make one an expert on the subject of patriotism?

As a writer or speaker you have an ethical responsibility to choose your supporting material honestly and accurately. When selecting testimony ask yourself these questions: Will the authority be acceptable to my audience? Is he qualified by training and experience? Is the statement I am using an accurate expression of the author's opinion?

COMPARISON AND CONTRAST

You might describe your history teacher as an intellectual Phyllis Diller, your new boy friend as a chubby Richard Harris, or your parents as the Mr. and Mrs. Archie Bunker of Roseville, Ohio. Comparison/contrast can be used in an exacting manner, as a statistical comparison of the infant mortality rate in civilized countries, or rather casually, i.e., your description of last night's date as "the battle of Bunker Hill revisited."

You were probably first introduced to comparison/contrast as a child. One of the best ways to teach the new or unknown to someone is to compare it to what is known. In answer to his child's question, "What does a zebra look like?" the parent replies, "Like a horse in striped pajamas." A teacher introducing her class to the concept of food as energy might compare food with the gasoline put in a car to keep it running.

Comparison

You would probably compare Shelley and Keats (both romantic poets of the same period) and contrast farm life with city life. Comparisons may be *literal* or *figurative*. A literal comparison describes similarities between things in the same category. Comparisons between infant mortality in America and infant mortality in Sweden, between unemployment rates in 1968 and 1970, or between Republican and Democratic candidates are literal comparisons. When we describe the similarities between things in different categories, we call this comparison figurative.

Examples of figurative comparison would be the comparison of communism to an ant colony, an occupied country to a canary in a cage, or a union-management bargaining session to a game of chess. Like all supporting devices, comparison can be used in communication to inform, entertain, or persuade. In his novel *Victory*, Joseph Conrad uses the technique of comparison to create for his reader a vivid picture of Heyst's tropical island.

> An island is but the top of a mountain. Axel Heyst, perched on it immovably, was surrounded, instead of the imponderable stormy and transparent ocean of air merging into infinity, by a tepid, shallow sea; a passionless off-shoot of the great waters which embrace the continents of this globe. His most frequent visitors were shadows, the shadows of clouds, relieving the monotony of the inanimate, brooding sunshine of the tropics. His nearest neighbour—I am speaking now of things showing some sort of animation—was an indolent volcano which smoked faintly all day with its head just above the northern horizon, and at night levelled at him, from amongst the clear stars, a dull red glow, expanding and collapsing spasmodically like the end of a gigantic cigar puffed at intermittently in the dark. Axel Heyst was also a smoker; and when he lounged out on his verandah with his cheroot, the last thing before going to bed, he made in the night the same sort of glow and the same size as that other one so many miles away.
>
> Joseph Conrad, Victory
> *(London: J.M. Dent & Sons Ltd., 1915), p. 3.*

Comparison is often used as a technique in persuasion. How many times have you heard or used arguments similar to these? "John's parents are letting him go and he's even younger than I am." "Oh, come on and try it. Everyone else is doing it. Why miss out on all the fun?"

It is also frequently used in combination with other supporting devices. The newspaper article below combines comparison, contrast, statistics, and explanation to inform the reader of the differing perceptions that blacks and whites have of each other:

THE HARRIS SURVEY:
MANY STILL HOLD RACE STEREOTYPES

While the stereotypes that whites carry in their minds about black people are gradually breaking down, substantial minorities of whites still cling to such attitudes. At the same time, blacks are developing a set of hardening animosities toward whites. This communication gap is at the root of today's racial tensions.

The number of blacks in the US who agree with the statement, "whites are really sorry slavery for blacks was abolished," has risen from 63 to 70% in the past year. A clear majority of blacks now believe that whites are less honest than blacks, physically weaker, and possessed of a "mean and selfish streak."

By contrast, the number of whites who hold stereotypes of blacks is gradually declining. For example, the number of whites who feel that "blacks have lower morals than whites" has decreased from 55 to 40% over the past 8 years; the number who said outright that blacks are "inferior" has dropped from 31 to 22%.

As reported previously by the Harris Survey, black confidence in white institutions in our society has reached a new low, and the number of blacks willing to adopt a more militant stance to achieve racial equality has risen in the past year.

Recently, a cross section of 1,200 black households was again asked: "Do you personally tend to agree or disagree with these statements?"

	Agree	
	1971	1970
	%	%
Whites feel blacks are inferior	81	81
Whites give blacks a break only when forced to	79	77
White men secretly want black women	76	74
Whites are really sorry slavery for blacks was abolished	70	63
Whites have a mean and selfish streak in them	68	65
Whites are physically weaker than blacks	65	55
Whites are scared that blacks are better people than they are	62	66
Whites are less honest than blacks	58	50
White people need to have somebody else like blacks to lord it over	52	49
Whites are more apt to catch diseases	49	44

In only one instance did the number of blacks agreeing with the point of view decline during the past 12 months. Taken together, these results indicate that blacks are giving whites far less benefit of the doubt in race relations these days. This hardening of hostility coincides with growing disenchantment with their lot in society, a condition probably influenced by such events as the recent killings at New York's Attica prison.

White attitudes on a parallel set of stereotypes about blacks have softened some since the Harris Survey began asking about them in 1963. A cross section of 1,445 whites was asked many of the same questions put to a comparable group eight years ago.

"Leaving aside the whole question of laws and civil rights, how do you feel as an individual? Do you personally tend to agree or disagree with these statements?"

	Agree	
	1971	*1963*
	%	%
Blacks are asking for more than they are ready for	55	X
Blacks have less ambition than whites	52	66
Blacks laugh a lot	48	68
Blacks smell different	48	60
Blacks have lower morals than whites	40	55
Blacks want to live off the hand-out	39	41
Blacks have less native intelligence	37	39
Blacks are more violent than whites	36	X
Blecks keep untidy homes	35	46
Blacks breed crime	27	35
Blacks care less for the family than whites	26	31
Blacks are inferior to white people	22	31

In every case where there is a trend line, the number of whites who agreed with derogatory statements about blacks has declined since 1963. One item on both lists points up the differing perceptions between the two races. A strong 81% of all blacks said they believe that "most whites feel blacks are inferior." Only 20% of whites admit to such prejudice.

Whites for the most part disclaim prejudice generally while documenting it in certain particulars. Blacks base their assessment less on what whites profess to be their views than on the actual injustices meted out by a society largely run by whites.

Harris Survey, *by Louis Harris.* © *1971 Chicago Tribune-New York News Syndicate, Inc.*
Reprinted with permission.

Contrast

While comparison points out similarities, contrast emphasizes differences. For example, there is an extreme difference between life in free and in totalitarian countries, between opera and acid rock, or between male and female (vive la différence!). The writer of the following editorial emphasizes the seriousness of our skyrocketing medical costs by contrasting a hospital visit in England with one in the United States:

WHAT A DIFFERENCE

A New York writer was in England last summer with his family. His four-year-old son became seriously ill, spent three nights in a private room in a hospital, had numerous tests and intravenous feeding. The boy's parents were given a room near him in the hospital.

Total cost was $7.80, for the parents' meals.

Foreigners in England are eligible, in emergencies, to receive the same treatment Britons get under their national health service.

On the other side of the coin—and the Atlantic—an Englishman visiting here last year was stricken and was rushed to a New York hospital. The hospital refused to admit him until it received a financial guarantee (he naturally had no private American health insurance coverage).

He died 16 days later. His wife received a bill for $12,000.

One point is not so much that a citizen of another country was treated shoddily here, bad as that is, but that many Americans would be in the same boat he was. The other point is that there are such things as health systems under which you can afford to get sick.

The Milwaukee Labor Press, November 18, 1971. With permission.

Contrast can be an effective attention-getter. Our language provides thousands of words which invoke striking contrasts. Life and death, love and hate, pleasure and pain, rich and poor, strong and weak, and fast and slow are just a few of the combinations that you have seen or heard. Charles Dickens uses the technique of sharp contrast in the opening paragraph of his novel, *A Tale of Two Cities*:

It was the best of times, it was the worst of times, it was the age of wisdom, it was the age of foolishness, it was the epoch of belief, it was the epoch of incredulity, it was the season of Light, it was the season of Darkness, it was the spring of hope, it was the winter of despair, we had everything before us, we had nothing before us, we were all going direct to Heaven, we were all going direct the other way—in short, the period was so far like the present period, that some of its noisiest authorities insisted on its being received, for good or for evil, in the superlative degree of comparison only.

EXPLANATION

As a student you are probably involved more with explanation than any other supporting device. The textbooks that you read are, for the most part, written for the purpose of making ideas clear. Your teachers are primarily explainers. The answers that you give in class or in essay examinations are explanations.

Definition

Explanation can take several different forms. It can include definition, analysis or description. One of the necessities in communicating is to be understood. If you plan to use a term that may be unfamiliar to your audience, either define it yourself or choose an appropriate definition by someone else. Do not fall into the habit of always using dictionary definitions; they are sometimes inappropriate for your specific context. If you can, keep your definition brief, clear, and geared to your audience's level of knowledge and experience.

For example, the definition of a "spinner" as "a cap that fits over the hub of an airplane propeller" would be more communicative and interesting to most people than the more technical definition of a spinner as "a ferric of paraboloidal shape which is fitted coaxially to the propeller and revolves with the propeller."

Malcolm X uses definition to clarify the word "revolution." Notice that in his definition he contrasts what revolution is with what it is not:

> This is a real revolution. Revolution is always based on land. Revolution is never based on begging somebody for an integrated cup of coffee. Revolutions are never based upon love-your-enemy and pray-for-those-who-spitefully-use-you. And revolutions are never waged singing "We Shall Overcome." Revolutions are based upon bloodshed. Revolutions are never compromising. Revolutions are never based upon any kind of tokenism whatsoever. Revolutions overturn systems. And there is no system on this earth which has proven itself more corrupt, more criminal, than this system that in 1964 still colonizes 22 million African-Americans, still enslaves 22 million Afro-Americans.

Quoted in George Breitman (ed.), Malcolm X Speaks, p. 50; copyright © 1965 by Merit Publishers and Betty Shabazz. Reprinted by permission of Pathfinder Press.

Analysis

Analysis is the technique of breaking an idea down into its parts and explaining each part separately. It is essentially a process of answering such questions as: Who? What? Why? When? Where? How?

You use analysis when you demonstrate how to do something. While organizing a speech on "Swimming More Effectively," you might divide your speech into three parts: (1) the crawl stroke; (2) the body position; and (3) the flutter kick. An essay on how to plant a tree would probably be organized according to the steps involved: (1) digging the hole; (2) preparing the soil; (3) placing the tree correctly; (4) covering the roots and watering them down.

Evaluation is a form of analysis. The following review uses the technique of analysis to comment on the Grand Funk Railroad:

GRAND FUNK: A GRAND FLUNKOUT

If dollars are votes, the most popular and successful rock group in the world today is Grand Funk Railroad. If they have ever been given a good review by a rock critic, it is a well-kept secret.

The trio of noisemakers has been branded "the world's biggest car radio" by Rolling Stone magazine and so consistently fails to make the musical grade that they would be better known as Grand Flunk.

Of their five albums to date ("On Time," "Grand Funk," "Closer to Home," "Live," and "Survival") all have been million dollar products. In July alone the constantly touring Flunk drew 55,000 to a New York City concert, then globe hopped to a universal appeal audience of 40,000 in Tokyo. The group made $5 million last year and is making a lot more this year.

The Flint (Mich.) group consists of Mark Farner, barechested guitarist with bicep length blond hair who writes and sings most of the songs; Mel Schacher, fuzzy-haired bass player who on stage acts as if he's being electrocuted; and drummer, Don Brewer, who is loud.

The Grandest Flunkout of them all is producer-manager, Terry Knight, whose figment of imagination the group is, who dictates their music and choreographs their every pelvic thrust at the audience.

Knight, a former top disk jockey but a failure as a rock musician, claims that the successful appeal of his group is in its identification with the audience, its open membership in a four letter word, revolutionary youth culture. Grand Funk, he says, is a politics that supersedes music.

Certainly, everything Grand Funk does is aimed at heightening a social experience—every hard rocking, loudspeaker crushing note, every swish of Farner's long locks, every hotfooted leap by Schacher, every stick snapping smash by Brewer is a carefully programmed event.

The result is a music and a show that appears spontaneous, that sounds raw, uncultured, sophomoric—high school sophomore level—and has an illusion of vitality and sexuality. Admittedly, after five albums and playing to live audiences almost every night (Grand Funk is perhaps the only group that charges $5 to $10 a seat to what should be billed as the world's longest running rehearsal), they are getting better. Farner's voice, for example, is really not a painful experience.

And, if it weren't for the Funk's overwhelming success, they might be a group that would warrant a critical "keep trying, you're getting better." But they are No. 1 with a kiddy car act and don't need to try harder.

What galls critics is not the group's mediocre music or political pretensions, but the fact that they have laid bare the weakness at the heart of the rock culture: The youth audience has no better taste than its beer bellied, boob tube addicted parents.

Grand Funk proves that a conscious, deliberate appeal to the lowest common public denominator is the most certain path to success for rock groups just as it is for top rated television series and winning presidential contenders.

The love generation is alas, no wiser than any other.

With permission of the writer, Pierre-Rene Noth, and the Milwaukee Journal. *From the October 10, 1971 issue of the* Milwaukee Journal.

Description

A third form of explanation, description, has been previously treated in Chapter 3. It makes use of the sensory appeals to give the reader or listener a clear picture of what is being communicated. The job of the writer or speaker who uses description as a form of support is to decide what to include and what to omit. Too much detail may bore your audience; too little may not communicate the picture you want conveyed.

The following excerpt from a TV speech delivered by President John F. Kennedy on October 22, 1962, makes use of each of the five supporting devices. The purpose of the speech was to persuade the audience that the steps the President was taking in regard to Cuba were prompted by sound reasoning and were consistent with this nation's principles. President Kennedy explained the situation to his audience, read the Soviet response to two separate protestations, reminded the audience of the lesson we learned from Hitler, indicated the steps to be taken, and dismissed the unacceptable alternative: submission.

1. *Explanation.* The President quickly moves to the business at hand. He explains that our promised surveillance of Cuba has revealed missile sites. These are *defined* as offensive missiles and *analysis* reveals that they provide a nuclear stroke capability.

1. This government as promised has maintained the closest surveillance of the Soviet military build-up on the island of Cuba. Within the past week unmistakable evidence has established the fact that a series of offensive missile sites is now in preparation on that imprisoned island. The purpose of these bases can be none other than to provide a nuclear strike capability against the Western Hemisphere.

2. *Explanation / Examples / Statistics.* The number and range of the missiles is indicated (statistics). The *description* is made

2. The characteristics of these new missile sites indicate two distinct types of installations. Several of them include medium-

more graphic by the use of familiar cities as *examples* of targets within the missiles' range.

range ballistic missiles capable of carrying a nuclear warhead for a distance of more than 1,000 nautical miles. Each of these missiles, in short, is capable of striking Washington, D.C., the Panama Canal, Cape Canaveral, Mexico City, or any other city in the southeastern part of the United States, in Central America, or in the Caribbean area.

3. *Explanation.* The President uses all three forms of explanation. He *defines* the uncompleted sites as intermediate-range ballistic missiles. He *describes* their strike capability, and he *analyzes* their presence as constituting an explicit threat to all the Americas.

3.   Additional sites not yet completed appear to be designed for intermediate-range ballistic missiles capable of traveling more than twice as far, and thus capable of striking most of the major cities in the Western Hemisphere. This urgent transformation of Cuba into an important strategic base by the presence of these large long-range and clearly offensive weapons of sudden mass destruction constitutes an explicit threat to the peace and security of all the Americas.

4. *Testimony.* President Kennedy's use of direct quotations enables the audience to hear *exactly* what the Soviet government said about the missile sites. Note that the quote carries an implicit threat of Soviet rocket potential.

4.   The Soviet Government, publicly stated on September 11, that, and I quote, the armaments and military equipment sent to Cuba are designed exclusively for defense purposes, unquote, that there is—and I quote the Soviet Government—there is no need for the Soviet Government to shift its weapons for a retaliatory blow to any other country, for instance, Cuba, unquote, and that—and I quote, the Government—the Soviet Union has so powerful rockets to carry these

nuclear warheads that there is no need to search for sites for them beyond the boundaries of the Soviet Union, unquote.

That statement was false.

5. *Testimony.* The President includes this second quote for the benefit of those who might reason that what a government says publicly and what it says privately are two different things. He quotes the Soviet Foreign Minister at some length to supply additional background information to his audience.

5. Only last Thursday, as evidence of this rapid offensive build-up was already in my hands, Soviet Foreign Minister Gromyko told me in my office that he was instructed to make it clear once again, as he said his Government had already done, that Soviet assistance to Cuba, and I quote, pursued solely the purpose of contributing to the defense capabilities of Cuba, unquote. That, and I quote him, "training by Soviet specialists of Cuban nationals in handling defensive armaments was by no means offensive," and that if it were otherwise, Mr. Gromyko went on, "the Soviet Government would never become involved in rendering such assistance."

That statement also was false.

6. *Comparison.* The comparison is drawn between this situation and Hitler's conquest of small countries in the thirties.

6. The nineteen thirties taught us a clear lesson. Aggressive conduct, if allowed to go unchecked and unchallenged, ultimately leads to war.

7. *Explanation.* President Kennedy defines our objectives in terms of our commitments.

7. This nation is opposed to war. We are also true to our word. Our unswerving objective, therefore, must be to prevent the use of these missiles against this or any other country; and to secure their withdrawal or elimination from the Western Hemisphere.

8. *Explanation.* After indicating his authority, the President combines description and analysis to explain the steps he will take to insure the withdrawal of the missile sites.

8. Acting, therefore, in the defense of our own security and of the entire Western Hemisphere and under the authority entrusted to me by the Constitution as endorsed by the resolution of the Congress, I have directed that the following initial steps be taken immediately: To halt this offensive build-up, a strict quarantine on all offensive military equipment under shipment to Cuba is being initiated. All ships of any kind bound for Cuba from whatever nation or port will, where they are found to contain cargoes of offensive weapons, be turned back. This quarantine will be extended if needed to other types of cargo and carriers.

9. *Psychological Proof.* The missiles are labeled as a clandestine, reckless, and provocative threat to *world* peace. Further, the missiles pose a direct threat to the *freedom* of every American. To back down on demanding a halt to this missile build-up would be like *surrendering*, which Americans never do.

9. I call upon Chairman Krushchev to halt and eliminate this clandestine, reckless, and provocative threat to world peace. Let no one doubt that this is a difficult and dangerous effort on which we have set out. No one can foresee precisely what course it will take, or what course or casualties will be incurred. The cost of freedom is always high, but Americans have always paid it. And one path we shall never choose, and that is the path of surrender, or submission.

Vital Speeches, XXIX:3 (November 15, 1962), p. 66.

EXERCISES

I. Below is an excerpt from a speech by Art Linkletter, delivered at the United Nations, September 14, 1971. Identify examples of all supporting devices discussed in this chapter.

1. Until two years ago my life was occupied principally in television and radio in the United States. My specialty was having fun with people. In fact, my best known NBC show for twenty years was called "People are Funny." My ability to talk with young children was featured on the CBS network five times a week, for twenty-five years.

2. My professional life as an entertainer kept me on the sunny side of the street, with happy detours to every part of the world visiting my "adopted" children. Over the last thirty years, Mrs. Linkletter and I, acting as "foster parents," have taken care of underprivileged and orphan children in France, Italy, Germany, Greece, China, Japan, the Philippines, Vietnam, and Peru. Our own five children learned to love their overseas brothers and sisters through visits, letters, and the exchange of presents.

3. Then, part of my life died in October 1969, when our beautiful daughter, Diane, was lost in the aftermath of LSD use. She would have been 21 years old that month. She was a victim of the reckless urge to experiment with hallucinogenic chemicals that became the fashionable thing to do among the young people of the world in the mid sixties. In Hollywood this insane desire to take pills, marijuana, and LSD swept through the film colony and many, many beautiful young sons and daughters of my friends have been ruined because of their teen-age yearning to be "part of the crowd."

4. That is why I am here today.

5. I am here to tell you something of what I have learned during these past two years.

6. Most of my generation had fixed ideas about drug addicts and dope that have been radically altered through research and knowledge based on fact—not myth. Until recently, we thought that marijuana was addictive and invariably led to narcotics. We thought all "pushers" were evil criminals sent to school yards to entice small children into becoming dope addicts. We thought that people who took any drugs for excitement and fun, or to forget their problems, were criminals and should be put in jail.

7. Today, we have learned that excessive users of psychotropic or narcotic drugs are sick people and only incidentally criminals. We have learned that pushers are often our own children searching for status or thrills or extra money. We have found out that you cannot stop drug abuse by making stricter laws, bigger jails, or by hiring more policemen. We have learned that drug abuse is a complex, perplexing subject that can never be simply, miraculously solved by some new drug or by some push-button method. And we have learned that it is not a passing fad that will go away with acid rock music or mod clothes. Drug abuse is on the doorstep of the world to stay. It is no new problem.

8. The late English writer Aldous Huxley, who knew whereof he spoke, wrote:

9. "In the course of history many more people have died for their drink and their dope than have died for their religion or their country. The craving for alcohol and the opiates has been stronger, in these millions, than the love of God, of home, of children, even of life. Their cry was not for liberty or death: It was for death preceded by enslavement."

10. Nations, in all parts of the world, continue to face serious problems related to drug abuse.

11. In England and Scotland, doctors have cut back on amphetamine prescriptions in reaction to what the British Medical Journal calls a "world epidemic of abuse."

12. In Hungary, with the highest suicide rate in the world, the drug alcohol has become a factor in twice as many suicides as 30 years ago.
13. Mexican authorities report that 10 tons of marijuana are used each week and that 15 percent of high school students use drugs.
14. In Hong Kong, one person in 50 is an opium user, and a habit there costs about $470 a year to support.
15. Figures are startling, and they point up the intensity of the problem. But the statistics themselves are really not important. What matters is that drug abuse respects no boundaries, obeys no political limits, holds firm to no territory.
16. Indeed, drug abuse respects no traditions. People everywhere are different, of course, and their lives run in different streams, but the human current throughout the world is now stained by some form of drug abuse. In America, the addict population has changed from what it was in the early 20th century, and now an emerging pattern of multiple drug use further complicates addiction.
17. Drug abuse is as complex and contradictory as it is damaging. It has been easy in the past to pose a simple cause-effect-solution syndrome. For example, we say, "The person took drugs. The person met with tragedy. Eliminate the drugs, and you have eliminated the possibility of tragedy."
18. I can report to you from my own tragic experience that such a simplistic model is invalid. There are too many factors at work, too much uncertainty about human behavior and human interaction to dismiss the drug abuse problem by talking only about the drugs.
19. The phenomenon of drug abuse touches our hearts, our minds, our courage, and our imagination. A simple answer simply will not do.

Vital Speeches, XXXVIII:1 (October 15, 1971, 22.

II. Choose one of the following statements and support it with a short example of each of the supporting devices:

"Wear a seat belt. The life you save may be your own."

"The U.S. should have a standard voting age of 18."

"Give yourself a break and quit smoking."

MODEL

The U.S. should adopt a system of national health insurance.

Comparison. **According to the U.S. Department of Health and Welfare, the cost of medical insurance in the U.S. has risen 165 per cent since 1960.**

Example. **Fred Feldman's wife entered the hospital in January and died six months later. The next day Fred was given a bill for $27,000.**

Statistics. **According to a 1970 survey by the U.S. Department of Health and Welfare, the average American pays over $1,000 per year in medical bills.**

Testimony. **The U.S. Surgeon General warns that unless something is done to halt the spiraling cost of health care, only the rich will be able to afford it.**

Ever wonder who buys them?

We did, too.

So we did some checking, and surprise! There were very few surprises.

People with 2.8 children

It came as no shock to find that an overwhelming number of people bought VW Station Wagons because they wanted a wagon that carried a lot and that was cheap to run.

But it was a surprise to learn that people really aren't taking advantage of the VW Station Wagon's enormous size.

The VW holds about 2/3 more than regular wagons: almost a ton. (The VW can hold up to 7 kids with no trouble at all.)

Yet the average family that buys one has only 2.8 children. (Maybe they all have big plans and aren't talking.)

Sometimes, all the extra space turns into a problem. "Once in a while I have to borrow somebody else's wagon," a man complained. "Because everybody else keeps borrowing my VW."

35% of the VW owners have no other car, so the VW Station Wagon gets used for all their driving.

The other 62% own more than one car, but 94% use the VW for most of their driving anyway.

"It's more fun," is the usual reason.

We were fascinated to find that some people (9%) own a great big conventional station wagon in addition to the VW. "I use the big one when I don't have too much to carry," a lady muttered.

There is also an astonishing number (17%) who drive both a Volkswagen Station Wagon and a Volkswagen Sedan.

"Why?" we asked.

"Why not?" we were answered.

65% are 2 or more car people

35% are 1 car people

The average income of our owners is a little over $300 a week.

But we get all kinds. About 1% of the owners earn less than $3,000 a year. And another 2% earn over $50,000.

So the VW is very democratic. The rich man saves as much money on gas, oil, tires and antifreeze as the poor man.

Volkswagen Station Wagon owners are pretty well educated: 6 out of 10 went to college and 4 out of 10 were graduated. (Which doesn't prove much, except that you don't have to be absolutely crazy to buy one.)

6 out of 10 are college people

We seem to have a high number of doctors, lawyers, teachers, foremen, etc. And they seem to be quite young: 34% of the owners are under 35.

Something that pleased us is that 79% bought the VW Station Wagon because we have a reputation for making a good product. (40%, in fact, didn't even consider buying anything else.)

On the other hand, it displeased us that not even 1% bought it because they thought it had good traction in mud and snow. (Evidently, nobody pays much attention to what we say in our ads.)

All in all, we were happy to learn that VW Station Wagon owners are such nice, sober, industrious citizens.

They think of their wagons (and themselves) as something special.

And they keep them for a long time because they hold up and stay in style. (A VW Station Wagon always looks exactly as preposterous as the day you drove it home.)

100% of the people who own Volkswagen Station Wagons couldn't care less.

Explanation. **If we had compulsory national health insurance, we could control doctor's fees and standardize practices for more efficient service.**

III. Shown is an ad that combines explanation and statistics to sell its product. Analyze this use of supporting material. Are the statistics documented? Who compiled them? Are they accurate? Should they be?

IV. Find an ad similar to the one shown and discuss the use of supports.

V. Indicate someone that most of your classmates would respect as an expert in each of the following fields: education, pollution control, space exploration, crime prevention, medicine, professional football, and politics.

VI. Find an example of effectively used statistics in a fairly current newspaper. Indicate why you think the statistics are effective.

7

effective sentence structure

SENTENCE VARIETY

The big league pitcher who threw nothing but fast balls would probably be batted out of the box in short order. A pitcher wants to keep the batter guessing, so he varies the pattern, throwing first a fast ball, then a curve, then a change of pace. The successful quarterback will, on occasion, throw the "bomb" when percentage dictates a power play into the center of the line. He, too, varies the pattern.

Sentence variety comes easily to the gifted writer. For those still striving to attain fluency, an understanding of different sentence classifications, both grammatical and rhetorical, will help to overcome the most common stylistic flaw in student writing—monotonous sentence structure.

GRAMMATICAL CLASSIFICATION

A clause is a word group containing both a subject and a predicate. A main clause makes sense when it stands alone. A subordinate clause is dependent upon, or subordinate to, a main clause. Sentence movement is largely determined by the relationship of clauses within a sentence or between sentences. An understanding of these relationships will enable you to recognize four basic sentence types: *Simple, compound, complex,* and *compound-complex.*

The *simple sentence* consists of one independent clause.

1. John went to a rock festival. (one subject, one verb)
2. John and Mike went to a rock festival. (compound subject, one verb)
3. John and Mike went to a rock festival and met some cute swingers. (compound subject, compound verb)

All three examples above are simple sentences. Don't be confused by compound subjects and compound verbs. If the sentence contains only one main clause, it is a simple sentence.

The *compound sentence* consists of two or more independent (or coordinate) clauses. In order for a compound sentence to be effective, the ideas expressed in the main clauses must be of equal rank.

1. The doorbell rang, and John answered it. The doorbell rang; John answered it. (two independent clauses, separated by a conjunction or semicolon)
2. "The hum of talk came to him dimly, his rage blood pounded in his ears, and he burst through and strode away." (John Steinbeck, *The Pearl*) (three independent clauses, separated by commas and a conjunction)

Do not use compound sentences to express ideas of unequal importance.

Ineffective: John is a technical engineering student, and he has won a full-tuition scholarship.

Improved: John, a technical engineering student, has won a full-tuition scholarship. (*Note*: This is a simple sentence because it contains one independent clause.)

The *complex sentence* consists of one main clause and one or more subordinate clauses. Because it enables us to combine ideas of unequal rank in the same sentence by subordinating one idea to another, it is the sign of a sophisticated writer.

1. My brakes are defective.
2. I don't have any money to replace them.
3. I won't be able to drive home between semesters.

We could coordinate these three independent clauses in a single compound sentence, but that would only result in three parallel strands with nothing emphasized. The best solution would be to subordinate the first two clauses to the last in a complex sentence.

Because my brakes are defective and I don't have the money to replace them, I won't be able to drive home between semesters.

The *compound-complex* sentence combines the principles of coordination and subordination; consequently, it consists of two or more independent clauses and one or more subordinate clauses. Used too frequently, the compound-complex sentence can result in a cumbersome style, but, on occasion, it is an effective means of connecting interrelated ideas.

1. Get dressed and have your breakfast while we load the gear.
   (two independent clauses)   (one subordinate clause)
2. When we went on our picnic, I left my camera in the car and Mike went back to get it.
   (subordinate clause)   (two independent clauses)

EXERCISES

DIRECTIONS: *Indicate whether the following sentences are: (1) simple, (2) compound, (3) complex, or (4) compound-complex. Be prepared to explain your answers in class discussion.*

1. When he smashed up his car, his wife became angry and the company cancelled his insurance.
2. Janet closed her eyes and rested her head on his shoulder.
3. George said he would return with the tickets, but I haven't seen him since noon.
4. My repeated attempts to talk him out of dropping English have fallen on deaf ears; nevertheless, I shall try again.
5. When the bell rings, leave quickly.
6. George Hays, the tallest player in the Conference, was dropped from the basketball team because of poor grades.
7. Before you report for your job interview, have your hair cut short and borrow your roommate's suit.
8. Jim's car, for which we couldn't obtain parts, had to be junked.
9. Before being wheeled into the operating room, the patient was given an anesthetic.
10. Being the only male in a class of nursing students must have its disadvantages, but I can't think of any.

Frequent use of complex sentences and an occasional compound-complex sentence can effectively link ideas of unequal importance. Our discussion of rhetorical classification will provide other equally effective techniques for achieving sentence variety. But before we proceed to this discussion, it would be well to pause and reflect upon the most basic type of sentence error: the inability to distinguish among complete sentences, run-on sentences, and sentence fragments.

Think back to your writing experiences in high school. Have your teachers ever commented on your inability to distinguish between a sentence and a nonsentence? Do you recall such symbols as *frag.* (sentence fragment) and *R.O.* (run-on sentence) in the margins of your compositions? If so, you may have a writing problem serious enough to affect adversely your chances for college and vocational success. Now is the time to resolve to correct that problem. Unless you plan to obtain remedial instruction, this will probably be your last classroom opportunity to learn to write a correct English sentence.

The following diagnostic test will measure your ability to distinguish among correct sentences, sentence fragments, and run-on sentences. If you achieve a score of 17 or better (out of a possible 20), you may skip the discussion of sentence fragments and run-on sentences and continue on page 114, beginning with *Rhetorical Classification*.

If you score below 17, review the material immediately following the Diagnostic Test, and then take the Post Test on page 114. (The Diagnostic Test and the Post Test may be used interchangeably.)

FORM A: DIAGNOSTIC TEST

DIRECTIONS: For each of the following word groups, indicate C for correct sentence, R for run-on sentence, or F for sentence fragment.

1. When the moon comes over the mountain.
2. The moon comes over the mountain.
3. Don't worry, we will work it out somehow.
4. Hoping to hear from you soon.
5. Go!
6. Sam Jones, who is the oldest student in the class and the best swimmer in the school.
7. While running to the bus stop, I fell.
8. After buying her one ounce of fine French perfume and taking her to the best restaurant in town.
9. Then we arrived at our destination.
10. The books were neatly arranged, however, papers were scattered all over the floor.
11. Jogging for two miles before breakfast was his usual routine.
12. He quickly glanced to his right, then he sprinted for the finish line.
13. This car needs new brakes and new tires, nevertheless, it's a good buy for the money.
14. Working out on the parallel bars for three full hours each day.
15. My job, however, leaves much to be desired.
16. Leaving his place of employment promptly enabled him to avoid the rush hour traffic.
17. Wondering whether the cute blonde in his English class would meet him later on for a sandwich and a coke.
18. The interesting scenery, however, makes the drive to school relaxing.
19. I just can't feel sorry for him flunking out of school was his own fault.
20. Rereading the chapter increased his understanding.

The Sentence Fragment

The word fragment means a part broken off or detached. A sentence fragment is a part of a sentence, as in the following examples:

Sentence Error	Analysis
Martha did poorly in her history examination. Although she spent all of last week studying.	**Although both italicized examples contain subjects and verbs, they are incomplete. The words** although **and because introduce subordinate clauses which require main clauses to complete the context.**
Because my parents and kid sister are driving up to visit. **I won't be able to have dinner with you tonight.**	**Combining the subordinate clause with a related main clause produces a complex sentence:**
	Martha did poorly in her history examination, although she spent all of last week studying.
	Because my parents and kid sister are driving up to visit, I won't be able to have dinner with you tonight.

Sentence Error	Analysis
	Deleting the introductory word of the subordinate clause results in a simple sentence consisting of one main clause: She spent all of last week studying. My parents and kid sister are driving up to visit. Review: **Use the following subordinate clauses in complete sentences:** After we finished our dinner Even though summer jobs are very scarce
Controlling exhaust emissions of the internal combustion engine. **This is one way of combating air pollution.**	**Phrases, unlike clauses, are word groups which do not contain subjects and verbs; therefore, they are not complete sentences.** **A phrase can function as the subject of a complete sentence:** Controlling exhaust emissions of the internal combustion engine **is one way of combating air pollution.** Review: **Use the following phrases as subjects of complete sentences:** **Watching televised football in color** **Studying for final examinations at the end of a busy day** **To play chess well**
To prevent loss of fuel vapors.	**A phrase can modify a main clause:** To prevent loss of fuel vapors, **the gas tank should always be tightly capped.** Review: **Use the following phrases to modify main clauses:** **In order to decide which extracurricular activities to participate in** **Working as quickly as he could**
Hoping to hear from you soon. Giving my best **whenever I compete.**	**A phrase can be converted into a main clause by adding a subject and verb:** **I hope (am hoping) to hear from you soon.** **I give my best whenever I compete.** **A phrase can complete an idea:** **I enjoy** walking in the rain.
Walking in the rain.	**I am** walking in the rain.

Sentence Error	Analysis
Jimmy Smith, the overwhelming choice for all-conference center.	**We have a subject,** Jimmy Smith, **and a modifying phrase,** the overwhelming choice for all-conference center, **but a verb is lacking.** **If we add a verb, perhaps as part of a complete predicate, our sentence would be complete:** **Jimmy Smith, the overwhelming choice for all-conference center,** has received **an offer to play professional football.** Review: **Convert the following fragments into sentences:** **Deciding what to do next Saturday night** **Discussing yesterday's lecture with two of his classmates** **The new Student Union, a massive combination of steel and concrete** **Mr. Halloway, the best English teacher I ever had**

On occasion, you may find professional writers using fragments punctuated as complete sentences. Grammatical rules, like most other rules, have their exceptions. An accomplished writer will sometimes *knowingly* write a sentence fragment in order to achieve a particular stylistic effect. When a student *unknowingly* punctuates a fragment as a complete sentence, he tells his reader that he is unable to distinguish a sentence from a nonsentence.

It is generally a good idea to avoid fragments early in your college writing career. Once you have achieved a measure of linguistic sophistication, you may feel ready to deviate from some of the rules.

The Run-On Sentence

A run-on **sentence contains two or more complete sentences punctuated as a single sentence. The two types of run-on sentences discussed in this section are the** fused **sentence and the** comma-splice.

Sentence Error	Analysis
Wait here we will see whether Tom is in his office.	**Two sentences are said to be** fused **when appropriate punctuation is omitted. This type of run-on sentence may be corrected as follows:** **1. Place a period after the first sentence**

Sentence Error

Analysis

and begin the next with a capital letter.

Wait here. We will see whether Tom is in his office.

2. Use a semicolon instead of a period if the two clauses are closely related.

Wait here; we will see whether Tom is in his office.

3. Formulate a compound sentence by separating main clauses of similar or equal rank with a conjunction.

Wait here and we will see whether Tom is in his office.

4. Formulate a complex sentence by changing one of the main clauses into a subordinate clause.

If you wait here, we will see whether Tom is in his office.

I purchased my cassette recorder many years ago it still gives me trouble-free service.

Correct this run-on sentence by using each of the four methods identified above.

Wait here, we'll see whether Tom is in his office.

When a comma is used to separate two complete sentences, the result is a comma-splice, **another type of run-on sentence.**

I purchased my cassette recorder many years ago, it still gives me troublesome service.

The comma is not a terminal mark of punctuation; therefore, it cannot take the place of a period or semicolon. A comma, like a yellow traffic light, is a signal to pause and proceed with caution. Periods and semicolons are the "red lights" of punctuation; they are used to stop sentences from running into one another.

Let's have dinner at the Nantucket, they serve the best Kansas City strip steak in town.

In order to correct a comma-splice, follow the procedure previously indicated for the fused sentence. (If the two main clauses are not of similar or equal rank, do not use the third technique, involving connection with a conjunction.)

This semester I am taking a reduced program, therefore, I must take two additional courses in summer schoool in order to graduate.

These two comma-splice sentences illustrate a particularly troublesome type of run-on sentence. They can be corrected as follows:

My suitcases are already packed, however, I still have a few things to take care of before we leave.

Separate the two main clauses by placing a period after the first sentence and beginning the next with a capital letter.

Sentence Error	Analysis
	This semester I am taking a reduced program. Therefore, I must take two additional courses in summer school in order to graduate. (You correct the second example.)

Use a semicolon instead of a period to indicate a particularly close relationship between the main clauses.

This semester I am taking a reduced program; therefore, I must take two additional courses in summer school in order to graduate. (Again, you deal with the second example.)

The words therefore and however in the sentences above perform similar functions. Because they modify or qualify the first main clause and relate it to a second clause, they are called conjunctive adverbs. Some common conjunctive adverbs are:

therefore	besides	consequently
however	then	furthermore

I lost my notes, therefore, I cannot study for the examination.
I have enough money to last until pay-day, however, I cannot afford to spend any of it foolishly.
The game was dull, besides, the weather was terrible.

Correct these italicized comma-splice sentences by separating the main clauses with periods or semicolons.

Sometimes a comma-splice sentence containing a conjunctive adverb can be corrected by placing a conjunction before the conjunctive adverb:

First we plan to have dinner together, and then we will see a play.

Do not confuse the conjunctions and, but, and or with conjunctive adverbs:

Correct: The tree in our yard is huge, but it doesn't provide much shade.

Incorrect: The tree in our yard is huge, however, it doesn't provide much shade.

Correct: The tree in our yard is huge; however, it doesn't provide much shade.

Study the following:

Most rules, however, have their exceptions.

The train was four hours late. The team, therefore, forfeited the game. These sentences are correct since each contains but one main clause.

FORM B: POST TEST

DIRECTIONS: For each of the following word groups, indicate C *for correct sentence,* R *for run-on sentence, or* F *for sentence fragment.*

1. After inviting him to dinner two consecutive Sundays and buying him a watch for his birthday.
2. Walking to Bill's apartment in this blizzard is folly.
3. Then we were ready to leave.
4. Losing his balance unnerved him.
5. Your directions were impossible to follow, otherwise I would have been here hours ago.
6. The extra money, however, paid for his tuition.
7. Jim Gibbons, who is the best punter and the fastest runner on the squad.
8. Because you aren't permitted to operate this machine without permission.
9. You aren't permitted to operate this machine without permission.
10. Conscientiously taking his medication after each meal enabled him to keep the problem under control.
11. Leaving me in charge of the automotive shop for the next three days.
12. Leave!
13. Try again, I'm sure you will be able to master the procedure shortly.
14. He said he would clean up after he finished the job, however, the house was a mess when he left.
15. Wishing you were here with me.
16. He checked his instruments and adjusted his helmet then he waited for the race to begin.
17. My plans, however, are still subject to change.
18. I hear the movie is excellent, besides, the concert has been sold out for more than a week.
19. Attempting to revise his plans so that he could visit his friend before the end of the semester.
20. Skating around the rink for the first time in years, I was surprised at how well I did.

RHETORICAL CLASSIFICATION

We have seen how the use of subordinate clauses in complex and compound-complex sentences help add variety to our writing. Our discussion of rhetorical classification will provide other equally effective techniques for achieving sentence variety. Sentences may be classified rhetorically as *normal, periodic, parallel,* and *balanced.*

The Normal Sentence

The *normal sentence,* so called because it occurs more frequently than any other type, consists of variations of the following subject-verb patterns.

Subject-Verb (**S-V**) In this sentence pattern the verb is *intransitive*, meaning it does not require an object to complete the predicate.

1. The boy fell. (S-V)
2. The boy fell (down the stairs). (S-V-M)
3. Mary sang. (S-V)
4. Mary sang (beautifully). (S-V-M)

Modifying phrases or words do not change the basic sentence pattern.

Subject-Verb-Direct Object (**S-V-O**) In this pattern the verb is *transitive*, meaning that it requires an object to complete the predicate.

1. Bill hit a home run. (S-V-O)
2. Janet bought a sweater for her boyfriend. (S-V-O)

The modifying prepositional phrase, *for her boyfriend,* does not change the basic sentence pattern.

Subject-Verb-Indirect Object-Direct Object (**S-V-IO-DO**) Sometimes S-V-O sentences also contain indirect objects. When this is the case, the direct object follows the verb, but precedes the direct object.

1. Mom bought Dad a new suit.
    S   V   IO   DO
2. Janet bought her boyfriend a new sweater.
    S   V   IO   DO

Subject-Verb-Complement (**S-V-C**) In this pattern a linking verb connects the subject to the complement. A complement functions like a direct object, but it always follows a linking verb.

1. Janet is a dental assistant. (S-V-C)
2. Mary is beautiful.
3. Jim felt bad.

To be is the most common linking verb. Other verbs often used to connect subjects to complements are *to become, to feel, to taste, to touch, to smell, to sound, to grow, to appear, to seem, to remain,* and *to become.* If in doubt about whether the verb is linking, try to substitute a form of *to be* for the verb in question. If the meaning of the sentence remains essentially the same, the verb is linking.

1. The swimming pool became (was) rusty.
2. The hamburger tastes (is) great.

Two other commonly employed normal sentence patterns are the *expletive* and the *passive*. The *expletive sentence* begins with *there*, and the verb precedes the subject.

1. There *is* a *stranger* at the door.
          V   S
2. There *have been* no more *tickets* available for two weeks.
          V   S

The *passive sentence* is a variation of the S-V-O sentence in which the subjects and objects are interchanged.

1. Bill hit the ball.   (S-V-O)
2. The ball was hit by Bill.   (Passive)
3. Tom met Mary at the dance.   (S-V-O)
4. Mary was met at the dance by Tom.   (Passive)

Modifying phrases do not change the basic sentence pattern.

· EXERCISES

DIRECTIONS: Basic patterns may stand alone in simple sentences or be combined in compound, complex, and compound-complex sentences. Using the following abbreviations, identify each of the lightface patterns.
    S-V S-V-O S-V-IO-DO S-V-C E P

1. Players from both sides swarmed onto the field.
2. Some players get nervous before a game; others keep their cool.
3. There are twenty students in class, **and** all of them seem to be shouting at once.
4. The house had been sold by Mr. Potter, **but** the agent didn't know the selling price.
5. If you give him the ball, he will make the first down.
6. Ernest Hemingway's novels brought him international fame.
7. A sentence containing a subordinate clause and a main clause is complex.
8. There are many good motels in town, **but** the Elgin is the best.
9. When anyone asks Jim a question, he becomes hard of hearing.
10. Our cousins from New York arrived by plane this afternoon.

Effective sentence combinations illustrate variations of these basic sentence patterns. Three rhetorical devices—modification, coordination, and subordination—help us to expand these basic patterns.

Modification Two of the eight traditional parts of speech, adjectives and adverbs, function as modifying elements in the sentence. In addition, phrases and clauses also function as modifying elements. This principle has been illustrated in various examples of basic sentence patterns. Modification is an effective means of avoiding the choppy, monotonous sentence structure that makes for ineffective writing.

> *Weak*: Dick Person is the first baseman for the Oshkosh Outlaws. He hit a home run on August 3. It was the longest home run ever hit in People's Stadium.
>
> *Improved*: On August 3, Dick Person, the first baseman of the Oshkosh Outlaws, hit the longest home run ever hit in People's Stadium.
>
> *Weak*: I have a new dog. His name is Willy. He is very intelligent.
>
> *Improved*: My new dog, Willy, is very intelligent.

Coordination Just as we combine independent clauses in a compound sentence, we utilize this same principle by coordinating subjects, verbs, objects, complements, and modifiers in any sentence to achieve economy of expression.

> *Weak*: My new dog, Willy, is very intelligent. He is a beautiful animal.
>
> *Improved*: My new dog, Willy, is intelligent and beautiful.

Subordination As previously defined, subordination provides us with the means of linking ideas of unequal rank in the same sentence.

> *Weak*: My brother is home on vacation. He attends the Milwaukee Area Technical College.
>
> *Improved*: My brother, who is home on vacation, attends the Milwaukee Area Technical College. (Or, depending on which idea is emphasized: My brother, who attends the Milwaukee Area Technical College, is home on vacation.)
>
> *Weak*: My new dog, Willy, is intelligent and beautiful. He is not as good a watch dog as Rusty. Rusty is my friend's dog.
>
> *Improved*: Although my new dog, Willy, is intelligent and beautiful, he is not as good a watch dog as my friend's dog, Rusty.

EXERCISES

DIRECTIONS: Combine each of the following sets of sentences into one sentence by coordinating, subordinating, and modifying the various elements.

1. Our regular English teacher is Mr. Simpson. He is ill with the flu. Mr. Hughes is a substitute teacher of English. He has been temporarily hired to teach senior English until Mr. Simpson returns.
2. My older brother lives in New York. His name is Ken. He is an engineer with Arco Industries. Last year we flew to New York to see him. We traveled via Northwest Airlines, landing at Kennedy Airport. Ken enjoyed our visit very much.
3. My little brother went to the store. He forgot to chain his bike to the railing. His bike was stolen. He was afraid to tell my father.
4. It was raining very hard. My windshield wipers were defective. My vision was severely hampered. My car swerved into the guard railing. I received a severe whiplash and I also broke my arm.

The Periodic Sentence

A *periodic sentence* must contain the rhetorical effect of building to a climax through a series of words, phrases, or clauses. Although the main idea of a periodic sentence is always withheld until the end, not every sentence in which the main idea is withheld is periodic. This somewhat confusing distinction might best be explained by example.

Not Periodic: When you go to the store, bring back some beer. (Although the main clause is withheld, the rhetorical effect of building to a climax is not present.)

Periodic: If you like authentic rock music, a sandy beach, picturesque Southern architecture, and lovely girls, you will love Fort Lauderdale.

Periodic sentences must be well-planned and properly executed if they are to be effective. They should be used more sparingly than any other rhetorical device if they are to add variety, rather than monotony, to your writing. The Reverend Martin Luther King, Jr., concluded his memorable *I Have a Dream* speech with the following periodic sentence:

And when we allow freedom to ring, when we let it ring from every village and hamlet, from every state and city, we will be able to speed up that day when all of God's children—black men and white men, Jews and Gentiles, Catholics and Protestants—will be able to join hands and to sing in the words of the old Negro spiritual, "Free at last, free at last; thank God Almighty, we are free at last."

Douglas MacArthur's 1961 speech commemorating Philippine Independence Day provides the following example:

In the effort to build a world of economic growth and solidarity, in the effort to build an atmosphere of hope and freedom, in the effort to build a community of strength and unity of purpose, in the effort to build a lasting peace of justice, the Philippines and the United States of America have become indivisible.

Shakespeare proves that a periodic sentence need not be lengthy to be effective.

To die, to sleep; to sleep, perchance to dream;
Aye, there's the rub . . . .

The Parallel Sentence

A *parallel sentence* is one which emphasizes coordinate elements—single words, phrases, or clauses—usually in a series. Anytime a coordinating conjunction (and, or, but) appears in a sentence, an element of parallelism is present. But for the purpose of our definition, a rhetorical effect different from that of a normal sentence must be achieved.

. . . and that government *of the people, by the people, for the people,* shall not perish from the earth.

Abraham Lincoln

We hold these truths to be self-evident, *that all men are created equal, that they are endowed by their Creator with certain unalienable Rights, that among these are Life, Liberty and the pursuit of Happiness.*

Declaration of Independence

"*Duty,*" "*honor,*" "*country*"—those three hallowed words reverently dictate *what you want to be, what you can be, what you will be.*

Douglas MacArthur

Frequently, the effect of parallelism is achieved by intentional repetition of key words or word groups through a series of sentences or paragraphs. Emphasis by repetition can be effective, if it is not overdone.

Dreyfus is innocent. I swear it. I stake my life on it. I stake my honor. In the presence of this Court, the representative of human justice, before all France, before all the world, I now solemnly swear that *Dreyfus is innocent.* By forty years of work, by the authority it has given me, I swear that *Dreyfus is innocent.* By the name I have made, by my contributions to the literature of France, I swear that *Dreyfus is innocent.* May all the results of my life melt away, may my work perish, if Dreyfus is not innocent. *He is innocent!*

Emile Zola

The Balanced Sentence

A *balanced sentence* emphasizes contrasting coordinate elements, usually two main clauses. It is similar to the parallel sentence in that it emphasizes coordination, but with one important distinction: the key to the balanced sentence is contrast. The conjunction "but" frequently serves as the fulcrum of the two contrasting ideas.

> The world will little note, nor long remember, what we say here, *but* it can never forget what they did here.
>
> *Abraham Lincoln*

> The true test of civilization is
> not the census,
> nor the size of the cities,
> nor the crops,
> no,
> but *the kind of man the country turns out.*
>
> *Ralph Waldo Emerson*

> Survival is still an open question—not because of environmental hazards, *but* because of the workings of the human mind.
>
> *Adlai Stevenson*

Notice how the elements of *parallelism* and *balance* are combined in the following example:

> It is time that we see this doctrine of guilt by association for what it is: not a useful device for detecting subversion, *but* a device *for subverting our constitutional principles* and practices, *for destroying our constitutional guarantees,* and *for corrupting our faith in ourselves and our fellow man.*
>
> *Henry Steele Commager*

A simple but striking method of achieving sentence variety is to vary sentence length. The paragraph from Zola (p. 119) is an excellent example. The sentences vary from three to twenty-six words. The shorter sentences at the beginning and end of the paragraph ring with finality. The longer periodic sentences in the middle build up to the same spirited conclusion—"Dreyfus is innocent."

We have touched on but a few of the many ways in which a writer may vary his sentence structure and thereby improve his writing. Because the sentence is our basic unit of communication, we have analyzed it, both grammatically and rhetorically, in the belief that this knowledge will enable the student to develop his own fluent and distinctive style.

8

effective paragraphing

Short story writers and novelists utilize similar techniques in developing a narrative. Similarly, the planning and execution of paragraphs and longer compositions have much in common. For this reason, the paragraph has been referred to as a composition in miniature. Because of its brevity, the paragraph is an ideal subject for careful analysis. The techniques of careful paragraphing to be developed in this section apply to longer compositions as well.

PURPOSEFULNESS

The principles of purposeful communication have already been detailed. Once your primary purpose is clear to you and you have tentatively selected your subject, you are ready to tackle the job of proper restriction. The brevity of most paragraphs makes adequate restriction particularly important. A subject not properly restricted invariably results in superficial writing. Having arrived at an adequately restricted subject, you should then formulate the main idea of your paragraph. Generally, this main idea is specifically stated in the paragraph; at times, however, it may be implied. The main idea of a paragraph is called the *topic sentence*. Here are some sample topic sentences:

1. Paperback textbooks are inexpensive and convenient.
2. A good dictionary is the most useful of all general reference books.
3. The phenomenal success of the instant 126 cartridge camera is due to its simplicity of operation.

ORGANIZATION

Applying one of four basic patterns of organization (or variations of these patterns) to your writing will result in a well-organized paragraph unit. The four basic patterns are general to specific, specific to general, chronological, and spatial. The following examples of organization are all taken from student writings.

General to Specific   Effective communication involves adequate generalization—support development. When the topic sentence stating the generalization or main idea appears at the beginning of the paragraph and the supporting details follow the topic sentence, a general to specific organizational pattern is employed.

Of the four basic organizational patterns, the general to specific is by far the most popular. Why? If you begin with your topic sentence and remain conscious of your main idea as you develop and support it, it is almost impossible to stray from your purpose.

MAIN IDEA **SUPPORT- ING DETAILS**	Although at first glance a final exam appears to be nothing more than a series of sloppily mimeographed, vaguely worded questions, *it is really a conspiracy aimed at students everywhere.* It is a third degree with no safeguard against self-incrimination, a mismatch with no time out between rounds, a sentence to solitary confinement without bread or water, and a parachute jump without a parachute. While purporting to test a student's knowledge of subject matter, the final exam measures, instead, his ability to withstand the ill effects of poor ventilation and bad circulation in an overcrowded classroom. It forces the student to sit between a rhythmic sniffer and a compulsive cougher while he is serenaded from behind by a nervous throat-clearer and carefully watched by a sadistic proctor. Temporary relief is just around the corner, but the establishment figure in charge views with suspicion the student who attempts to relieve the tension through the only avenue open to him: a brief, but glorious visit to the John.

Specific to General   At times you might attempt to achieve a specific stylistic effect by beginning your paragraph with a series of details which lead up to your generalization. When the main idea or topic sentence is withheld until the end of the paragraph, a specific to general organizational pattern is utilized.

SUPPORT- ING DETAILS **MAIN IDEA**	Do you often take in a movie or watch television when you should be doing assigned reading? Do you enjoy having bull sessions with your friends into the early hours of the morning when you should be getting your rest? Would you rather tackle a ski slope on a winter afternoon than crack a novel assigned by your English instructor? Do you prefer a burger, fries, and a Coke to a well-balanced meal? Are you more interested in campus social life than you are in the pursuit of knowledge? Do you view a college degree as a passport to the good life? Have you puffed on an occasional joint and given some thought to the hard stuff? Are you frequently bored and occasionally stimulated by class lectures? If so, cheer up; *like thousands before you, you're college material.*

Chronological   When you employ a chronological pattern of development, you relate a series of incidents according to the order in which these events actually occurred. Narration and exposition are the two forms of discourse not frequently organized chronologically.

NARRA-
TION

Just before sunrise I awoke, quietly dressed, shook Mike, my son, and went outside to start the coffee. A few minutes later Mike came bounding out of the tent raring to go. We had decided the night before to get some fishing in before breakfast. After shoving off we maneuvered our raft into the deep water. Mike got a bite almost as soon as his bait struck water. Seconds later, the tip of my pole went down under the weight of a catch at the end of my line. When I reeled in the line and started to pry the hook from the walleye's mouth, Mike started to laugh. As I looked up I noticed that we had drifted back to shore. The gentle breeze had carried our anchorless raft halfway across the lake. Mike baited my hook, as I paddled back to the deep water.

Our morning was busily occupied by the activities of catching fish, rebaiting, and paddling back to the deep water. After this cycle had been repeated many times, I noticed my wife waving us in to shore. As we headed for land, Mike and I held up our stringers of fish and Mike proudly hollered, "This should make a delicious breakfast." "Breakfast," my wife exclaimed; "it's time for lunch!"

EXPOSI-
TION

The phenominal success of the instant loading 126 cartridge camera is largely due to its simplicity of operation. First swing the back open and insert the cartridge into the camera. Then close the camera and advance the lever clockwise, repeatedly, until it locks. You are now ready for your first exposure. Compose your picture carefully, using either a horizontal or vertical format, whichever better suits your subject. Then squeeze the shutter release, taking care not to jerk the camera. Continue to advance the lever, compose carefully, and avoid excessive camera movement for your remaining exposures. Provided your lighting is adequate, a series of pleasing snapshots will be your reward.

Spatial An organizational pattern is spatial when the progression of details is arranged according to some logical arrangement in space. Placing gravel, plants, and ornaments in your new aquarium, arranging an attractive floral display, and describing a place with which you are familiar are subjects that would lend themselves to this pattern of development.

MAIN
IDEA

Tucked away on the north east corner of our unpretentious second story flat, *my 10' x 12' room houses all my possessions, treasured and otherwise.* As I enter the room my maple bed, placed adjacent to the north wall, is immediately evident. My matching nightstand, to the left of my pillow, supports my clock radio, a recent birthday gift, and a hand-me-down lamp

SUPPORT-
ING
DETAILS with a battered pirate ship for its base. The remainder of the
west wall surrounds the only window in the room, my window
of the outside world. There I sometimes sit for hours watching
the early morning traffic entering the city or the late afternoon
traffic returning to suburbia, thinking thoughts, dreaming
dreams of life styles so very different from my own. Beneath
the window sits my desk, antiqued blue years ago by my father.
The cigarette burns and chipped corners are usually hidden
from view by the ever present textbooks and clutter of papers.
Opposite the window my mirror-topped dresser is placed in the
middle of the east wall, surrounded by the sports banners and
autographed pictures of my youth. My black wrought iron
bookcase, covering the two feet of wall space between the door
and the closet of the south wall, is crammed with the paper-
backs, magazines, and records that enable me to escape, if only
temporarily, my commonplace surroundings.

ADEQUATE DEVELOPMENT

Have your papers ever been returned with such comments as "support your
judgments" or "further development needed"? Failure to support and develop your ideas adequately is an all too common characteristic of student
writing. There are two main causes of inadequate development:

1. The writer *assumes* that his readers have knowledge about the subject that they do not, in fact, actually possess.
2. The writer *intends* to provide a more complete explanation than he
   does, but because of laziness or the inability to support his judgments, he fails to do so.

During the planning, execution, and proofreading of your writing, consider your readers and provide them with sufficient information to receive
your message. Whether you are relating an incident from personal experience or dealing with a subject you have researched, it is incumbent upon
you, as the expert, to supply sufficient details. If you must err, it is better
to provide too much detail rather than too little.

See Chapter 6 for a detailed treatment of the five major supporting devices: Examples, Statistics, Testimony, Comparison Contrast, and Explanation. It would also be desirable to review the late President Kennedy's
televised speech concerning the Cuban Crises for an analysis of how
these supporting devices are incorporated into a finished manuscript.
The preceding pages contain examples of student writing which illustrate
adequate generalization—support development.

Depending upon your approach to your subject, you might decide to use a combination of supporting devices or only one extended example. The quality of a communication cannot be judged by the number of supports used. One well-developed example of a heavy smoker who developed lung cancer because of his habit might be far more effective than a series of statistics and explanations.

Paragraph Models (A)

It is 6 a.m. of a winter Sunday in Putney, a crossroads town in southern Vermont. There is a foot of new snow, but lights go on in the houses as families arise and start to pack picnic lunches. Minutes later the lights go off, doors open and laughter fills the crimson dawn. Toddlers, kids and adults snap onto narrow touring skis and, bodies bent and arms swinging, glide off through the fields. As the sun rises and twinkles on icy peaks, more people join the parade. Children call to each other as they disappear into the silent forest, their voices muted by the powdery snow.

Excerpt from "The Magic of Ski Touring," by Jean George, The Reader's Digest, February 1972. Copyright 1972 by the Reader's Digest Assn., Inc.

ANALYSIS

1. Which organizational pattern is employed?
2. Locate a simple sentence, a compound sentence, and a complex sentence.
3. Locate a parallel sentence.
4. Show how two of the sentences in the paragraph illustrate the principle of modification.
5. Is the paragraph effective? Explain your answer.

EXERCISE: Describe a seasonal scene, organizing your answer chronologically.

Model (B)

Frequently, some belligerent, anti-law enforcement elements of our society refer to police officers as "pigs." Obnoxious four-letter words are shouted at policemen, and the familiar chant, "Off the Pigs," meaning "Kill the Police," is a prominent cry wherever these groups assemble. Further, cartoons and publications depicting police officers as pigs are common fare, even for children. The ridiculous statement, "The only good pig is a dead pig," is a slogan of violent protesters. Such deplorable epithets can be gratifying only to little minds.

By J. Edgar Hoover. Reprinted with permission of the FBI Law Enforcement Bulletin.

ANALYSIS

1. Identify the topic sentence and the organizational pattern.
2. Hoover describes policemen as "officers," a term having a favorable connotation, while bemoaning the fact that certain elements in society refer to them as

"pigs." Complete the following table, supplying favorable and unfavorable terms for the neutral words given:

Favorable	Neutral	Unfavorable
Officer	Policeman	Pig
_____	Teacher	_____
_____	Lawyer	_____
_____	Housewife	_____
_____	Student militant	_____
_____	Salesman	_____
_____	Politician	_____

3. How do connotative words reveal the attitudes and values of the communicator?

EXERCISE: Write a paragraph giving your point of view about a word having a strong connotation, either favorable or unfavorable. Use either a general to specific or specific to general organizational pattern.

Model (C)

Fashions in what society considers proper fluctuate wildly. A number of words Chaucer used in the *The Canterbury Tales*, one of the great masterpieces of the language, couldn't possibly be printed today in a book like this one, and though they have only very recently again been permissible in contemporary fiction, they have also helped set off controversy about the "degeneracy" of the modern novel. In contrast, our Victorian forbears were "proper" in public to a degree that seems fantastic to us today. "Legs" were unmentionable, for instance. The decent word for them, especially on ladies, was "limbs," but it was no doubt preferable not to have to mention them at all. It was during this era that the "breast" of chicken became "white meat," to avoid any unpleasant suggestivity in mixed company. At about the turn of the century Owen Wister wrote a story entitled "Skip to My Loo," set in Texas, in which much is made of the disapprobation of the local people for names like "boar," "stallion," "rooster," and "bull," euphemisms being employed in their stead. I myself have heard an old timer refer to a bull as a "he cow." (Incidentally, dancing was frowned on as quite sinful by the people in this story, though they enjoyed a game set to music, remarkably like dancing, which was called Skip to My Loo, and hence the name of the story.) I remember that during my boyhood something of this attitude lingered on in the more primitive backwaters of the West, where I was raised, and I was punished once for using the word "belly" and again for calling my younger brother a "liar." In this latter instance it wasn't my attitude toward my brother that was considered wrong—calling him a "story teller" would have been all right—but the coarse, bald, ugly word "liar" itself.

Ray Past, Language as a Lively Art (Dubuque: Wm. C. Brown Co., 1970), p. 274.

ANALYSIS

1. Identify the topic sentence and the organizational pattern.
2. Identify and illustrate the methods of support.
3. Explain the "controversy about the 'degeneracy' of the modern novel" referred to in the paragraph. Does this controversy extend into other art forms?
4. What is a euphemism? Give at least three examples not found in the paragraph.
5. How does the author's point about euphemisms relate to the preceding Hoover paragraph?
6. Give three examples (other than those mentioned in the paragraph) of words that have graduated to positions of respectability.

EXERCISE: In a paragraph relate an experience, preferably personal, involving the changing nature of the English language. Employ whatever organizational pattern you deem appropriate.

Model

Contrary to the widespread notion that people go through a divorce with a minimum of psychic disturbance, divorce is generally an emotionally, psychologically, and socially traumatic experience, which leaves its marks and scars on the personalities involved. To begin with, many individuals experience a sense of personal rejection, which is painful. Even when there is mutual agreement that the divorce is necessary, each may feel that he was not wanted or desired by the other. Furthermore, there may be a profound feeling of having failed in a personal sense. It is as though the couple "should have made it work" in spite of any obstacles in their path. The extent to which one is disturbed by a divorce is frequently increased when one member of the former marriage decides to remarry. For the remaining individual the remarriage of his former spouse may prove to be rather traumatic. This is particularly so when one member of the relationship continued to hope, as many do, that somehow even after the divorce "they would get back together." Sometimes these people become martyrs, waiting for the mate to return. In other instances they may desperately plunge into a new relationship prematurely in order to prove that they are still lovable and desirable.

Herman R. Lantz and Eloise C. Snyder, Marriage: An Examination of the Man-Woman Relationship *(New York: John Wiley & Sons, Inc., 1962), p. 410.*

ANALYSIS

1. Identify the topic sentence and the organizational pattern.
2. Identify the principle method of support. Are any other supporting devices employed?
3. Do you agree that a "widespread notion that people go through divorce with a minimum of physic disturbance" really exists? Discuss.
4. Define in context: physic, traumatic, martyr.
5. Discuss the effectiveness of the foregoing paragraph.

EXERCISE: Take issue with a commonly held belief, employing a general to specific organizational pattern.

Model

In a troubled corner of the country, something vaguely subterranean is welling up. It seems, at once, an apprehension of the final catastrophe or the huge breathing of a vast organism, or perhaps the anonymous mobility of some mute ghost that yearns to make itself known. The American South—a land of labored fables, shared glories, soil, blood, brassy vanity and souls spun tight together in patterns of tradition—remains an intricate, fugal overlay of clashing passions: Gentility and violence, humanism and hatreds, beliefs and brutalities, obscurities, incongruities, cadenzas of humor, Sweet Jesus and unknowable madness. Add to this an infinitude of traumas and small transformations, multiply by 38 million whites, 11 million blacks plus every possible variable of the past, the present, the climate and the terrain, and you extract today a place where nothing whatever is the same. Yet you draw from this, too, a people who in being forced to find pragmatic new realities of their own, may well forge prophetic insights into the very root of all human hearts.

With permission of Cowles Communications, Inc.

ANALYSIS

1. Which sentence best expresses the main idea of the paragraph?
2. As what part of speech is *welling* used in the first sentence? The word *well* is an excellent example of *functional shift*, meaning that a word shifts its function or part of speech in different contexts. With the help of your dictionary, indicate how *well* can be used as five different parts of speech. Then illustrate each use in a separate sentence.
3. Define in context: subterranean, mute, fugal, humanism, incongruity, cadenza, pragmatic, prophetic.
4. Identify and illustrate the methods of support.
5. State the purpose of the paragraph.

DIRECTIONS:

I. In a paragraph, give your impression of a place with which you are thoroughly familiar: a neighborhood, a favorite hangout, a vacation retreat, a school, a place of employment. As in the foregoing example, provide your readers with insights into the people who occupy the place you describe.

II. Supply a caption for each of the following photographs. Then, using one of the captions as your subject, write a paragraph or a longer essay, as your instructor directs.

Used with permission of the photographer, Elliot Schnackenberg.

Used with permission of the photographer, Elliot Schnackenberg.

Used with permission of the photographer, Arnold Gore.

Used with permission of the photographer, Samuel Gansheroff.

9

speech
evaluation

If you are like most students, you probably face the thought of getting up to deliver a speech in front of a group of classmates with some apprehension. Perhaps you are not entirely clear as to how to develop an effective speech. You might be concerned with whether what you want to say will be interesting to your audience. You could be afraid that you will forget part of your speech, or say the wrong thing, or say it badly. You might even feel, "Why should I learn how to deliver a formal platform speech? I'll probably never have occasion to deliver one."

Although you may be called upon to make a formal public speech only a few times in your entire lifetime, the same skills are indispensable to effective face-to-face communication. People generally tend to equate ability to speak well with ability to think well. Therefore, the impression you make on others, even your own circle of friends, depends upon your ability to express yourself clearly and effectively in an easy, natural way.

Although there is no single formula that must be followed to be effective as a public speaker, two broad guidelines can help insure success: (1) say something worthwhile, and (2) say it in an easy, natural way.

SAY SOMETHING WORTHWHILE

When you prepare a speech, you are concerned with two things: what you want to say, and how you want to say it. What you say is called the *content* of the speech, which includes the subject, the way you organize your material, the types of attention factors you choose, and your word choice. While you should choose a subject from your own area of interest so that you know what you are talking about and have some enthusiasm for it, you must do so with your audience in mind. An audience will find your speech worthwhile if it is either interesting or useful to them. If the subject you choose has little to offer your audience in terms of usefulness and is not interesting of itself, your job is to make it interesting by handling your material in an imaginative and attention-getting way. It should be noted that although you are often free to choose any subject for a speech, the less interesting or useful the subject, the more difficult it will be to make the speech interesting. For example, unless you were in a class of music students, a speech on classical opera would require more imagination and effort than a speech on sky diving. The latter means daring, danger, thrills, and excitement to many; while opera might evoke similar responses in a few, it does not have nearly as broad an appeal.

Similarly, your classmates would be more inclined to see the usefulness of a speech on how to take a better snapshot than one on how to tune a guitar. Almost everyone takes snapshots, and most of us do not do so as effectively as we might. Consequently, a speech on how to improve this ability would be useful. On the other hand, probably the only person who would see the value of learning to tune a guitar would be someone who has just started learning how to play one. Anyone who knows how to play a guitar knows how to tune one, and the person who neither plays the guitar nor has a strong interest in learning to play couldn't care less.

SAY IT IN AN EASY WAY

The way in which you say something is called *delivery*. Delivery includes such things as platform manner, voice, eye contact, and facial expression. Effective delivery should seem easy and natural. Other than an increase in volume for a larger audience, the *principal difference* between platform speaking and ordinary conversation should be in content. Since a platform speech is more carefully prepared than everyday conversation, your subject will, no doubt, be handled more imaginatively and your words chosen more carefully. Be sure to avoid using language with which you are unfamiliar. Use your own vocabulary, but eliminate words which might be inappropriate to the occasion.

An advantage to using your conversational style of delivery in front of an audience is that you will feel comfortable with it. If you try to change your way of speaking, your style will seem stilted and unnatural. The key to effective delivery is to be yourself, as natural as possible. At first this might seem difficult—how do you get up in front of your classmates, many of whom you haven't met before, and be yourself? You will probably meet most of your fellow students during the semester on an individual basis anyway. Meeting others casually involves spontaneous, unplanned conversation. By delivering a carefully thought-out speech that deals with your own area of interests, you show your classmates your best side. When listening to them, you get to know something about their interests. Both of you have, in effect, put your best foot forward, which should result in a clearer understanding of each other.

Presented below are a number of characteristics of both content and delivery that your audience will consider in evaluating your speech. While it isn't necessary that you excel in every one of these areas, it is wise for the beginning speaker to try to do as well as he can in all of them.

PLATFORM MANNER

In a broad sense, platform manner can include all of the speaker's non-verbal communication—the way he walks up to and away from the platform, his facial expression, posture, gestures, and attire. The speaker who approaches his audience in a positive way says to his listener, "I have something to offer that I think you will find rewarding." An audience begins evaluating a speaker as soon as he comes into their line of vision. If you want to create the right impression, walk to the speaker's platform in a firm, energetic way. Good posture projects alertness and self-confidence. After you have reached the lectern, pause briefly and look out at those in your audience in a friendly, interested manner. If a smile is in order, by all means smile. The important thing is that your facial expression should be appropriate to your subject matter; it should set the mood for your speech.

It is usually a good idea to maintain good posture when addressing an audience. Speakers who slouch over the lectern or affect too casual a pose tend to receive an indifferent response.

There will be times when it will be necessary for you to move around in front of your audience, to walk to a chalkboard or map, to demonstrate a way of doing something, or simply to move closer to them to develop a more intimate mood. There is one simple rule to follow when you are in front of an audience. Anything you do, whether it is sitting on your desk or walking to the window, is acceptable as long as it does not call attention to itself. A movement is unacceptable when the audience thinks, "I wonder why he's doing that?"

Gesture is another characteristic of platform manner. In casual, relaxed conversation we habitually employ a wide range of gestures. We nod our heads, shrug our shoulders, wrinkle our brows, or wave our hands to emphasize what we have to say or to describe something.

If, when presenting your speeches, you find it difficult to use gestures successfully, wait until you feel the urge to use them. To be effective, gestures must come naturally and instinctively. A beginning speaker is often overly conscious of his audience. It is better to wait with your gestures until you are more relaxed in the speaking situation, since an awkward gesture is worse than no gesture at all.

The clothes worn by a speaker should suit the occasion. For a classroom speech, wear what you would normally wear to class; for a more formal occasion, dress accordingly. In both cases your clothes should be cleaned, pressed, and in good repair. Clothing which does not call attention to itself is always the best choice.

The conclusion of your speech should be carefully planned so that you can finish with your eyes fixed on the audience. After a brief pause, leave the speaker's platform with the same air of confidence with which you approached it. Don't indicate by your facial expression or gesture that you were at all dissatisfied with your performance. Let your audience evaluate you.

EYE CONTACT

Good eye contact is an aid in holding attention, and necessary for feedback from the audience. In general, your eye contact will be effective if you look slowly from one individual to another; if your eyes dart rapidly from person to person, the effect will be shifty or unnatural. Although it isn't necessary to look at each individual in your audience, be careful to include persons from all parts of the group. Do not develop the habit of looking mostly to one side of the room or at just those nearest you.

Eye contact is an aid to holding your audience's attention for a number of reasons. First, we indicate our interest in others by looking them in the eye. One of the most important things a speaker can do is to convince each listener that he is addressing him as an individual. An audience will tend to respond to a speaker who demonstrates that interest.

Second, eye contact is thought of as an indication of straightforwardness and honesty. We look people right in the eye when we are open and aboveboard, and avoid someone's eyes when we are saying something dishonest or embarrassing. Looking your audience right in the eye will convince them of your honesty and sincerity.

Third, we speak to our audience nonverbally as well as verbally. We say a great deal to them with our facial expression, especially the eyes. Facial expression can aid greatly in making meanings clear, giving emphasis, and expressing moods. Obviously, an audience will have difficulty seeing your facial expression if you are staring out the window or at your notes.

The final reason for establishing eye contact is to obtain feedback from the audience. We look at people while communicating to them because we are interested in their reaction to what we are saying. They indicate this through changes in facial expression, posture, and gestures. This feedback tells us how well we are communicating, whether our listeners are interested or bored, clear or confused, and friendly or hostile, thus giving us the opportunity to respond appropriately.

VOICE

The very least a listener can expect of a speaker is that he speak in a voice loud and clear enough to be heard and understood. It takes too much effort to listen to a speaker who mutters or speaks too softly. However, if you want to be an effective speaker, you must do more than the bare minimum. Your voice must be an asset to you; it must help to make what you say more interesting and meaningful. The different characteristics which express meaning and add variety to your voice are: volume, rate, articulation, quality, and pitch.

Volume

Volume refers to the loudness or softness of your voice. Obviously, you must increase your volume to be heard in a large room or in a situation with a high degree of surrounding noise. Don't be misled by the fact that you can hear yourself adequately. If it takes effort on the part of the listener to hear you, you are probably not communicating effectively.

Rate

Rate, the speed at which a person speaks, is dependent upon two elements —duration and pause. Duration is the length of time a word is prolonged. It is an effective way to emphasize, and is often used in conversation, particularly to accentuate modifiers, e.g., "He has a *fabulous* record collection —we had a *fantastic* time." Pause, together with duration, determines the rate at which a person speaks. If a person cuts his words off short and allows little pause, his rate will be rapid. Most beginning speakers tend to speak faster than they should, because a person tends to increase his rate when he is nervous or excited. In addition, many people tend to associate pause with nonfluency, with the idea that a person pauses because he does not know what to say. Ironically, this attitude toward pause as an indicator of nonfluency is often formed while a child is being taught to read in the primary grades. The child who reads slowly and haltingly, pausing before words with which he is unfamiliar, is thought of as a slow learner. The child who reads at a fairly rapid rate with few pauses is considered bright and given praise. The result is that the student is taught to avoid pause.

Articulation

We learn to speak by imitating the speech of those close to us. Consequently, our habits of speech often resemble the speech habits of those we have imitated. If we are lucky, and those we learn from speak distinctly, we tend to speak distinctly. However, if those we learn from tend toward indistinct speech, the chances are that our speech will also be indistinct. Unless the problem is physical, indistinct speech is caused by poor articulation, which is the process of forming the consonant and vowel sounds of words. It is a necessity for successful communication, since if you fail to articulate your words clearly, you will be difficult to understand.

The two most common errors of articulation are substituting one sound for another and leaving off the endings of words. For example, "this" becomes "dis," "student" becomes "stoont," and "asked" becomes "ast." An audience forms an unfavorable impression of a speaker who says things in a careless way. If the impression you give to others is important to you, make sure your articulation is precise.

Improving your articulation may not be easy if bad habits are ingrained in your speech. The first thing you must do is become aware of your weaknesses. What are your specific problems—running words together? Leaving off word endings? Substituting sounds? Although you can become aware of your problems by listening carefully to yourself as you speak, it is preferable, if you have the opportunity, to record your voice with a tape recorder or video tape. Tape yourself not only while practicing your speech but during ordinary conversation as well. Once you have determined your problems, make a list and study them.

Quality

A pleasant voice is free from undue harshness, huskiness, hoarseness, breathiness, and nasality. Unless a person has some problem caused by a disease or physical defect, he should be able to speak in a voice which is pleasant to listen to. Serious speech problems should be handled by a trained speech therapist. For those with minor difficulties, Jeffrey and Peterson make the following suggestions:

1. The speaker should learn to hear his voice as others hear it. An almost universal reaction of persons upon hearing a recording of their voice for the first time is, "That's not me. There must be something wrong with the recorder." But, of course, there is nothing wrong with the recorder and the recording, as classmates or friends will verify, is a faithful reproduction of the individual's speech. The speaker's initial reaction reveals that most people do not hear themselves as others hear them. This is in part because some of the sound is carried from the voice box to his ears through the cheek and neck bones. But it is also in part because most people have become so accustomed to hearing their own voice that they really do not listen to themselves carefully or analytically.

   Quite clearly, the first step in learning to hear one's voice as others hear it is for the speaker to record and listen to his speech frequently. The second step is to develop an awareness at all times of how it sounds.

2. To avoid strain, one should speak at a comfortable pitch level.
3. The speaker should maintain adequate breath support.
4. He should remain relaxed while speaking.
5. If strain or hoarseness occurs regularly, the speaker should consult a speech correctionist.

Robert C. Jeffrey and Owen Peterson, Speech: A Text with Adapted Readings *(New York: Harper & Row, Publishers, 1971), pp. 385–86.*

Pitch

Pitch refers to the highness or lowness of a speaker's voice. Everyone has a natural pitch level at which he can speak most comfortably. Problems in pitch can occur when a person tries to speak at a pitch which is higher or lower than his natural level. Suppose, for example, that a young man with a natural tenor voice feels that a bass voice is more masculine. His attempts to speak in a lower voice result in a husky and rasping sound. Instead of his natural, resonant voice, he produces a voice with an unpleasant quality, lack of adequate volume, and monotony in pitch. The size and length of your vocal chords determine the tone of your voice. If you want to avoid problems with your voice, speak at your most comfortable pitch level.

A natural conversational style is characterized by a variety of pitches. In normal conversation, these inflections come spontaneously. The best way to insure that your inflection will be interesting and meaningful is to choose a subject which you desire to communicate to your listeners. When you are concerned with expressing your true feelings, your inflection will come naturally.

ORGANIZATION

The function of organization is twofold. First, an audience can more easily understand and appreciate a message that is set in a clear framework. Second, an organizational pattern helps the speaker to eliminate wordiness, i.e., material that is unnecessary to the realization of his purpose. All speeches are divided into three parts—the introduction, the body, and the conclusion. The introduction should direct your audience's attention to the subject and make them want to listen. The body should communicate your ideas in a clear, meaningful way, and the conclusion should tie these ideas together in a neat package.

Introduction

The introduction to a speech has much to do with its success or failure. If a speaker fails to capture the attention of his audience in the introduction, he has little chance of regaining their interest. An introduction can have three purposes: (1) getting the audience's attention, (2) indicating the usefulness of the subject, and (3) indicating the purpose of the speech and its main idea. Although an introduction will often include all three of the above, at times one or two of them may be omitted.

Besides fulfilling these purposes, a good introduction has other characteristics. It must be appropriate to the purpose and main idea of the speech. A humorous introduction to a serious speech, for example, might cause the audience to feel that the speaker was not sufficiently concerned with his intentions. The introduction must lead naturally and easily into the body of the speech. Because your job is not only to get the attention of the audience but to hold it throughout the speech, a transition should be provided between the introduction and the body. Finally, an introduction should make an audience want to listen to the rest of your speech. The first impression you make is very important, so develop your introduction with your audience and subject in mind.

Body

The body of a speech develops the speaker's ideas in detail. It should contain a restatement or clarification of the main idea, and supporting material which clarifies or reinforces the main idea. The body of the speech has been developed effectively when the listener can see clearly the relationship between the main idea and the supporting material.

Conclusion

No matter how short your speech is, it must have a conclusion to round it off. Many experienced speakers feel that the conclusion is the most important part of the speech, since it leaves the listener with his final impression.

An effective conclusion should leave an audience with a sense of completeness. Usually involving a summary or restatement of the main idea, a conclusion should be brief, to the point, and developed in the same style as the rest of the speech. Both the language and mood of the introduction and body must be continued in the conclusion. (A humorous conclusion to a serious speech would reflect on the sincerity of the speaker.)

One final note. New material should never be introduced in the conclusion. Such an action will give your audience the impression that you have failed to plan your speech carefully and have added the new material as an afterthought.

AUDIENCE ANALYSIS

The process of communication involves four elements: a sender, a message, a receiver, and a response. Whenever a breakdown in communication occurs, it is at one or more of these points. Breakdowns in speech communication often occur when the speaker fails to consider carefully both the receiver and his response. As a result, too many speeches end up with the speaker talking about matters of self-interest, with little regard for the needs or interests of his audience. An effective speech must be audience-directed. Man is basically a self-centered creature; nothing interests him so much as himself. He relates to others in terms of their concern for him. A speaker whose purpose is simply self-expression or personality enlargement has little chance of holding the interest of his audience. He must show his listeners that he is concerned with their interests and needs.

Knowledge of your audience will help you plan a speech designed specifically for them. Find out as much as you can about them: their age, sex, educational background, and common interests. The more you know about an audience, the more likely you will be to establish a common ground of interest and information.

Contrast, for example, an audience of college students with an audience of golden-agers. College students tend to be liberal, objective, willing to take a chance, interested in performance sports, and familiar with the language, music, personalities, and problems of their own generation; golden-agers are more likely to be conservative, cautious, subjective, interested in spectator sports, and more concerned with problems of security and health than with current issues. A subject that would be highly interesting to one group might be quite boring to the other. Chapter 4, which deals with the subject of audience analysis, will help you plan a speech with a specific audience in mind.

STYLE

The manner in which a person expresses himself in language is called his style. This book has stressed the use in speech of conversational style, with its frequent employment of the personal pronoun, which gives it an air of familiarity, as if the speaker were talking to close friends. To achieve a conversational style, make frequent use of the terms "us," "we," "our," and "you and I." Think of your speech as talking "with" your audience, not "to" them.

The level of usage in conversational style will vary according to the occasion. In general, the more formal the occasion, the more formal will be the language of the speech. However, regardless of the language used, a style, to be effective, must be communicative. A communicative style has three characteristics: clarity, interest, and appropriateness.

Clarity

Communication does not take place unless the listener understands the message. Too many speakers are concerned with what the audience will think of them rather than with whether they are communicating. By using multisyllabic words and flowery phrases, they try to project what they feel is the image of a successful orator. This is a mistake, because the effective speaker never tries to impress the audience with his vocabulary; he communicates with a common vocabulary, whenever possible. If you want an effective speech style, choose terms that are appropriate and easily understood. If too much of what you have said is missed or misinterpreted, communication has failed.

For example, if a writer uses the word "exigency" in an essay, the reader unfamiliar with it can look it up; a listener has no such opportunity. Unless he knows the word or can determine its meaning from the context, he misses part of the message. This is avoided by the speaker who chooses a more familiar word, such as "urgency."

Unless you are delivering a formal speech, you should present your ideas in relatively short, uncomplicated sentences. Today's listeners won't spend the time or effort to search for your meaning. For example, a half century ago, when one-hour sermons were common, congregations were impressed with the verbal gymnastics of their clergy. Today the average sermon lasts about 15 minutes because the modern churchgoer demands directness and simplicity.

Interest

Clarity and interest are closely related to each other, since a listener or reader is more inclined to pay attention to a message that he can easily understand. To insure clarity a speaker must explain abstract terms which are important to the understanding of his subject. While this can be accomplished through definition, a more interesting way is through illustration or comparison. Note how interestingly Martin Luther King clarifies the abstract concept of equal opportunity by comparing it to a paycheck:

> In a sense we have come to our nation's capital to cash a check. When the architects of our republic wrote the magnificent words of the Constitution and the Declaration of Independence, they were signing a promissory note to which every American was to fall heir. This note was a promise that all men, yes, black men as well as white men, would be granted the unalienable rights of life, liberty, and the pursuit of happiness.
>
> It is obvious today that America has defaulted on this promissory note in-so-far as her citizens of color are concerned. Instead of honoring this sacred obligation, America has given the Negro people a bad check, which has come back marked "insufficient funds."
>
> But we refuse to believe that the bank of justice is bankrupt. We refuse to believe that there are insufficient funds in the great vaults of opportunity of this nation. So we have come to cash this check—a check that will give us upon demand the riches of freedom and the security of justice.

From "I Have a Dream," reprinted from Rhetoric of Racial Revolt *(Denver, Colorado: Golden Bell Press, 1964), by permission of the publisher.*

Another way of achieving clarity and interesting style is to choose the specific rather than the general. This is especially important in description. When the word "dog" is mentioned, what comes to mind? A collie? A poodle? A St. Bernard? Obviously, you can respond in various ways. With the more specific term "boxer" you get a clearer mental picture which can be improved even more with added modification, e.g., "Cruncher, the boxer next door." If you want to be clear and interesting, be specific. Don't say, "a man came toward me," if he "staggered," "lurched," "ran," "stumbled," or "crawled."

Sometimes a word can appear to be specific and yet be difficult to visualize. Words that deal with statistics or measurements fall into this category. For example, it is estimated that last year 37 million people died of starvation, most of them children. Although it is specific, this figure is difficult to visualize. To say, "10,000 people die each day" is more vivid, since the number is easier to comprehend. An even more vivid and, therefore, more interesting image, is provided by saying, "While you hear these words, seven people have died of starvation."

Appropriateness

You must use language appropriate to your audience. It would be obviously inappropriate to use medical terminology in presenting a speech on cancer research to a group of laymen. Not so obvious would be the use of technical terms (even though simple) in discussing carburetor adjustment to a general group of students. Since most people are unfamiliar with auto mechanics, you would probably be confusing some in your audience.

In most cases, it is best to avoid off-color stories or profanity. Although modern novels and movies tend to belie this, most listeners will consider the speaker who uses off-color material guilty of poor judgment. While you might draw the attention of your audience with the startling use of a four letter word, any advantage you gain will be negated if some find the word offensive.

Finally, unless it is apparent that you are deviating for deliberate effect, observe the rules of good grammar. An audience will probably overlook or even miss an occasional grammatical slip, but if your speech is filled with errors, they will think less of you. Whether they are justified or not, an audience tends to judge a person's intelligence by his use or misuse of language.

The sample of the speech evaluation form which follows is designed for both student and instructor evaluation. It lists those characteristics of delivery and content which should be considered when evaluating a speaker.

SPEECH EVALUATION SHEET _____
GRADE

NAME_____ DATE_____ 1972

SPECIFIC PURPOSE_____

(DELIVERY)

PLATFORM
MANNER _____

EYE
CONTACT _____

VOICE
_____

(CONTENT)

ORGANIZATION _____

AUDIENCE
ANALYSIS
_____

LANGUAGE
_____

WORK ON:

It is important that a speaker be able to evaluate his performance objectively. Fill out a self-evaluation form after each speech you deliver. This will help you to clarify your strengths and weaknesses as a speaker.

```
┌─────────────────────────────────────────────────────────────────┐
│                                                                   │
│                    SELF—EVALUATION FORM                           │
│                                                                   │
│                                                                   │
│   NAME_____ DATE_____ GRADE_____  │
│                                                                   │
│   SPECIFIC PURPOSE_____ │
│                                                                   │
│                                                                   │
│   _____ │
│                                                                   │
│   STRENGTHS                                                       │
│                                                                   │
│                                                                   │
│   _____ │
│                                                                   │
│   WEAKNESSES                                                      │
│                                                                   │
│                                                                   │
│   _____ │
│                                                                   │
│   AUDIENCE RESPONSE                                               │
│                                                                   │
│                                                                   │
│   _____ │
│                                                                   │
│   WAYS TO IMPROVE                                                 │
│                                                                   │
│                                                                   │
│   _____ │
│                                                                   │
│   COMPARE YOUR EVALUATION                                         │
│   WITH EVALUATION OF THE                                          │
│   INSTRUCTOR AND OTHERS    _____ │
│                                                                   │
│   DID YOU FULFILL                                                 │
│   YOUR PURPOSE?                                                   │
│                                                                   │
│   _____ │
│                                                                   │
│                                                                   │
└─────────────────────────────────────────────────────────────────┘
```

10

speech delivery

You have finished the hardest part of your job when you have developed the content of your speech. However, the work you have done in analyzing your subject and organizing your material may be wasted if you fail to deliver your speech effectively. Good delivery demands preparation and practice. There are four principal methods of delivery: (1) manuscript, (2) memorized, (3) impromptu, and (4) extemporaneous.

While the way in which you present your speech will vary according to audience and occasion, the best method for most occasions is the extemporaneous speech, spoken with preparation but not written out or memorized. Let us consider each of these methods of delivery separately.

MANUSCRIPT

In formal situations, where the oral presentation must be very precise, you may find it best to read your manuscript verbatim. Be careful to avoid overusing the manuscript speech. While this method offers security to the speaker afraid that he will forget what he wants to say or say it badly, it has three disadvantages: (1) it is difficult to maintain eye contact with the audience while reading, (2) it takes skill and practice to read a speech in a spontaneous and convincing manner, and (3) it is almost impossible to change the language or content of a manuscript speech to fit the mood or reaction of an audience.

Although you may be tempted to accept these disadvantages in return for the security of a manuscript speech, the best advice is to read a speech only when its content demands exact word order, as would research papers and technical data. To deliver a manuscript speech effectively, consider the following suggestions:

1. Edit your speech by reading each sentence aloud. Avoid overly long or involved sentences. No matter how complex or technical your material, it must be communicated clearly.
2. Type the manuscript speech in capital letters, triple-spaced to allow easy reading. Type on only one side of the paper.
3. Become familiar with your material by practicing it aloud; this will help you to obtain maximum eye contact. Even though you are reading, you must read "to people."
4. Indicate pauses and places of emphasis.
5. Use gestures and bodily action to enliven your delivery.

MEMORIZED

While the memorized speech appears to offer ease of eye contact along with the advantages of a manuscript speech, it has two distinct weaknesses:

(1) it takes a skillful actor to present memorized material in a natural, spontaneous way, and (2) the speaker who delivers his speech from memory runs the risk of forgetting. Unless you have complete confidence in your ability to deliver a speech naturally without losing your place, memorizing a speech is a risky method.

IMPROMPTU *not prepared*

An impromptu speech is one developed on the spur of the moment. Since it seldom allows opportunity for advance thought or preparation, it demands a great deal of the speaker. Unlike the writer of an impromptu theme, who can rephrase a clumsy sentence, the speaker finds it awkward to correct himself once he has said something. His audience receives his message the moment it is delivered. He has little time to analyze his subject, audience, or occasion, and must think on his feet as he chooses and organizes his material. While the impromptu method can often impart directness and spontaneity to the speaker's delivery, handling material that is not carefully thought out can often result in a rambling presentation. Experience in the planning, preparation, and delivery of extemporaneous speeches will provide guidelines for greater effectiveness in impromptu situations.

When you are called upon to deliver an impromptu speech, consider the following advice: (1) make sure that your central idea and specific purpose are absolutely clear to your audience, (2) keep your speech short and to the point, and (3) handle only one main point.

EXTEMPORANEOUS *prepared*

Like the written or memorized speech, the extemporaneous speech is carefully planned and rehearsed with the difference that the speaker does not deliver the speech in a predetermined word order. He decides on his exact wording at the moment of delivery. Thus, the extemporaneous method offers the same directness and spontaneity as the impromptu method without the danger of the speaker rambling off the point or repeating himself unnecessarily. When you prepare an extemporaneous speech, follow the steps dealt with in previous chapters for preparing any communication. After you choose and restrict your subject: (1) determine your purpose; (2) formulate a statement of specific intent and a main idea statement, if needed; (3) choose material adequate to develop your main idea and supporting points; (4) develop an introduction that captures attention, clarifies the main idea, and relates the subject to your audience; and (5) develop a conclusion that will emphasize what you have accomplished in the speech. At this point you are ready to prepare your speech for delivery.

PREPARING THE SPEECH FOR DELIVERY

An extemporaneous speaker delivers his speech from notes which include his main ideas and supporting materials. Many experienced speakers put their individual ideas on separate note cards rather than together on the same page. An individual note card isolates an idea so that it can be seen at a glance; after the speaker has dealt with the idea, he can move on to the next card. Whether you work from individual cards or an outline, be sure that you can read your notes easily. Notes are easy to read when they are typed in capital letters, and double- or triple-spaced. Use only one side of the paper, since turning over your notes is both awkward and time-consuming. Each note card or page should be clearly numbered to prevent you from losing your place.

Avoid writing your notes in too much detail. Coming to the speaker's platform with an overly detailed guide may tempt you to read your speech, thereby defeating the whole purpose of the extemporaneous method. Below are a delivery outline and some sample note cards. Create similar copy for your own speech to see which is most effective for you.

Delivery Outline

COULD YOU HAVE DIABETES

Introduction

The story of Uncle George who has that middle-aged run-down feeling and finally sees a doctor. The diagnosis is diabetes-mellitus.

Body

I. Susceptibility to diabetes
  A. No one immune
  B. High risk groups
    1. Those over 40
    2. Those related to diabetics
    3. Those overweight
II. Characteristics of diabetes
  A. Symptoms
    1. Weight loss
    2. Visual difficulty
    3. Excessive fatigue
    4. Frequent urination
    5. Constant hunger
  B. Types
    1. Adult
    2. Juvenile
  C. Causes
    1. Lack of insulin
    2. Pancreas deficiency
    3. Excess sugar

III. Treatment for diabetes
   A. Physical activity
      1. Maintain proper weight
      2. Establish muscle tone
      3. Improve circulation
   B. Diet
      1. Food exchange
         a. Milk (skim, buttermilk, evaporated)
         b. Vegetable (list A & B)
         c. Fruit (low calorie)
         d. Bread (spaghetti, cakes)
         e. Meat (cheese, eggs)
         f. Fat (cream, butter, bacon)
      2. Variation in planning
         a. Eating out
         b. Packing lunches
         c. Exact measurement
   C. Medication
      1. Insulin
      2. Oral drugs

Conclusion

Now Uncle George feels better than ever. He stays healthy by:
1. Staying under doctor's care
2. Taking medicine in exact amounts prescribed
3. Following his meal plan carefully
4. Exercising

Sample Note Cards

```
(1)
UNCLE GEORGE   RUN-DOWN   DIABETES
    SUSCEPTIBILITY   NO ONE IMMUNE
HIGH RISK   OVER 40   RELATED   OVERWEIGHT
SYMPTOMS: WEIGHT   EYES   BOWELS   FATIGUE
         HUNGER   URINATION
```

```
(2)
TYPES   ADULT/ JUVENILE   HEREDITARY
     GOOD CONTROL   BUT NO CURE
       CAUSES   LACK OF INSULIN
PANCREAS SUGAR/ ENERGY BLOOD/URINE
```

```
(3)
 TREATMENT   MEDICATIONS  CIRCULATION
PHYSICAL ACTIVITY   WEIGHT   MUSCLETONE
                      MILK        BREAD
DIET   FOOD EXCHANGE   FRUIT       MEAT
                      VEG         FAT
      VARIETY   KEEP ON SCHEDULE
```

> **(4)**
> *UNCLE GEORGE   BETTER THAN EVER*
> *DOCTOR'S CARE   TAKING MEDICINE*
> *MEAL PLAN   EXERCISE CONTROLLED*
> *ANYONE CAN HAVE   EVEN YOU!*

Preparing the Speech

The key to effective delivery is practice. Few experienced speakers would deliver an extemporaneous speech without practicing at least two or three times. Practice offers an additional benefit to you as a beginning speaker. While practicing in a relaxed atmosphere to improve a specific speech, you can take stock of your strengths and weaknesses as a speaker.

After you have practiced your speech a few times, deliver it as if you were in front of an audience. Doing your best in practice will give you a good idea of the quality of your ultimate performance. If possible, deliver your speech to someone who can evaluate it objectively. If it is possible to tape record or videotape yourself, by all means do so. Self-evaluation is a prerequisite to improvement.

Delivering the Speech

Although your audience expects you to use notes in an extemporaneous speech, you should do so unobtrusively. Remember, anything that calls attention to itself can distract from what you are saying. Note cards are much easier to handle if you must deliver the speech without a lectern. You can hold them in one hand and still be able to gesture freely. However, in most platform situations a lectern will be available to you. Once you have reached the lectern, put your notes down and leave them there; notes are to remind you of what to say, not to read verbatim. When you finish with a note card, move it to one side as unobtrusively as possible.

There is one instance when you should call attention to your notes. When reading a direct quotation, hold your notes up so that your audience can see that you are taking special care to be accurate.

Finally, don't let the fact that you are using a guide inhibit your gestures or facial expression. Spontaneous, convincing delivery requires bodily action and expressiveness.

SPEAKING ASSIGNMENTS

Following the suggestions given on the preceding pages, prepare and deliver whichever of these assignments that your instructor chooses.

READING A COMMERCIAL

DIRECTIONS: Read a one-two minute radio or TV commercial that you have written yourself or picked up from a local broadcaster. Study it carefully to decide how best to indicate meaning and emphasis. Practice it so that you can deliver it easily and naturally.

DELIVERY: It is important that you communicate sincerity to your audience. You can do this best by using a conversational style. Be yourself. Try to inject color and feeling into your words and phrases by being enthusiastic about the product. Smile when you speak.

Model

MISTER DONUT
ESTABLISH & FADE BACKGROUND FOR ANNOUNCER
ANNCR: Before he opens his own shop, each MISTER DONUT owner goes through a rigorous 5-week training course on how to make the finest and freshest donuts a man can buy. That's why they're able to make over 100 varieties of fresh donuts ... honey dips, chocolate, bavarian cream, toasted coconut ... even fancy pastries like eclairs and bismarks and blueberry bursts. Why, these fellows have such good looking fancy donuts, some of them look as good as miniature wedding cakes. Come on in to Mister Donut and buy a dozen ... for the kids, or your guests or the gals at the office.
Visit the Mister Donut Shop, at 3151 South 92nd Street ... or ... the Mister Donut Shop, at 9230 West Capital Drive ... in Milwaukee.
MUSIC TO FILL

*Used with the permission of Mister Donut of America, Inc.
and The Sycamore Corporation.*

A LETTER TO THE EDITOR (An expression of viewpoint; 2-3 minutes)

DIRECTIONS: Write to the "Letters to the Editor" column of one of our local newspapers expressing a point of view. It will be helpful if you familiarize yourself with these columns in order to be aware of the rules and format to follow. A reader will judge you on your style and grammatical correctness. A simple, to the point style must still be interesting.

DELIVERY: This speech will be delivered in manuscript method of presentation. Remember, the successful speaker reads as though he were speaking extemporaneously. Practice to deliver this speech in a spontaneous, convincing manner.

Suggestions

1. If you are writing in response to a published letter, read it so that your audience is clear as to what you're disagreeing with.
2. Write as if you were speaking—in an informal, direct way.
3. Read the letter aloud to a friend or two.

4. Become familiar enough with the letter to develop good eye contact.
5. Proofread your letter to eliminate weaknesses in style and grammatical errors.

Model

ABANDONED CARS A HAZARD

To The Journal: Why doesn't the city of Milwaukee do something to remove all of the abandoned autos from vacant lots and even private property? These vehicles are not only an eyesore but they are potentially dangerous to our children. Children have been locked in cars, trunks, and have been injured by sharp steel edges and glass from playing in these deserted vehicles.

I think the city should impose a strict fine on the owner of the abandoned auto, or the property owner for such negligence.

If these danger traps are not removed within two weeks from the date of notification, both the owner and the property owner should be deemed financially liable.

Failure to comply with this procedure should allow the city to invoke a $500 fine on the parties involved. Furthermore, the city should be authorized to remove the abandoned auto at the owner's expense. This certainly would help to beautify our city and make it safer for children.

Phil Mrozinski
Appeared in the Milwaukee Journal, Wednesday, Nov. 17, 1971.
Used with the permission of the writer.

READING PROSE OR POETRY

DIRECTIONS: Choose a selection of prose or poetry. Study it carefully in regard to meaning and mood. Practice it until you can deliver it effectively. In order to read well, a person must understand the meaning and mood of the material, and be able to convey that meaning and mood to his audience.

SUGGESTIONS

1. Choose your reading carefully. **Pick something interesting that you can handle intelligently.**
2. Time your reading. **Your selection must fall within a two-three minute time limit.**
3. Insure understanding. **Preface your reading with any information that will contribute to your listener's understanding.**
4. Use effective speaking techniques. **Speak clearly and distinctly, using variations in rate, pitch, and volume to convey the author's meaning and to make the reading more interesting. Know your selection well enough so that you can maintain adequate eye contact with your audience. It might be a good idea to copy your selection double-spaced on note cards or half sheets of paper.**

Model

The reader's job here is to communicate the attitudes of the two speakers in the poem.

SLOW DOWN?

Slow down, black man, you tell me,
You're moving much too fast
At the rate you're going
You surely cannot last.
You're entitled to your rights,
You're going to get them too.
But, you're rushing things too fast
And, that ain't good for you.
Sure you're demonstrating,
You're picketing and such
I know you want your rights.
But, you're crowding things too much.
Slow down, black man, Slow down.
Heed the words I say
You're injuring your cause
This is not the way
Things will be all right.
You haven't got to worry.
But, slow down, black man. Slow down
Don't be in such a hurry.
I get the Message white man.
It's coming in loud and clear.
But, you ain't saying nothing.
It's like, Mister, I can't hear.
How long you been a black man?
How long you been a "boy"?
What rights does the nation have
That you cannot enjoy?
It's easy for you to say,
"Black man, take it slow."
But, do you know segregation?
Have you ever met "The Crow"?
You don't fool me, Mr. White Man.
You ain't dealing from the top.
You don't mean "slow down."
You mean, damn it, "NIGGER"
STOP! Slow down, black man, you tell me.
Man you got your gall.
You've never cried for justice
You don't understand at all.
Have you ever lost a brother
To the fury of a mob?

Has the color of your skin
Stopped you from getting a job?
Slow down, black man, you tell me.
Well, mister, that's all right.
It's easy for you to say.
Who've never known a slight.
I have been going slow
For more than five score years
And yet and still I know
The same old hate and fears.
Have your brethren been lynched?
For the crime of being white?
Have you seen your mother tremble
When the klansmen rode at night?
I've been patient, Mr. White Man.
The Lord knows I have been
But, I ain't as good as Job
My patience has an end.
You bomb my house of worship.
You kill my babies, too.
Slow down, black man, you tell me.
Well, man, that's up to you.
I'll slow down, Mr. White Man.
I promise you I will,
When jimcrow is interred—
And we stand on freedom hill.

Ben Anderson
With permission of the author, Ben Anderson, Mt. Vernon, New York.

A SPEECH OF CRITICISM

DIRECTIONS: Deliver a two–four minute speech or write a 250–500 word essay in which you criticize a person, policy, or organization. Pick a subject that really annoys you. Express your views in a direct, to the point manner, emphasizing your annoyance with the language you use. If you deliver this as a speech, underline your irritation with facial expression, gestures, and tone.

DELIVERY: This speech should be delivered extemporaneously. The more spontaneous and direct you are in your presentation, the more clearly you will communicate your conviction and sincerity to the audience. This is an expression of your viewpoint. Indicate your attitude with emphasis, intensity, and force.

SUGGESTED TOPICS

1. Let's end our hypocritical attitude toward (censorship, segregation, communism, religion, etc.).

2. Welfare is another word for stealing.
3. People who brand all long-haired teenagers as hippies are ignorant.
4. Let's get the bigots out of our judicial system.
5. When are we going to stop kidding ourselves about America being a free country?
6. Allowing students to protest is undermining the principles upon which our colleges and universities were founded.

Model

WHERE DOES THIS HERO REST?

Mr. Conyers. Mr. Speaker, not too long ago a young black American named William Terry volunteered to serve in the U.S. Army. Proudly he assumed the uniform of his country, and willingly took his training and was sent to Vietnam.

Private First Class Terry wore his uniform proudly, even though it may have been woven by a company which would not have hired or promoted him. And he fought for his country, even though he and 24 million of his countrymen were denied the rights due to them as full-fledged American citizens. And, not long afterwards, Private First Class Terry, only 20 years old, gave his life to his country—killed in action in defense of a government that renounced the same freedoms he was told he was fighting for.

Bill Terry did not think of the slave ships, the auction blocks, Jim Crow, or Judge Lynch. He did not allow himself to be swayed by those who would destroy the dreams of himself and his fellows, by those who would segregate his schools, isolate his jobs, hurl threats, or even bombs at his doorways. Instead, he thought only of what he conceived to be his duty to his country. He fought for what he thought right and he died for it.

And then, in a Government-issue coffin, he came home to his family—in Birmingham, Ala.

His family asked that he be buried in Birmingham, in a place called the Elmwood Cemetery. But the Elmwood Cemetery said no, only white people could be buried there. So, because he was black, Bill Terry was buried in another cemetery outside of Birmingham, where only blacks were interred. And he was buried in an unmarked grave.

Just as it is a source of pride to relatives of others who lie with him that he is there, so it is a source of shame to our country that he was forced to lie there. What was he to America, even in death? What was his family to America? And now, what is America to them?

In recent days we have heard much of patriotism and our country. Many speeches have been delivered. With all those flags flapping in the breeze, I wonder whether all those speakers included Bill Terry in their thoughts. Did they count him in? Did they care?

Maybe Bill Terry even heard them, there in that place where he rests.

Congressional Record. *Speech given by Hon. John Conyers, Jr., of Michigan in the House of Representatives, November 25, 1969.*

RELATING A PERSONAL EXPERIENCE (To entertain)

DIRECTIONS: Deliver a two–five minute speech or write a short narrative of 300–500 words in which you relate a personal experience. Describe the situation in enough detail to create a mental picture for the reader or listener. Develop your material informally, with emphasis on details of action.

DELIVERY: This speech should be delivered extemporaneously. An audience will expect you to have almost total eye contact when talking about your own experiences. The more spontaneous and relaxed you are, the more your audience will enjoy your presentation.

SUGGESTED TOPICS

1. My last day on the job
2. A visit to the Internal Revenue Service
3. My uncle George
4. A brush with death
5. A day in Vietnam
6. My first date
7. My most embarrassing experience

Model

One day, a few friends and I were in my basement playing cards and drinking beer. One of them was an avid parachutist. I don't recall how it happened, but I soon found myself making a bet with this skydiver, Tom, that I would not be afraid to jump. The deal was, if I would jump, he would pay for it but if I didn't jump, I would pay him five dollars. I asked him where we would be jumping and he said "out at the airport."

We left the next morning for what I thought would be a major airport. It wasn't. It was a shabby pasture with one beaten down path for a runway and a rundown shack. I had figured on this jump being highly supervised by qualified personnel. Now that I saw where we were going, the tension started building.

We went up to the shack, and Tom started pulling out a number of chutes and helmets, trying to decide which ones he was going to use. I went into the building to pay the five dollars for the ride up. I asked the man at the desk for my parachute, and he directed me to a dusty corner where a pile of packed chutes were. I picked up a chute and he said, "No, not that one, that one don't work." So I picked up another one and he said, "Yah, that's a good one." I said, "Well are you sure?" He said, "Yah, don't worry, that one works." So I picked it up and I noticed a clean spot underneath it, amid all the dust. Now I was really getting nervous.

We got over to the plane and it was obvious that it wasn't one of the latest models. In fact, it almost looked obsolete. The pilot started the engine, and it wasn't the soft purr of a finely tuned engine that I had expected. It sounded like an old, oil burning, sputtering piece of junk. It was running for about a minute, and then of all things, it conked out. I thought to myself, "Aw this is ridiculous." The pilot was cursing and trying to start the plane again, and I noticed a hole in the back wall of the plane. I said to Tom, "what happens if this plane conks out up there?" And he says, "Well we'll just glide down." I said, "No Tom, if that plane conks out up there we're going straight down." Then he said "Ah, don't worry, nothin'll happen."

The pilot got the plane started again and we piled in, me first, because I was to jump last. Next, I found myself in the back of the plane with four people pressing against me, right next to that hole that I saw from the outside. There was no doubt about it now—my knees were shaking and I was scared.

Well up we went. When we got to about 6,500 feet the first three guys jumped. With each jump the plane rocked and swayed. The wind was rushing in my face as I hung on to my back corner seat with an iron grip. Tom told the pilot that he wanted to go up another thousand feet, and I began to think that my friend was nuts. When we got to the right altitude, Tom asked me to come over to the open door and view the target. We were so far up that I couldn't even see the airport. Tom got out on the wing, smiled at me, and down he went . . . just like a bullet. I never saw anyone drop so fast. He was doing summersaults, both forwards and backwards with the seconds going by. He kept falling and falling and I started to think that he had better open that chute pretty soon. Finally, he popped his chute, and I thought to myself, "This is nuts." When the pilot looked back at me and asked me if I wanted to go up another thousand feet, I said, "Hell no, I want to go down."

By the time we landed, Tom was floating to the ground. I walked up to him, gave him the five dollars, and never went near the place again.

Robert Wojs
Used with permission of the speaker.

RELATING A PERSONAL EXPERIENCE (To persuade)

DIRECTIONS: Deliver a two–four minute speech or write a short narrative of 300–500 words in which you relate a personal experience to persuade. Describe the material in enough detail to create a mental picture for the reader or listener. Develop your material informally, with emphasis on details of action. A personal story is an excellent means of reinforcing or clarifying your ideas.

DELIVERY: This speech should be delivered extemporaneously. An audience will expect you to have almost total eye contact when talking about your own experience. The more spontaneous and relaxed you are, the more your audience will enjoy your presentation.

SAMPLE TOPICS

1. Getting involved can pay off
2. Don't depend on the other driver
3. The grass is always greener on the other side
4. Sometimes it pays to be ignorant
5. A first aid course could save a life

Model

I used to feel that a lot of what people learned in classes at school was unnecessary. I remember thinking that about a course in first-aid that I had to take as part of my naval reserve requirement. That all changed one evening about four years ago. I was sitting in our living room with my uncle George, watching the Wednesday night fights on television. During a particularly exciting round I heard a thud. Looking around I saw that my uncle had fallen to the floor.

I rushed over to him and found that he wasn't breathing. Remembering what I had been taught in first-aid, I immediately rolled him on his back, put his head on a pillow and to the side and loosened his collar after I checked to see if he had anything in his mouth. I rushed to the phone and called the rescue squad. When I returned to my uncle I found that he was not only not breathing but that his heart had stopped too. I began giving him mouth-to-mouth resuscitation and external heart massage at the same time. Almost miraculously I remembered the instructions for both as if they were being given to me by the instructor again. "Exhale into the person's mouth and push down sharply on the sternum, release, count to ten and begin again." Finally, after what seemed like an eternity, uncle George responded and began breathing. By the time the rescue squad arrived, some of the color had returned to his cheeks and he had regained consciousness.

To this day whenever I think of a course as being of doubtful value, I think of my uncle George and work at it a little harder.

SPEECH TO INFORM USING A VISUAL AID

DIRECTIONS: Choose a subject whose effectiveness will be increased by use of a visual aid. Studies indicate that a person learns more readily when he is given the opportunity to see as well as hear what is being explained. Visual aids may consist of charts, diagrams, maps, pictures, photographs, models, film strips, projectors, records, physical gestures—in short, whatever provides an extra audio or visual dimension to the words the audience hears.

DELIVERY: This speech should be delivered extemporaneously. The speaker must be free to move to his map, chart, or diagram, or to use both hands in demonstrating a technique.

SUGGESTIONS

1. Keep visual aids out of sight when not in use. **Don't display your aid until you are ready to use it, and remove it as soon as you are through with it.**
2. Visual aids should be easily seen. **Be sure that the aid is large enough to be seen by all. Stand to the side of an aid so that you can speak directly to the audience.**
3. Visual aids should be clear and relevant. **Unless an aid is easy to understand and related to the subject, it can confuse rather than clarify. Don't use a visual aid just for the sake of appearances.**
4. Practice using your visual aid. **When you practice your speech, have your visual aids ready and use them. If possible, practice using your aid in the room in which you will be speaking. Make sure that the necessary equipment is available. Stand at the back of the room to insure that your aid can be clearly seen or heard.**

SAMPLE TOPICS

1. Mark Twain, America's great wit
2. The laser beam
3. The art of tree dwarfing
4. How to beat the stock market
5. Automobile lubrication

Model

I am a member of the Mid-Continent Railway Historical Society of North Freedom, Wisconsin. We are a non-profit organization, whose sole purpose is to acquire, restore, and operate vintage steam locomotives and rolling stock. To pay for the restoration of this equipment, our organization has become a tourist carrying railroad.

Our railroad line is a 4½ mile spur contected to the Chicago & Northwestern RR. line. It was first built in 1903 to ship iron ore out of a small mining town called La Rue, Wisconsin. (slide) By 1908 the rich ore petered out and the mines were shut down.

With WWI beginning, blast furnaces were needed for steel. Hard quartzite rock is required to line them. A mile past La Rue was a deposit of this rock and by 1918 the rails extended to this pit. (slide)

The quarry closed in 1962 and by 1963 we bought the spur for $25,000.00. At that time all there was (slide), was just one single track covered with weeds. In the last ten years we have improved this quite a bit. (slide) These shots of the museum from the air were taken out of an old bi-plane. (slide, slide) We also have our own office, in town, the old bank of North Freedom, donated to us by the town.

Our members are railroad workers on the weekend, but are doctors, carpenters, and students during the week. (slide) All their labor (slide) is volunteer. Now lets take a closer look at our machines; we have 12.

(slide) The 6-spot is the 1923 switch engine (slide), which carries its water and coal on the engine. (slide) The 6 came to us in 1963.

(slide) The Dardenelle & Pusselville #9, built in 1884—rebuilt in 1904 (slide), is an active engine on our roster. (slide) She is now due for extensive repairs.

(slide) These engines are due for display (slide) and some for operation purposes. (slide) The #4960 is the engine that pulled the Circus Train in 1965–66.

Our #1 (slide) is from the Western Coal & Coke Co., from Lethbridge Alberta, Canada. Built in 1913, she was bought and shipped to us (slide) on flat cars, back in 1965. (slide) She weighs 55 tons and nearly everything was rebuilt. (slide) In 1967 she looked like this. But by 1970 she rolled fresh out of the shops, looking like this. (slide)

The first locomotive to operate on our line (slide) was a 120 ton C. & NW. freight engine. In 1964 she was put to rest and worked on. (slide) She'll be ready in July of 1972.

We also have over 85 pieces of rolling stock from cars (slide) to reefers (slide) to (slide) cabooses.

Our passenger car fleet also requires many years of restoration. (slide) Here is the Copper Range #25 built in 1903, she looked like this (slide) when we got her. The car's latest re-paint job looked like this. (slide) Wisconsin Central (now Soo Line) (slide) was built in 1905 and put into train service (slide) last summer. Last fall we started to restore G.N. coach (slide) x-791. slide) Here are some shots of the progress (slide, slide, slide).

We recently bought two more coaches from the Burlington Northern and just a few months ago, 4 more from the Erie-Lakawanna. (slide, slide)

This is just a preview of what there is up at the museum. I invite you to come up some time, during the summer, where you can ride behind a steam locomotive in a turn-of-the-century coach, and hear (slide) to whistle on the wind.

Jeff B. Haertlein
Used with permission of the writer.

SPEECH TO INFORM

DIRECTIONS: Choose a subject in which your main job as a speaker is to present information. Present your material in such a way as to hold and maintain audience attention so that they can readily understand and remember.

DELIVERY: This speech can be delivered either with manuscript or extemporaneously. Keep the pattern of development simple so that you move from one idea to another in a clear, meaningful manner.

SUGGESTIONS

1. Decide whether your audience is listening to the information out of curiosity or need.
2. Present material that is unknown by relating it to what is known.
3. You may need to summarize from time to time to make your points absolutely clear.

SAMPLE TOPICS

1. The Koala bear
2. Today's average student
3. The real story of Howard Hughes
4. Planting a garden
5. The native American

Model

BLACK HISTORY WEEK

Mr. Anderson of California. Mr. Speaker, the black man's history in the United States, although often neglected in our history books, is one of great achievement and accomplishment. The record shows that black men and women have been in the forefront of our progress as a Nation. Whatever our history has been; whatever our future brings; the black man has made outstanding contributions toward making this world a better place to live.

This week, February 13 through February 19, is Black History Week—an occasion which has been observed in Los Angeles for a number of years. In view of this observance, I would like to take a few moments to recount just a few of the accomplishments of these Americans whose participation in our Nation's development began in 1619.

Due to the publicity and public adulation received by sports heroes and celebrities, the accomplishments of black athletes, musicians, and singers have often overshadowed the accomplishments of black scientists, inventors, educators, businessmen, and religious leaders.

However, throughout the history of the United States, the black American has made his mark and helped determine the outcome of events. Thus, any history of America must include black Americans.

Jean Baptiste Point DuSable, a black pioneer, founded the settlement of Chicago. Another black pioneer, Matthew Henson, was with Adm. Robert E. Perry when he discovered the North Pole in 1907.

Some 5,000 Negroes served in the Continental Army and Navy during the American Revolution. The first American to die in the cause of freedom was Crispus Attucks, a black man shot by the British at the "Boston Massacre" in 1770.

Nearly a quarter of a million black soldiers and sailors served in the Union forces during the Civil War. Twenty of these men were recognized for valor and received the Nation's highest medal for heroism—the Congressional Medal of Honor.

There were more than 5,000 black cowboys in the Old West. A black man, Bill Pickett, invented the art of "bull-dogging." James P. Beckworth was a black frontiersman who excelled in trapping and hunting.

The first black physician in America was James Derham, who established a prosperous medical practice in Philadelphia. The first doctor to perform open heart surgery was black—Dr. Daniel Hale Williams.

Dr. Charles Drew, a black surgeon, invented the blood bank and became the world's greatest authority on blood plasma.

The achievements of Booker T. Washington and George Washington Carver are well known to students, but how many Americans have read the works of Alexander Dumas, the author of "The Count of Monte Cristo," and realized that he was of African descent as was Samuel Coleridge-Taylor, and Alexander Pushkin. Black Americans such as Paul Laurence Dunbar and Charles Waddell Chestnutt have left their mark in the literary annals of America.

Black men have prospered in the field of business. C.C. Spaulding developed an insurance company that had assets worth $33 million when he died. S.B. Fuller set up a firm in Chicago that manufactures toiletries and cosmetics and distributes them by door-to-door salespeople. The Fuller Products Co. is one of the largest black-owned businesses in America.

Leaders in the movement for civil rights have admired such leaders as Frederick Douglass, and, of course, the outstanding leader, the late Martin Luther King, Jr.

The residents of Los Angeles know the fine architecture of Paul Williams, who designed the Beverly Wilshire Hotel, a Saks Fifth Avenue store, office buildings, and mansions. He ranks high among architects of the world.

The list of accomplishments by black men and women in the sports and entertainment field is endless.

The steps that have been taken toward the goals and the quality of life which we all seek have been made by Americans of all races. Let us never forget those giant steps made by black men and women, and let us take pride in the rich heritage which has been left to us and to future generations by the black pioneers.

Congressional Record. *Speech given by Hon. Glenn M. Anderson of California in the House of Representatives, February 16, 1972.*

SPEECH TO ENTERTAIN

DIRECTIONS: Either describe a stimulating experience of yours (i.e., an exciting event, a memorable trip, an unforgettable performance) which you feel would be interesting to the class, or deliver a speech in which you use humor to entertain your audience. You may, for example, treat a serious subject lightly or a light subject seriously. Contact is very important; speak directly to your audience. The more clearly the audience can visualize what you describe, the more effective will be your speech.

DELIVERY: This speech should be delivered extemporaneously. Maintain as much eye contact as possible. Your facial expression and gestures should indicate that you are enjoying yourself. Remember, enthusiasm is contagious.

SUGGESTIONS

1. Use vivid, colorful language to stimulate the senses of the audience.
2. Organize your material in a simple rather than complex pattern.
3. Be friendly and relaxed. Avoid being overresponsive to your own humor.
4. Read such authors as Art Buchwald, Dick Gregory, Al Capp, and Dorothy Parker to get an idea of effective satirical style.

SAMPLE TOPICS

1. How to wash a bull elephant
2. How to get a fair share of the government "giveaway"
3. A moment I'll always remember
4. Camping can be fun, for bears
5. My first and last day on the job

Model

Love is a wonderful thing, but, like anything worthwhile, it often has its ups and downs. For about six years prior to our meeting, my husband had been sequestered in the religious life. I knew very soon in our friendship that I was stimulating his interest in women but I could also tell he wasn't very versed in the art of courting and when it came to kissing—YUK!!! Forget it!

His kisses started out as quick stolen little pecks on the cheek and progressed to quick stolen little pecks on the lips. As his kisses increased in length, I saw that some things had to change. First there was the pucker—Now, puckers are fine for babies and grandmothers, but for me—No Sir! Well the pucker soon changed to the tight lipped method—That was just as bad as the pucker. Another thing was his approach. He wasn't quite sure of whether to jump right in and grab or to slowly sidle up and nonchalantly start kissing. What he didn't realize then was that you don't just attack with a passionate kiss, but that you work up to the really big one with tender little loving kisses.

One particular evening we were standing at the kitchen counter, just talking and drinking iced tea. I figured there was no particular limitation as to time or place, and after all practice makes perfect, so I made the approach this time. Well right in the middle of this fit of passion, just as I was marveling to myself of his improvement, I heard a strange noise, the sound of an iced tea glass being slid—klunk klunk—across the tiled counter. So I opened one eye—and curled one lip from the full press—and quietly said "Did you want a drink of iced tea?" As you can imagine it completely broke the two of us up. It seems I caught him off guard and he was just trying to put the glass back so he could get a better grip. That was the icebreaker, because from that time on it was clear sailing for my Romeo.

Pat Kiley
Used with permission of the speaker.

THE IMPROMPTU SPEECH

DIRECTIONS: Deliver a two–four minute impromptu speech. Your purpose may be to inform, persuade, or entertain. You will either be given a subject or allowed to choose one from a list made available to you shortly before you will begin speaking.

DELIVERY: Use the limited time available to you to decide on your purpose and specific intent. Make sure that both are absolutely clear to your audience. Keep your speech short and to the point. Handle only one main point in the body and restate your central idea at the conclusion.

SAMPLE TOPICS

1. Honesty as the best policy
2. My views on socialism
3. The ideal wife
4. The most useful profession
5. If I had it to do over again
6. What I consider a good movie
7. City versus country living
8. The most useless profession
9. A day I would like to forget
10. Thirteen, my lucky number

PERSUASION TO CONVINCE

DIRECTIONS: Deliver a three–five minute speech or write a 300–500 word essay supporting one point of view in regard to a controversial subject. Analyze the audience beforehand to determine their attitude toward your point of view. Man takes great pride in the fact that he is a rational creature. He has a high regard for intelligence and problem-solving ability. Appeal to your reader or listener's desire to know the truth in order to modify his existing attitudes. Rely chiefly on logical materials to obtain mental agreement from your audience.

SUGGESTIONS

1. Don't attempt to do too much in this assignment. You will be successful if you change, even if only to the slightest degree, the attitudes and opinions of your audience.
2. Present your material objectively. An audience will react negatively to a reader or speaker who is overly biased.
3. Show that there is need for a change.
4. Show that your proposal is practical.
5. End with a statement of support for your proposal.

Model

THE TRAGEDY OF VIETNAM

Suppose we took gigantic bulldozers and scraped the land bare of trees and bushes at the rate of 1,000 acres a day or 44 million square feet a day until we had flattened an area the size of Rhode Island, 750,000 acres.

Suppose we flew huge planes over the land and sprayed 100 million pounds of poisonous herbicides on the forests until we had destroyed an area of prime forests the size of Massachusetts or 5½ acres.

We've Done This to South Vietnam

Suppose we flew B-52 bombers over the land, dropping 500 pound bombs until we had dropped almost 3 pounds per person for every man, woman and child on earth—8 billion pounds—and created 23 million craters on the land measuring 26 feet deep and 40 feet in diameter.

Suppose the major objective of the bombing is not enemy troops but rather a vague and unsuccessful policy of harassment and territorial denial called pattern or carpet bombing.

Suppose the land destruction involves 80% of the timber forests and 10% of all the cultivated land in the nation.

We would consider such a result a monumental catastrophe. That is what we have done to our ally, South Vietnam.

While under heavy pressure the military finally stopped the chemical defoliation war and has substituted another massive war against the land itself by a program of pattern or carpet bombing and massive land clearing with a huge machine called a Rome Plow.

The huge areas destroyed, pockmarked, scorched, and bulldozed resemble the moon and are no more productive.

This is the documented story from on the spot studies and pictures done by two distinguished scientists, Prof. E. W. Pfeiffer and Prof. Arthur H. Westing. These are the same scientists who made the defoliation studies that alerted Congress and the country to the grave implications of our chemical warfare program in Vietnam, which has now been terminated.

The story of devastation revealed by the movies, slides, and statistics is beyond the human mind to fully comprehend. We have senselessly blown up, bulldozed over, poisoned and permanently damaged an area so vast that it literally boggles the mind.

Horror Defies Adequate Description

Quite frankly, I am unable adequately to describe the horror of what we have done there.

There is nothing in the history of warfare to compare with it. A "scorched earth" policy has been a tactic of warfare throughout history, but never has a land been so massively altered and mutilated that vast areas can never be used again or even inhabited by man or animal.

This is impersonal, automated and mechanistic warfare brought to its logical conclusion—utter, permanent, total destruction.

The tragedy of it all is that no one knows or understands what is happening there, or why, or to what end. We have simply unleashed a gigantic machine which goes about its impersonal business destroying whatever is there without plan or purpose. The finger of responsibility points everywhere but nowhere in particular. Who designed this policy of war against the land, and why? Nobody seems to know and nobody rationally can defend it.

Strategists, Victims Are Worlds Apart

Those grand strategists who draw the lines on the maps and order the B-52 strikes never see the face of that innocent peasant whose land has been turned into a pockmarked moon surface in 30 seconds of violence without killing a single enemy soldier because none were there.

If they could see and understand the result, they would not draw the lines or send the bombers.

If Congress knew and understood, we would not appropriate the money.

If the president of the United States knew and understood, he would stop it in 30 minutes.

If the people of America knew and understood, they would remove from office those responsible for it if they could ever find out who is responsible. But they will never know, because nobody knows.

By any conceivable standard of measurement, the cost-benefit ratio of our program of defoliation, carpet bombing with B-52's, and bulldozing is so negative that it simply spells bankruptcy. It did not protect our soldiers or defeat the enemy, and it has done far greater damage to our ally then to the enemy.

These programs should be halted immediately before further permanent damage is done to the landscape.

The cold, hard and cruel irony of it all is that South Vietnam would have been better off losing to Hanoi than winning with us. Now she faces the worst of all possible worlds with much of her land destroyed and her chances of independent survival after we leave in grave doubt at best.

This has been a hard speech to give and harder to write because I did not know what to say and how to say it—and I still do not know. But I do know that when the members of Congress finally understand what we are doing there, neither they nor the people of this nation will sleep well that night.

For many reasons I did not want to make this speech but someone has to say it, somewhere, sometime.

Gaylord Nelson
Congressional Record. *Speech given by Hon. Gaylord Nelson of Wisconsin in the U.S. Senate, April 19, 1972.*

11

persuasion

Never before in our society has the technique of persuasion been so important or profitable. Advertising ranks among our nation's billion dollar enterprises. Political candidates pay staggering amounts to public relations firms to insure election. Motivational researchers make millions telling manufacturers how to sell their product. Few in our society are paid more than the effective salesman. As a result of this, we are constantly bombarded with appeals to "get with it," to "come alive," to enjoy a new "taste sensation." We are the unceasing target for those who would persuade us to buy their product, to accept their viewpoint, or to support their cause. It is obvious, therefore, that because of the intensity of this competition for our money, our time, or our support, we must have an understanding of persuasion if we are to choose wisely.

A WORKING DEFINITION

Persuasion is *the conscious attempt to influence the thought or behavior of others through the use of personal, logical, and psychological appeals.*

The emphasis on persuasion as a "conscious" attempt to influence is important. The more aware you are of exactly what you want done, the more likely you are to be successful. Persuasion must be intentional. A good informative speech or paper may also persuade, but if its primary aim is to inform, then the persuasion is accidental. The persuader must deliberately attempt to influence.

However, you don't have to sell your product immediately to be successful. You don't have to change someone's mind on the spot. Persuasion can be a long-range process which modifies thought or behavior a little at a time. In some cases it might take a series of speeches, editorials, and meetings to change an existing policy or law.

Suppose that shortly after getting a driver's license you want to use the family car. If your father says, "No, you're not ready yet," you must convince him that you are. Although you might point to your success in passing the driver's test, or an "A" in a Driver's Education course in school, convincing your father that you are ready to take on this new responsibility will probably involve your driving the car a number of times while he is with you. Since you know that each time you do a good job you are influencing him to respond in the way you desire, you are careful to do your best when he is your audience. In this case, as you can see, it will take a series of these demonstrations of your ability to persuade your father to see things your way.

In most cases you will be more successful in persuading your parents or friends than you will be in persuading others. This is because you have a

—Hesse in the St. Louis Globe-Democrat

"Daddy, could your $750 exemption have the car?"

Hesse in the St. Louis Globe Democrat.

better understanding of those you know; since you are sensitive to their likes and dislikes, you know how to handle them.

Now go back to the example above. You have convinced your father that you should be allowed to use the family car for occasional dates, but you want it on a night when he was considering using it. Getting the car will be difficult. The first thing you must do is to approach him when he is in a good mood. This might be after you have given him his pipe and slippers and turned on his favorite TV program. If Mom has more influence with Dad than you have, you make your appeal to her. In any case, you are sensitive to the situation and attitudes of the person or persons to whom you are making the appeal. You are in effect a salesman trying to sell yourself or your ideas. The cash register rings when the response is favorable. If you fail to make a sale, you learn from the experience and try a new approach the next time. As indicated in our definition, there are three appeals or types of proof you can use in selling your product more effectively: personal, logical, and psychological.

PERSONAL PROOF

What your audience thinks of you has a definite effect on their reaction to your persuasion. When we like a person we find it easy to do what he asks of us; when we dislike him, we might even enjoy refusing him.

This same concept relates directly to your credibility as a speaker or writer. Ideally, you want your audience to see you as an intelligent person with integrity and goodwill.

Intelligence

Everyone admires the person who appears to know what he is talking about, the person who, because of education or experience, can get the job done. To be an effective persuader you must show your reader or listener that you have thought the problem over carefully, considered all the evidence, and decided on the best course of action. A well-organized, fluent presentation is the mark of a competent communicator.

Your audience also judges your intelligence by the language you use. The effective persuader chooses words that will convey his meaning accurately, grammatically, and forcefully. He chooses words to communicate, not to display his vocabulary.

Integrity

Even though you are skilled in presenting your ideas, your audience must feel that you are worthy of their trust and respect. In today's society, with its credibility gaps and hypocrisy, the honesty of a writer or speaker is of major concern to his audience. Careful preparation and documentation will help to indicate your sincerity and honesty. Remember, you are judged by what you do and say. Be sure that your audience finds your comments and behavior desirable.

Goodwill

It is important that you indicate goodwill for your audience. Treating them with respect will help you to demonstrate your goodwill toward them. Greet them with enthusiasm. Give them credit for having intelligence and ability.

In a March 23, 1775 speech to the House of Burgesses, Patrick Henry faced the difficult task of supporting a resolution of war against strong opposition by rich planters who feared an uprising even more than they feared oppression from the crown. Note how tactfully he compliments those with whom he disagrees.

MR. PRESIDENT:
No man thinks more highly than I do of the patriotism, as well as abilities, of the very worthy gentlemen who have just addressed the house. But different men often see the same subject in different lights; and therefore, I hope it will not be thought disrespectful to those gentlemen, if, entertaining as I do opinions of a character very opposite to theirs, I shall speak forth my sentiments freely and without reserve. This is no time for ceremony. The question before the house is one of awful moment to this country. For my own part, I consider it as nothing less than a question of freedom or slavery. And in proportion to the magnitude of the subject ought to be the freedom of the debate. It is only in this way that we can hope to arrive at truth and fulfill the great responsibility which we hold to God and our country. Should I keep back my opinions at such a time, through fear of giving offense, I should consider myself as guilty of treason toward my country, and of an act of disloyalty toward the Majesty of Heaven, which I revere above all earthly kings.

The Image

Public relations men, advertisers, and motivational researchers are constantly involved in image building. They are acutely aware of the image of their product held by potential customers. They have come to realize that to a great extent it is this image which sells the product. In order for the speaker or writer to gain acceptance of his ideas, he must project an image of himself that will be favorably received by his audience. The manner in which this image is projected is shown in the diagram on page 174.

Note that a person projects his image to others by what he says, what others say about him, and what he does. (He has to back up his words with actions.) Probably no group is more concerned with the image they project than the politicians.

For years presidential candidates traveled around the country on whistle-stop tours in an attempt to drum up votes. They wanted to demonstrate that they were men of goodwill who were honestly interested in the people. The idea was that the more hands they shook and the more babies they kissed, the greater was their chance of being elected. Then came television.

Suddenly the candidate was offered an opportunity to meet millions of people face to face at one time. This was the perfect means of communication for the politicians. But they found that they couldn't compete with shows produced by the experts, so the experts were called in and the

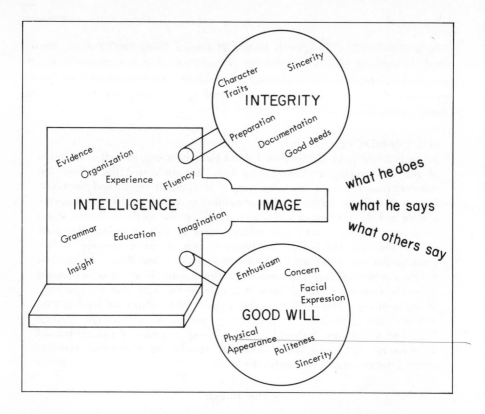

changes began. The half hour political speech was discarded in favor of the five minute spot commercial. The ideal spot was the last five minutes of a popular show. Since most of the people watching would feel that it was too late to switch to another channel, the candidate would have essentially a captive audience.

The purpose of these five minute spots was to project a compelling image to the audience. The effectiveness of this Madison Avenue approach can be demonstrated by the success of Nixon's 1968 presidential campaign.

In 1960 Richard M. Nixon won the Republican presidential nomination on the first ballot. Shortly thereafter he faced his Democratic opponent, Senator John F. Kennedy, in four nationally televised debates. Vice President Nixon's performance in the first of the debates, said to have been affected by a painful knee injury, poor lighting, and poor makeup, was believed to have helped Kennedy. On election day Mr. Nixon was defeated.

In 1962 Mr. Nixon decided to seek the governorship of California. In the general election, he lost to the Democratic incumbent, Governor Edmund Brown, 2,740,351 to 3,037,100. Six years later Richard M. Nixon was elected President of the United States. Why?

Although it would be an oversimplification to attribute Richard M. Nixon's political success entirely to the emergence of a new image, the seasoned advertising and TV professionals hired by the Nixon team made a significant contribution. Joe McGinniss's controversial best seller, *The Selling of the President, 1968,* gives a disturbing firsthand account of how a political candidate is packaged and sold to the public through adroit manipulation of the mass media.

> Price[1] suggested attacking the "personal factors" rather than the "historical factors" which were the basis of the low opinion so many people had of Richard Nixon. "These tend to be more a gut reaction," Price wrote, "unarticulated, nonanalytical, a product of the particular chemistry between the voter and the image of the candidate. We have to be very clear on this point: that the response is to the image, not to the man. . . . It's not what's there that counts, it's what's projected—and carrying it one step further, it's not what he projects but rather what the voter receives. It's not the man we have to change, but rather the received impression. And this impression often depends more on the medium and its use than it does on the candidate himself."
>
> So there would not have to be a "new Nixon." Simply a new approach to television.
>
> "What, then, does this mean in terms of our uses of time and of media?" Price wrote. "For one thing, it means investing whatever time Richard Nixon needs in order to work out firmly in his own mind that vision of the nation's future that he wants to be identified with. This is crucial. . . ."
>
> So, at the age of fifty-four, after twenty years in public life, Richard Nixon was still felt by his own staff to be in need of time to "work out firmly in his own mind that vision of the nation's future that he wants to be identified with."

From Joe McGinniss, The Selling of the President, 1968
(New York: Trident Press, 1969).

According to Price, it is the image that the voter has of the candidate which determines his reaction to what is said. With this in mind, analyze the following statements to see which are in keeping with your concept of the people who made them.

1. I'm not going to be the first President to preside over an American defeat.
2. The black man's pride is the white man's hope.

President Richard Nixon

1. We will have to repent in this generation, not merely for the vitriolic words and actions of the bad people, but for the appalling silence of the good people.

[1]Price, Raymond K., a former editorial writer for the New York Herald Tribune, who became Nixon's best and most prominent speech writer in the campaign.

2. **There will be neither rest nor tranquility in America until the Negro is granted his citizenship rights.**

Dr. Martin L. King

1. **If a free society cannot help the many who are poor, it cannot save the few who are rich.**
2. **As President of the United States, I am determined upon our system's survival and success, regardless of the cost and regardless of the peril.**

President J. F. Kennedy

1. **There is only one word to describe the federal judiciary today. That word is "lousy."**
2. **And my prayer is that the Father who reigns above us will bless all the people of this great sovereign state and nation, both white and black.**

George Wallace

1. **I'm opposed to censorship of television, of the press in any form.**
2. **If you've seen one slum, you've seen them all.**

Vice President S. Agnew

Credibility

If you are like most people, one statement in each of the preceding pairs of statements more clearly fits your concept of the person who made it. Why? Because people judge what a person has to say by their image of him. The better a person's image, the more likely we are to believe what he says. The term *credibility* refers to the extent to which we believe what someone tells us. A person who has a good image also has high credibility. Conversely, a person with a poor image has low credibility.

As you can see from the chart on page 174, image projection is a complex process. People form judgments about others on the basis of a variety of factors. Furthermore, these judgments can be made by evaluating what a person does, what he says, and what others say about him. Because of this complexity, the image that a person projects may or may not be an accurate representation of what he actually is.

The society in which we live can often have a decided effect on the image that we develop. A person usually tries to develop an image of which others will approve, and the advertisers try to set the standards. We are told that "blondes have more fun," that a "thinking man" smokes a particular brand of cigarette, and that we should "grab as much out of life as we can," because we only go around once. And we respond. In 1970, the cosmetic industry in this country grossed over 3 billion dollars. Countless more billions are spent each year by Americans to keep in step with the latest fashion or style. It is "in" to belong to a certain group, and this group often determines a person's outward appearance, his speech, his code of ethics, and his conduct. He tries to be what the group wants him to be, and yet, in some cases, what he appears to be is not what he is at all.

Some psychologists feel that this projection of a false image has much to do with our high divorce rate. Two people are often attracted to each other because they believe they see traits that they admire. Then, when they get married, what they thought they saw isn't actually there. The husband, who seemed considerate and charming, was actually selfish and dull. The wife, who appeared self-assured and insightful, was, in fact, withdrawn and insensitive. After the first few months of marriage, when their physical attraction no longer overshadows their daily routine, they find that the one they thought they married does not really exist.

As we have seen, a person often tends to evaluate what someone says in the light of his projected image. If the impression is good, his credibility is high; if it is bad, his credibility is low. The following cases indicate how credibility is related to this received impression.

TOM'S FATHER

Tom's father, the owner of a small factory, is a highly respected member of his community. He goes to church regularly, contributes generously to charity, and belongs to several civic and fraternal organizations. He is considered by many people to be a man of intelligence, integrity, and goodwill, and consequently he enjoys a high degree of credibility with them. Tom, however, has a different image of his father. He has heard his father say that it was "good for business" to be seen at church on Sunday or to give to charity. He has heard his father brag about the "tax loopholes" and "payoffs" that he enjoys, and he strongly suspects him of infidelity on business trips. For this reason, Tom's father possesses little credibility in Tom's eyes, particularly in dealing with issues regarding morality.

JOHN AND HARRY

John and Harry both attend a small, midwestern junior college. They share a small two bedroom apartment and get along very well together although their style of dress and appearance are entirely different. John has shoulder length hair, rimless glasses, a full beard, and wears beads, levis, and an old army jacket. Harry, on the other hand, has a crewcut, black framed glasses, is clean shaven, and usually wears neatly pressed slacks and a sports coat. When rapping with fellow students who are little influenced by their manner of dress, their credibility is about equal. However, this changes markedly when speaking to their landlord, a middle class businessman. Harry enjoys rather high credibility, while John's credibility is quite low. The landlord generally listens to Harry's opinions thoughtfully, while almost always dismissing John's as radical. He allows Harry to put up his "sister" over the weekend but threatens to call the police when John brings his girl home for a midnight snack.

Relationship of Image to Credibility

We have seen that what your audience thinks of you has a definite effect on their reaction to your persuasion. Tom's judgment of his father is based on knowledge that others do not possess. Because the landlord has a preconceived picture in his mind of both John and Harry, he is unable to react to them objectively. Although John had apparently done nothing to warrant it, the landlord responded negatively to him. He formed an image of John on the basis of outward appearance. The image *he perceives* of John is poor; therefore John's credibility is low.

This relationship of image to credibility can be seen clearly in advertising. The job of the advertiser, simply stated, is to convince the consumer that his product is better than that of his competitor. As one advertiser put it, "What makes one product different from another is how people feel about it." Therefore, the advertiser must make the customer feel kindly disposed toward his product. In a marketplace jammed with competitive goods, this poses a problem. How, for instance, do you outsell your competition in an area as overcrowded as cosmetics, liquor, or cigarettes? The answer is to create an image of the product that will appeal to the public. Joseph Seldin analyzes the relationship between cigarette advertising and image building.

As the advertising pages were converted into an image-building Donnybrook, the cigarette companies entered with some of the most virile-looking males ever to squint at the consuming public. First came the Marlboro Man with a crew haircut, squared-off jaw and provocative hand tattoo who was supposed to erase from the public mind that the Marlboro cigarette was a tainted female brand. The Marlboro Man soon had rugged company in the Viceroy Man who thought for himself, the L&M Man who lived modern, the Chesterfield Man who liked his pleasure big, and the Lucky Strike Man who knew a real smoke. It became almost a physiognomical impossibility to tell what brand the craggy character was smoking on TV until he announced his allegiance after a satisfying puff at the cigarette. But he undoubtedly entranced millions of desk-bound white-collar males and females with the immense benefits of the great outdoors.

Among the farmers, truck drivers, cabbies, steelworkers, divers, jet pilots, loggers, construction workers, ski patrolmen, Coast Guardsmen, firemen, and cowboys who puffed satisfyingly on one brand or another, the cowboys seemed to emerge for the tobacco companies as the epitome of American manhood. Indeed the cowboys seemed destined to become the leading authorities on whiskeys, automobiles, and many other products, as they became the hired hands of an increasing number of advertisers. A staff columnist on *Advertising Age*, who patently took advantage of his anonymity to criticize the rugged cowboys, objected to their aggrandizement in U.S. life. The particular cowhands he had met, the columnist said, had excited

him chiefly for their resemblance, intellectually, to the animals they hus-
banded. They were no doubt an outstanding symbol of masculinity—at its
worst and lowest form. Considering their exaggerated pleasure in personal
ornamentation, drinking, brawling, and regarding females largely in the
herd, the columnist wondered how "civilized" admen could parade them
before America as individuals "whose habits are worthy of copying."

From Joseph J. Seldin, The Golden Fleece (New York: The Macmillan Company, 1963).
Reprinted with permission.

We have thus far talked primarily about image building by professionals
in politics and advertising. But what about your image? Your credibility?
How does this relate to you? You project an image to others by what you
say and do, and by what others say about you. You have seen how important this image can be, how it, in effect, sells the product. Improve your
image and you will sell yourself and your ideas more effectively. The first
step toward improving your projected image is to improve your self-image.
This can be accomplished by getting to know yourself better.

Personality Development

We develop our personalities largely as a result of our relationships with
others. We learn to communicate by imitating those around us. Our views
on life are shaped by those with whom we come in contact. We often mir-
ror the attitudes and sentiments of our parents and friends. Our speaking
habits are usually similar to the habits of those closest to us as we grow up.
Problems like mispronunciation and unclear diction can usually be traced
to parents or friends with the same difficulties.

The reaction of others to us as we are growing up also has an effect on
our personalities. People tell us by their responses whether we are important or unimportant, good or bad, smart or dumb, and we develop a picture
of ourselves accordingly. Furthermore, we tend to act like the person we
conceive ourselves to be. Thus, a child who developed the self-concept of
being unimportant because of his parents would probably respond by being
withdrawn and unfriendly. The child who was thought of by his classmates
as being dull and a troublemaker would probably live up to this label.

The first step to personality improvement is careful self-appraisal. Obviously, the more accurate a picture a person has of himself, the more clearly
he can see how to improve himself, how to develop his strengths and eliminate his weaknesses. If, for example, John is strongly attracted to Jane but
sees himself as being inferior to her in terms of personality and attractive-
ness, he is apt to communicate this attitude to her in uneasy, superficial,
and, therefore, nonproductive conversation. On the other hand, if John can
see his own strengths and weaknesses in their proper perspective and recog-

Who cares if these boys have good homes to grow up in?

Equitable cares. For countless children, home is cracked plaster, broken plumbing, dingy rooms. Equitable thinks children deserve better. We're trying hard to make sure they get it. From Seattle to Birmingham, we've invested over $95,000,000 to build better housing for those who need it most.

As a company deeply involved with helping people build a better life, we feel it's our responsibility to do what we can to rebuild our cities.

We're glad so many of our agents feel the same way. By getting involved with urban renewal projects in their own communities, they're helping make life better for all of us.

THE EQUITABLE

Courtesy of the Equitable Life Assurance Society.

nize his own self-worth, he will be more likely to communicate his interest to Jane.

The key to John's success with Jane is self-worth. Before anyone else can like you, you first have to like yourself. Communicate this attitude of self-worth to others by the careful preparation and practice of your speeches and the critical proofreading and rewriting of your papers and you will project a more effective image.

Good writers and speakers are not born; they are developed as the result of commitment and hard work. Before you can become proficient at either skill, you have to want to work at it. It took John Steinbeck six years to complete his novel, *East of Eden.* Ernest Hemingway once said, "The first four times I write a paragraph it reads like any one else's writing. It's the fifth time that it becomes Ernest Hemingway." "Getting by" wasn't enough for them. If you want to project a good image, it can't be enough for you either.

EXERCISES

I. The advertisement on page 180 is designed to project an image of Equitable Company to the reader. Indicate in a speech or essay how the advertiser tends to humanize the company for the audience. How, for example, is the reader shown that the company possesses a strong sense of social responsibility or contributes to the common good?

1. What character traits are possessed by the boy feeding the baby? Explain.
2. Why weren't adults included in the picture?
3. What is the reason for using white and black models? Are they friends? What attitude does the boy watching the feeding have?
4. Does this picture say something about Equitable's attitude toward equal opportunity? What?
5. Is there any special reason for specifically mentioning Birmingham?
6. How does this ad tend to humanize the Equitable Life Assurance Society in the public mind?

II. In a eulogy at his brother Robert's funeral, Edward Kennedy projects an image of his dead brother by telling his audience what his brother said and did, and what others thought about him. Read the speech carefully and make a list of character traits that the speech indicates Robert Kennedy possessed.

A TRIBUTE TO HIS BROTHER

Your Eminences, your excellencies, Mr. President. In behalf of Mrs. Kennedy, her children, the parents and sisters of Robert Kennedy, I want to express what we feel to those who mourn with us today in this cathedral and around the world.

We loved him as a brother and as a father and as a son. From his parents and from his older brothers and sisters, Joe and Kathleen and Jack, he received an inspiration which he passed on to all of us.

He gave us strength in time of trouble, wisdom in time of uncertainty and sharing in time of happiness. He will always be by our side.

Love is not an easy feeling to put into words. Nor is loyalty or trust or joy. But he was all of these. He loved life completely and he lived it intensely.

A few years back Robert Kennedy wrote some words about his own father which expresses the way we in his family felt about him. He said of what his father meant to him, and I quote:

"What it really all adds up to is love. Not love as it is described with such facility in popular magazines, but the kind of love that is affection and respect, order and encouragement and support.

"Our awareness of this was an incalculable source of strength. And because real love is something unselfish and involves sacrifice and giving, we could not help but profit from it."

And he continued:

"Beneath it all he has tried to engender a social conscience. There were wrongs which needed attention, there were people who were poor and needed help, and we have a responsibility to them and this country.

"Through no virtues and accomplishments of our own, we have been fortunate enough to be born in the United States under the most comfortable conditions. We therefore have a responsibility to others who are less well off."

That is what Robert Kennedy was given.

What he leaves to us is what he said, what he did and what he stood for.

A speech he made for the young people of South Africa on their day of affirmation in 1966 sums it up the best, and I would like to read it now.

"There is discrimination in this world and slavery and slaughter and starvation. Governments repress their people. Millions are trapped in poverty, while the nation grows rich and wealth is lavished on armaments everywhere.

"These are differing evils, but they are the common words of man. They reflect the imperfection of human justice, the inadequacy of human compassion, our lack of sensibility towards the suffering of our fellows.

"But we can perhaps remember, even if only for a time, that those who live with us are our brothers, that they share with us the same short moment of life, that they seek as we do nothing but the chance to live out their lives in purpose and happiness, winning what satisfaction and fulfillment they can.

"Surely this bond of common faith, this bond of common goals, can begin to teach us something. Surely we can learn at least to look at those around us as fellow men. And surely we can begin to work a little harder to bind up the wounds among us and to become in our own hearts brothers and countrymen once again.

"The answer is to rely on youth, not a time of life but a state of mind, a temper of the will, a quality of imagination, a predominance of courage over timidity, of the appetite for adventure over the love of ease. The cruelties and obstacles of this swiftly changing planet will not yield to the obsolete dogmas and outworn slogans; they cannot be moved by those who cling to a present that is already dying, who prefer the illusion of security to the excitement and danger that come with even the most peaceful progress.

"It is a revolutionary world which we live in, and this generation at home and around the world has had thrust upon it a greater burden of responsibility than any generation that has ever lived. Some believe there is nothing one man or one woman can do against the enormous array of the world's ills. Yet many of the world's great movements of thought and action have flowed from the work of a single man.

"A young monk began the Protestant Reformation. A young general extended an empire from Macedonia to the borders of the earth. A young woman reclaimed the territory of France, and it was a young Italian explorer who discovered the New World, and the 32-year-old Thomas Jefferson who explained that all men are created equal.

"These men moved the world, and so can we all. Few will have the greatness to bend history itself, but each of us can work to change a small portion of events, and in the total of all those acts will be written the history of this generation.

"Each time a man stands for an ideal, or acts to improve the lot of others, or strikes out against injustice, he sends forth a tiny ripple of hope.

"And crossing each other from a million different centers of energy and daring, those ripples build a current that can sweep down the mightiest walls of oppression and resistance. Few are willing to brave the disapproval of their fellows, the censure of their colleagues, the wrath of their society. Moral courage is a rarer commodity than bravery in battle or great intelligence. Yet it is the one essential vital quality for those who seek to change a world that yields most painfully to change.

"And I believe that in this generation those with the courage to enter the moral conflict will find themselves with companions in every corner of the globe.

"For the fortunate among us there is the temptation to follow the easy and familiar paths of personal ambition and financial success so grandly spread before those who enjoy the privilege of education. But that is not the road history has marked out for us.

"Like it or not, we live in times of danger and uncertainty. But they are also more open to the creative energy of men than any other time in history. All of us will ultimately be judged and as the years pass, we will surely judge ourselves, on the effort we have contributed to building a new world society and the extent to which our ideals and goals have shaped that event.

"Our future may lie beyond our vision, but it is not completely beyond our control. It is the shaping impulse of America that neither faith nor nature nor the irresistible tides of history but the work of our own hands matched to reason and principle that will determine our destiny."

There is pride in that, even arrogance, but there is also experience and truth, and in any event it is the only way we can live. That is the way he lived. That is what he leaves us.

My brother need not be idealized or enlarged in death beyond what he was in life. He should be remembered simply as a good and decent man who saw wrong and tried to right it, saw suffering and tried to heal it, saw war and tried to stop it.

Those of us who loved him and who take him to his rest today pray that what he was to us, and what he wished for others, will some day come to pass for all the world.

As he said many times, in many parts of this nation, to those he touched and who sought to touch him:

"Some men see things as they are and say why. I dream things that never were and say, why not."

Vital Speeches XXXIV:18 (July 1, 1968), pp. 546–47.

STEREOTYPES: FORM A

INSTRUCTIONS: Below are descriptions of three different people. Based on the information given, what is your best guess about their personalities? Place a checkmark somewhere on the rating scale. For example, if you think Jane is probably very friendly, put a checkmark at or near the 1 point on the scale. If you think she is probably very unfriendly, then place the checkmark at or near the 5 point on the scale. If you have absolutely no opinion, place the checkmark at the 3 point on the scale. Remember that there are no right or wrong answers; this is not a test, merely a survey of your opinion.

1. Jane is 18 years old and a freshman college student. She is five feet, two inches tall and has red hair. She makes average grades, and dates about once a week. She probably is:

FRIENDLY	1	2	3	4	5	UNFRIENDLY
INTELLIGENT	1	2	3	4	5	STUPID
EASYGOING	1	2	3	4	5	HOT TEMPERED
CONCEITED	1	2	3	4	5	MODEST
ATTRACTIVE	1	2	3	4	5	UNATTRACTIVE

2. James Winthrop is 48 years old, is a college professor, is married, and has four children. He probably is:

FRIENDLY	1	2	3	4	5	UNFRIENDLY
INTELLIGENT	1	2	3	4	5	STUPID
ALERT	1	2	3	4	5	ABSENT MINDED
FAIR	1	2	3	4	5	UNFAIR
LAZY	1	2	3	4	5	AMBITIOUS

3. George Smith is 30 years old, a Black, married, a high school graduate, and works at a gas station. He probably is:

FRIENDLY	1	2	3	4	5	UNFRIENDLY
INTELLIGENT	1	2	3	4	5	STUPID
SUPERSTITIOUS	1	2	3	4	5	UNSUPERSTITIOUS
LAZY	1	2	3	4	5	AMBITIOUS
SERIOUS	1	2	3	4	5	HAPPY-GO-LUCKY

Reprinted by permission of Terrence Adams.

FORM B

INSTRUCTIONS: Below are descriptions of three different people. Based on the information given, what is your best guess about their personalities? Place a checkmark somewhere on the rating scale. For example, if you think Jane is probably very friendly, put a checkmark at or near the 1 point on the scale. If you think she is probably very unfriendly, then place the checkmark at or near the 5 point on the scale. If you have absolutely no opinion, place the checkmark at the 3 point on the scale. Remember that there are no right or wrong answers; this is not a test, merely a survey of your opinion.

1. Jane is 18 years old and a freshman college student. She is five feet two inches tall and has dark hair. She makes average grades, and dates about once a week. She probably is:

FRIENDLY	1	2	3	4	5	UNFRIENDLY
INTELLIGENT	1	2	3	4	5	STUPID
EASYGOING	1	2	3	4	5	HOT TEMPERED
CONCEITED	1	2	3	4	5	MODEST
ATTRACTIVE	1	2	3	4	5	UNATTRACTIVE

2. James Winthrop is 48 years old, is a TV repairman, is married, and has four children. He probably is:

FRIENDLY	1	2	3	4	5	UNFRIENDLY
INTELLIGENT	1	2	3	4	5	STUPID
ALERT	1	2	3	4	5	ABSENT MINDED
FAIR	1	2	3	4	5	UNFAIR
LAZY	1	2	3	4	5	AMBITIOUS

3. George Smith is 30 years old, married, a high school graduate, and works at a gas station. He probably is:

FRIENDLY	1	2	3	4	5	UNFRIENDLY
INTELLIGENT	1	2	3	4	5	STUPID
SUPERSTITIOUS	1	2	3	4	5	UNSUPERSTITIOUS
LAZY	1	2	3	4	5	AMBITIOUS
SERIOUS	1	2	3	4	5	HAPPY-GO-LUCKY

Ibid.

EXERCISE: Choose a political candidate you support, and in a short speech or essay indicate those character traits that he or she has demonstrated which provide personal proof to that candidacy.

EXERCISE: Compile a list of character traits, in order of importance, that you think would be desirable for a member of the opposite sex. Compile a similar list for your own sex.

12

logical proof

We humans are rational creatures who take a great deal of pride in the fact that we have the ability to reason, to analyze, to think things out for ourselves. We are appreciative of intelligence and the ability to solve problems, and being adept at problem-solving is important to us. Throughout our lives we use reasoning to decide what to buy, what to wear, what school to attend, or what to contribute in terms of time and money to our church or charity. In order to protect our self-image we must be able to justify our beliefs to others. We must rationalize our behavior to ourselves and defend it to our loved ones and friends. Therefore, an understanding of logical reasoning is imperative.

ARGUMENTATION

Reasoning is the process of drawing conclusions from evidence. When the relationship between the evidence and the conclusion is communicated to others in an attempt to influence belief, it is called argumentation.

In its simplest form argumentation consists of two statements, a premise and a conclusion drawn from that premise. The statements below are arguments in which the italicized conclusion is drawn from the premise.

1. John has been sent to the office three times this week for causing disturbances in class. Therefore, *he is a troublemaker.*
2. John is a member of the SDS. Therefore, *he is a troublemaker.*

Both of these arguments involve a premise-conclusion relationship. In the first example the conclusion was drawn from an examination of three individual situations: "John has been in the office three times. Therefore, he is a troublemaker."

When we examine individual cases and draw a conclusion, we are using *inductive reasoning.* The following situations involve the inductive process:

1. A poll predicting the winner in an upcoming election.
2. Tests conducted on a group of people to determine the effectiveness of a new vaccine.
3. The decision to put a traffic light on a street corner after a series of accidents.
4. A student deciding to become a college business major on the basis of previous interest and high school performance.

In each instance, the reasoning proceeds from specific cases to a general conclusion. In the first example, pollsters take a random sampling from a cross section of the voting population. On the basis of the results of this survey they conclude that the voting preference of the cross section will be typical of the vote of the entire group involved. The second example is similar: If the vaccine is effective for 95 per cent of the test group, it will probably be effective for 95 per cent of the total population. The third example—the decision to install the traffic light—also demonstrates movement from specific instances to a general conclusion. In the fourth case, the student considers experiences in his background before reaching a conclusion about his future. The movement in all of these cases has been from specific, individual experiences to a general conclusion.

Now let us return to the second of the two arguments concerning John: "John is a member of the SDS. Therefore, he is a troublemaker." It has been concluded that John is a troublemaker, not because he has been seen in individual situations in which he has caused trouble, but because membership in a certain group carries with it that label. You have come to some previous conclusion about members of the SDS being troublemakers. Since John is a member of that group, he, according to your stereotype, is a troublemaker. Reasoning in this manner, from a general rule to an individual (specific) case, is called deductive reasoning.

As you have seen, reasoning can take two forms—inductive and deductive. To test your understanding, indicate whether the following are examples of inductive or deductive reasoning.

1. I knew as soon as she walked into the room that tall skinny girls shouldn't wear miniskirts.
2. That's the last party I go to at a fraternity house. Boy, male college students are wolves.
3. We can't have pork for supper tonight. The Cohens are coming and they're Orthodox Jews.
4. I'll never learn to drive, mother; today I backed the car into our sunken living room.
5. We can't let our daughter marry him. He has longer hair than she has.
6. I'm not bowling anymore. That's the third time I dropped a ball on my foot.
7. Looks like Senator Harris will win again. The Gallup poll gives him a two to one edge.
8. Don't go around with those Jones boys, son. Their father is an ex-con.

THE PROCESS OF INDUCTION

As a result of an examination of specific cases, the writer or teacher comes to a general conclusion on the basis of his observations. The three principle forms of induction are those of generalization, causal relation, and analogy.

Generalization

We generalize when we examine examples from a class and then draw conclusions about the whole class. We conclude that characteristics true of the cases examined are also true of similar cases not examined. For example, if we have had good service from three Buicks, we might come to the conclusion that a Buick is a good car to own. If we have done poorly in English throughout high school, we might conclude that English courses are not our "cup of tea."

As you can see, generalization is an often-used form of reasoning in our daily lives. Testing the reliability of generalization may be summed up in these questions.

1. Are the instances examined sufficiently large to warrant the generalization? The number of instances examined depends upon the proposition. For example, you might be justified, on the basis of only one or two observations, in concluding that overly fat women should avoid wearing slacks. Coming to a conclusion in this way is called an *inductive leap*, and in some instances it is warranted. However, if you were investigating the protective qualities of a new vaccine, you might have to examine thousands of people before you could justify a conclusion. If in doubt, a good rule of thumb is the more cases examined, the more reliable the generalization.

2. Are the instances examined typical? The examples in a generalization must be representative of those in the class which are not examined. For example, an adverse conclusion about teenagers based on a few newspaper stories would probably be slanted, since many newspapers generally deal with the sensational rather than the commonplace. All possible care should be taken to insure that the examples used are typical. The best method of doing this is to choose examples at random. A random sample is one selected entirely by chance, as in choosing the first and last name on every page in the phone book.

3. Is the information used true? We do not limit examples used in generalization to those we examine personally, but also include instances we hear or read about. In a court of law, hearsay evidence is usually inadmissible as testimony. It is important that the evidence used be accurate.

4. Are there any negative instances which invalidate the conclusion? A negative instance will not invalidate a generalization if it can be shown to be an exception to the rule. Suppose you conclude that people on welfare are living in extreme deprivation. Someone points out that a man receiving welfare payments was also working full time. If you can show that documented statistics indicate that less than 1 per cent of welfare cases involve fraud, you will explain why the above case is an exception to the rule.

Causal Relation

Reasoning from causal relation is based on the principle that every cause has an effect. Causal reasoning may move from effect to cause or cause to effect. In either event, we reason from a known to an unknown. For example, in effect-to-cause reasoning, we see an increase in illegitimacy, and we infer an increase in promiscuity. We read of the high drop-out rate for students at a particular university, and we infer that the school has rigid academic standards. We begin with a known effect and attribute it to a probable cause. In cause-to-effect reasoning, we read about a tax increase on beer and infer a rise in beer prices. We observe a new school being built in our district and anticipate an increase in next year's taxes.

Cause-and-effect relationships can be most clearly shown in a carefully controlled scientific experiment in which a control group is used to determine whether there are other causes operating in such a way as to contribute to the alleged effect. For example, suppose that researchers are interested in developing a vaccine for prevention of a new variety of Asian flu. They would use the control group method. Ideally, the control group should be composed of subjects matched in every pertinent way with those in the experimental group, except that the experimental group receives the vaccine while the control group does not. If the two groups are alike in every respect other than the isolated variable (the vaccine), we can conclude with some confidence that any effect in regard to immunity to this strain of flu is due to the vaccine.

When using cause-and-effect, be careful to include the important links in the chain of causation, or else your reasoning may be unclear. Notice how a series of events which develops a logical cause-and-effect relationship can be made unclear because of poor communication.

A student was late for his first hour class because he shut his alarm clock off and fell asleep.

When he finally re-awoke, he glanced in horror at the time, hurriedly dressed, and ran to his car.

In his rush to get to school, he exceeded the speed limit considerably.

He noticed a truck at an approaching crossroad too late to avoid a collision.

When questioned by the police as to why the accident had occurred, he replied, "Because I shut the alarm off and went back to bed."

Had the student explained the series of events as outlined above, his reply would have constituted a logical causal relationship. Instead, his brief reply,

omitting essential links in the chain of causation, probably caused the policeman to wonder whether his reasoning had been affected by the accident.

Cause-and-effect relationships are more difficult to establish where strict
controls cannot be implemented. This is especially true in the area of social
problems, where causes may be so many that causal relation is almost impossible to define.

Analogical Reasoning

Use of analogy is a popular and colorful way of supporting a point. It assumes that if things are alike in known respects, they will also be alike in
unknown respects. We conclude that a son who has been trustworthy when
he was home will also be trustworthy when he is away at school. We reason
that if there is discontent among ghetto area residents of one city, there will
be discontent in the ghetto area of another city of similar size, population,
job opportunity, and city management. For analogical reasoning to be
persuasive, the points of similarity must clearly outweigh the points of
difference.

It is important to examine carefully the essential comparative features in
the analogy. Remember, the strength of the similarity is more important
than the number of similarities found. As was true in regard to cause-and-
effect relationships, it is difficult to make valid comparisons between people
and between groups of people, because of the complexity of the problem.
For example, in the analogy that a student will be unsuccessful in college
because he got lower than average grades in high school, suppose that the
student spends a number of years working before he enters college, and is
thus highly motivated to succeed. This significant difference might outweigh
the similarities and render the analogy invalid.

EXERCISE

*DIRECTIONS: Indicate whether the inductive reasoning used is generalization,
cause-and-effect, or analogy.*

1. This is my eighth marriage. Boy, women sure are a bunch of losers.
2. I always got good grades in high school. The fact that my college grades are
   low proves that there is something wrong with the college.
3. Last month I read three nineteenth-century novels, and they were lousy. After
   this I stick to the twentieth century.
4. I didn't go to church yesterday. Watch me lose at cards.
5. If you can't get the money from your own dad, how can you expect to get
   it from a friend?
6. You had better take an umbrella along. Look at those black clouds.
7. I'll never be at ease with a girl. Everytime I talk to one alone I get "all
   clutched up."

8. I'm taking Mr. Simpson's literature course. I had him for freshman English and he was tremendous.
9. Sure, I flunked English, Dad. Mr. Simpson only likes the girl students.
10. Fred and I will never get along, mother. That's the third fight we've had this week.
11. What man of you, if his son ask him for bread, will give him a stone? Or if he asks for a fish, will give him a serpent? If you, then, who are evil know how to give good gifts to your children, how much more will your God who is in heaven give good things to those who ask him?
12. I don't think Myron is going to do well in college. He got lost again this morning trying to find the school.

THE PROCESS OF DEDUCTION

Deduction is that form of reasoning which proceeds from a general truth to a particular conclusion. It is typically expressed in a three step pattern known as the *syllogism*. The three statements are so arranged that the last can be inferred from the first two. They are known as the major premise, minor premise, and conclusion. The most often used type of syllogism is the categorical, as in the following example:

Major Premise (general proposition about a category)	All cows	eat grass.
Minor Premise (falls within the category)	Bessy is a cow	
Conclusion (what is true of the category is true of all parts of the category)	Therefore, Bessy eats grass.	

As can be seen, the conclusion is simply a statement of what is clearly implied in the major and minor premises. If we know that all cows eat grass and that Bessy is a cow, we know that Bessy eats grass because eating grass is a characteristic of a cow.

There are two tests used to determine validity in deduction. The first applies to the major premise, which is a statement about a category and must be stated in a universal sense; that is, "all" or "every" or "none" of the things in the category have a particular characteristic. If there are exceptions which cannot be explained, you begin with an inaccurate assumption which invalidates the conclusion.

Some cows eat grass.
Bessy is a cow.
Therefore, she might/or might not eat grass.

Second, if the subject of the minor premise does not belong to the category referred to in the major premise, the conclusion will be invalid.

My cat eats grass.
All cows eat grass.
Therefore, my cat is a cow.

For some experience in recognizing validity in categorical syllogisms, examine the following premises in order to see what conclusions can be drawn from them. Keep in mind the tests discussed above.

M.P. Some college instructors are bald.
m.p. My English teacher is a college instructor.

No conclusion can be drawn from these premises since the term used is "some," not "all." Remember, the distribution in the category must be universal, or, if there are exceptions, they must be satisfactorily explained.

M.P. All college instructors are bald.
m.p. My English instructor has long flowing hair.

The conclusion is that my English teacher is not a college instructor. If he is not bald, he does not qualify, according to the major premise.

M.P. No college professor is bald.
m.p. My English instructor is bald.

The conclusion is that my English teacher is not a college instructor. His baldness rules him out of the category, according to the major premise.

M.P. All college instructors are bald.
m.p. My mother-in-law is bald.

No conclusion can be drawn from these premises. The major premise does not say that all people who are bald are college professors; it says only that all college professors are bald. Remember, a deduction can draw only those conclusions implied in the premises.

EXERCISE

DIRECTIONS: Read the following syllogisms. Indicate which are valid and which are invalid. When a syllogism is not valid, briefly explain why.

1. All good citizens vote. Eldridge Cleaver voted. Therefore, Eldridge Cleaver was a good citizen.
2. No Pandas have wings. This creature has wings. Therefore, this creature is not a Panda.
3. All athletes eat Whams for breakfast. Jerry is an athlete. Jerry eats Whams for breakfast.
4. Men of distinction drink Carlsberg beer. I drink Carlsberg beer. I am a man of distinction.
5. Some persons like cats. George is a person. Therefore, George likes cats.
6. Any golfer who makes a hole in one is lucky. Sam made a hole in one. Sam was lucky.
7. No nice person uses vulgar language in public. He uses vulgar language in public. He is not a nice person.
8. Anyone who reads Karl Marx is a communist. Mr. Schwartz reads Karl Marx. Mr. Schwartz is a communist.
9. All communists read Karl Marx, Mr. Schwartz reads Karl Marx. Mr. Schwartz is a communist.

How do these ideas relate to the persuader? The idea is to get your audience to agree with your premises. If they accept the premises as true, and if the premises are set up properly, then they must logically accept the conclusion. Some of the premises above, from which a conclusion could be drawn, were not acceptable, e.g., "All college instructors are bald." This premise is false (fallacious). A syllogism may be fallacious and still valid, since validity refers to the structure of the syllogism.

Faulty deduction often occurs when people accept generalizations about classes of people as being general truths. Such generalizations are called stereotypes and are generally wrong when used as the major premise in a categorical syllogism. We develop stereotypes of the "conservative," "liberal," "communist," "Catholic," "Protestant," "stockbroker," "Jew," "Black," "college instructor," and so on. The following stereotypes are stated as general rules from which people have reasoned incorrectly:

All Negroes are shiftless.
All politicians are dishonest.
All effeminate males are homosexuals.
All college professors are intellectual.
All members of S.D.S. are troublemakers.
All teenagers are rebellious.

Although these statements are all incorrect, you can find those who use them as general truths from which to reason. Take the first, "All Negroes are shiftless." A racist employer might reason this way and never hire a black person. The syllogism is valid, since it is structurally sound, but fallacious because the major premise is untrue. In order to be reliable, deduction must start from true premises.

EXERCISE

DIRECTIONS: Some of the syllogisms below are valid and others are not. If the syllogism is invalid, briefly explain why. If you think that a valid syllogism is fallacious, briefly explain why.

1. All hippies have long hair. He has long hair. He is a hippy.
2. Jewish people may not eat pork. He is Jewish. He may not eat pork.
3. No full-blooded Indian can grow a beard. He has a beard. He is not a full-blooded Indian.
4. All welfare recipients who are physically able to work and do not are lazy. She is physically able to work. She is lazy.
5. Anyone who goes to church regularly is charitable. He goes to church regularly. He is charitable.
6. Anyone who believes in premarital sex relations is promiscuous. She believes in premarital sex relations. She is promiscuous.
7. All policemen are oppressive. He is a policeman. He is oppressive.
8. Anyone who is promiscuous believes in premarital sex relations. She believes in premarital sex relations. She is promiscuous.
9. All Scotsmen are tight-fisted. He is a Scotsman. He is tight-fisted.
10. All college professors are well-qualified in the subjects they teach. He is a college professor. He is well-qualified in the subject he teaches.

FALLACY

Fallacious reasoning can be the result of faulty induction or deduction, or the acceptance of misleading argumentation. Some of these fallacies occur so often that they have been isolated and labeled. The most common of these are treated below.

Unwarranted or Hasty Generalization

A generalization is fallacious when it is based on insufficient or unfair evidence, or when it is not warranted by the facts available. For example, "all hippies are dirty," "all welfare recipients are lazy," and so on.

Errors in Causal Induction

Fallacy in causal induction occurs when there is no logical relationship between a cause and an effect. Two most common cause-and-effect fallacies are *post hoc* (after this, therefore, because of this) and *non sequitur* (it does not follow).

Post Hoc   *Post hoc* is the fallacy of thinking that an event which follows another is necessarily caused by the other. Thus, you might conclude that the Democratic Party promotes war, that television viewing increases juvenile delinquency, and that an easing of censorship causes an increase in immorality.

The error in post hoc reasoning occurs because the reasoner ignores other factors which may have contributed to the effect. A survey of former college debaters revealed, for example, that they were considerably more successful in their chosen field of work than their nondebating counterparts. To assume from this that their experience as debaters was the cause of their success would be fallacious. Other factors must be considered: Students who become debaters usually possess superior verbal ability, have keen analytical minds, and are highly motivated by competition. No doubt these factors, which led them into debate, also contributed to their success.

Non Sequitur   In this fallacy the conclusion reached does not necessarily follow from the facts argued. The argument that because a man is kind to animals he will make a good husband ignores the possibilities that the man may make a bad husband, drink excessively, cheat, or beat his wife.

Begging the Question

An argument begs the question when it assumes something as true when it actually needs to be proven. For instance, the declaration that "these corrupt laws must be changed" asserts the corruption but does not prove it, and consequently the conclusion is not justified.

Begging the question also occurs when we make a charge and then insist that someone else disprove it. For example, to answer the question, "How do you know that the administration is honest?" would put the respondent in the position of trying to disprove a conclusion which was never proven in the first place. Remember, whoever makes an assertion has the burden of proof.

Ignoring the Question

Ignoring the question occurs when the argument shifts from the original subject to a different one, when the argument shifts from the proposition to the character or personality of the opponent, or when the argument appeals to some emotional attitude which has nothing to do with the logic of the case. An example of the first would be a man replying, "Haven't you ever done anything dishonest?" when accused of cheating on his wife. He ignores the question of his infidelity by shifting to a different argument. The argument that attacks the man rather than the issue is called *argu-*

mentam ad hominem. "I wouldn't trust him. His best friend is a homosexual" or "You're not going to believe a former convict?" are examples of this fallacy. An argument that appeals to the emotional attitudes of the reader or listener would be the statement, "No good American would approve of this communistic proposal."

False Analogy

To argue by analogy is to compare two things which are alike in germane known respects and to suggest that they will also be alike in unknown respects. This method is accurate if the things being compared are genuinely similar: "George will do well in graduate school; he had an excellent academic record as an undergraduate." It is likely to be fallacious when they are dissimilar: "There's nothing to handling a snowmobile; it's just like riding a bicycle."

Analogies are more difficult to prove when the comparison is figurative rather than literal. In a political campaign, the incumbent might admonish the voter "not to change horses in the middle of the stream," while the opponent replies that "a new broom sweeps clean."

EXERCISE

DIRECTIONS: Identify the following fallacies by employing these identifications: hasty generalization, inadequate causal relation, false analogy, begging the question, ignoring the question.

1. My English grades were always good in high school. The fact that I got a D in English proves that there is something wrong with this English course.
2. Because he doesn't smoke, drink, or swear, he'll make some woman a wonderful husband.
3. There's no sense in not spanking your children. The neighbors on each side of me are opposed to physical punishment and their kids are monsters.
4. We wouldn't have all this crime and immorality if people would return to the church.
5. Would you listen to a man who spent a year behind bars?
6. Giving to charity is like throwing your money down a sewer.
7. No one with any brains would vote for him.
8. Of course it's true. I read it in a book.
9. I had an automobile accident yesterday morning on the way to school, but I wasn't surprised. As I was approaching Wisconsin Avenue, a black cat crossed in front of me.
10. No, I didn't quit smoking. But neither did you.
11. She couldn't be his mother-in-law. She's too nice.
12. The theatres are full of nothing but movies about sex. In last night's paper, for instance, there were six X-rated movies advertised.
13. This unfair law should be abolished.

14. This communistic proposal would be unacceptable to any real American.
15. Girls who smoke marijuana never amount to much. I have known this to happen a number of times.
16. "I told you, honey, I can't afford to buy a new car." "I don't see why not. Sandy's husband bought her a new car. I should think you love me as much as he loves her."
17. He's a Ph.D., isn't he? He must know what he's talking about.
18. Me, vote for a divorced man for governor? If he couldn't keep his marriage together, how can he run our state government?
19. I didn't go to church Sunday; watch me lose my shirt.
20. He'll make a fine senator; he's a good Christian.

EXERCISES

DIRECTIONS:

I. Give an example other than those mentioned in this chapter of the following fallacies: (1) hasty generalization, (2) error in causal relationship, (3) begging the question, (4) ignoring the question, (5) false analogy.

II. Select an editorial or short essay which supports or criticizes an organization, program, or policy. Comment on its effectiveness as persuasion. Indicate whether the reasoning used is inductive or deductive.

III. Deliver a two to three minute speech or write a two to three hundred word essay in which you support or refute a stand taken on a controversial campus issue. Develop your communication inductively or deductively.

13

psychological proof

Logical proof appeals to the reason of the audience. Psychological proof, on the other hand, makes its appeal to the audience's attitudes and motives. People do things as a result of two factors, motive and desire. We are predisposed to act in certain ways because of goals, attitudes, sentiments, and motives which we have developed as part of our personality. When the desire to satisfy this "inner drive" becomes strong enough, we act.

ATTITUDES

Through learning and experience we build up reaction tendencies, which cause us to respond in predisposed ways to situations, people, values, and events. These reaction tendencies are called *attitudes*. Our attitudes are developed from our own experiences and from information handed down to us by parents, teachers, and friends. Thus, we form attitudes toward religion, LSD, mothers-in-law, Blacks, sex, liquor, and so on. These attitudes give direction to our behavior, causing us to react in positive or negative ways. Keep in mind the fact that attitudes direct behavior—motives stimulate it. The following example should help you to see the difference between attitudes and motives:

A young girl is attacked by a man wielding a knife. She is stabbed repeatedly while a number of people watch. When the knife-wielder leaves, one or two run forward to aid the dying girl. The others hang their heads, ashamed that they stood by while this horror occurred. All of the people who watched had attitudes which were in sympathy with the victim. Why didn't they help? Probably because they were held back by motives related to their own safety which were stronger than those motives which would have caused them to act.

MOTIVES

As you have just seen, *motive* is the inner drive or impulse that stimulates behavior. If we look at attitude as the directive force of behavior, we can call motive the driving force. All of us have certain physical and social desires and wants. The inner force which moves us to satisfy these wants is called a motivating force. Motive is defined, therefore, as an impulse or drive which causes a person to act in a certain way. There are two basic types of motives: (1) Physical motives—hunger, thirst, self-preservation, shelter, and sex; and (2) social motives—security, approval, popularity, success.

Physical Motives

All of us have essentially the same basic physical wants. We try to eat when hungry, rest when tired, and protect ourselves when threatened. The more money we have, the more we spend to achieve the greatest possible comfort. We put money aside to escape heat in the summer and cold in the winter. We buy heated swimming pools, air-conditioned cars, and remote-controlled appliances to insure the comfort and protection of our most priceless possession, ourselves. We are, to a considerable degree, creatures of the body. Few could imagine how many business deals or sales have been made to clients who have been put into the right mood with a steak dinner and all the trimmings.

Hunger and Thirst Although, one and a half billion people in the world exist on a starvation diet, few Americans know what it is to go hungry. Therefore, advertisers do not attempt to satisfy the hunger or thirst of an audience, but to create desire which will cause them to want to eat or drink. In short, the persuader attempts to stimulate the appetite of his audience in order to sell the product. We read of a product's "delicious goodness," "enticing aroma," "frosty freshness," or "tantalizing taste," and if we are sufficiently motivated, we buy.

A typical ad shows a group of men working in the heat of the summer sun. Near them, on a table in the shade, is a tray with four ice-cold schooners of beer.

The caption reads:

It's hot and sticky and you've been working hard. You need a little lift and you know nothing will cool you off the way the refreshing taste of_____beer does. So get with it. Grab a taste of gusto and cool off.

Self-Preservation No drive is stronger in man than the drive for survival. Any account of the unbelievable horror and pain that men have endured in prison camps, in hospitals, or on the battlefield in an effort to stay alive testifies to the strength of this drive. The persuader who appeals to this basic want tries to create a need on the part of the reader or listener. Slogans like "Drive carefully; the life you save may be your own," and "Stop smoking; it's a matter of life and breath," direct themselves to establishing this need. Note how the Christian Children's Fund ad points out that the person willing to become a sponsor will save the life of the child.

Reprinted from Better Homes and Gardens, *October 1970, with permission of the Christian Children's Fund, Inc.*

Sex No appeal is used more widely in advertising than the appeal to the sex drive. Our society is supersaturated with sex in advertising to sell everything from spark plugs to corporate image. The degree of subtlety employed in advertising based on sex appeal depends upon the specific audience the ad is intended to reach. The General Cigar Company designed this ad to sell its product to the readers of *Playboy* Magazine.

Should a gentleman offer a Tiparillo to a marine biologist.

You're scuba-ing along, admiring a purple parrot fish and a red coral reef when you spot something truly breathtaking.

A pink leg.

A marine biologist. Discovering new things under water. Maybe, you muse, she'd like to discover a Tiparillo®. Or a Tiparillo M with menthol.

She could classify them as the slim, elegant cigar with neat tip. Mild taste? Well...she'd have to try one, wouldn't she?

But should you offer her one? Or shouldn't you?

Think fast, mate. Your face mask is steaming up.

With permission of the General Cigar Company and Playboy Magazine.

A typical TV commercial shows a skinny, bespectacled young lad approaching a football stadium in his new car. He is met by a campus beauty walking arm in arm with a football player, a magnificent physical specimen who appears to be the hero of the game. When the girl sees the car, she pushes the hero aside and hops into the front seat with love in her eyes. Moral: When you buy Mustang, you buy sex appeal.

Shelter While some in our society live under deplorable conditions of poverty, most of us live in relative comfort. For this reason, advertisers make their most of us live in relative comfort. For this reason, advertisers make their appeal to man's drive for shelter in terms of the "desire for comfort" which is evident among most Americans. An air conditioned restaurant on a sweltering July day might be more inviting than a sign promising excellent cuisine. The additional cost of building a fireplace in a new home is offset by the thought of sitting in front of its warm blaze on a chilly evening.

There are, however, times when the persuader must make an appeal on behalf of those who are in such desperate circumstances that the audience, having little experience of hardship themselves, would lack a basis for grasping fully the seriousness of the problem. It is then up to the persuader to make the situation as real as possible for the audience. The picture and story of little Margaret is designed to make the reader feel what it must be like to go without adequate food or care.

Putting one's self in another person's place is called empathy. When we cry or are saddened because of another person's grief, or when we are happy because another person is happy, we are responding empathically to that person. In order to get your reader or listener to respond in a desirable way, you must make your description real enough to produce empathic response.

Social Motives

The physical drives we have talked about thus far are called basic drives and are common to all higher forms of animal life. However, while animals conform only to the law of the jungle, man is a social being and must live within the framework of the group. Even in the most primitive society, man has values, mores, and customs to which he must adhere in order to avoid the condemnation of his fellows. If he would live in harmony within his society, man must satisfy his physical drives in socially acceptable ways.

Early in life you learned to conform to certain rules if you wanted to maintain the approval of those around you. As you grew older and came in contact with more people, you found that this "code of conduct" became more complex. In order to achieve satisfaction and still conform to the rules, you developed a set of secondary, social motives. We list these motives as security, approval, popularity, and success. They seldom operate singly, but frequently combine to effect behavioral response.

Different groups within the society have different codes of expectations. Therefore, in discussing values and customs we will be talking about those common to most Americans. It is our belief that, in order to survive, every free society must have a common set of values to which most of its members ascribe.

"Bastards!"

Reprinted from True *Magazine, copyright June 1969, Fawcett Publications, Inc.*

Security Foremost among man's social motives are those that provide for his survival. These include desire for money, property, health care, provision for loved ones.

The force of this drive for security is clearly evident in today's world. The effect that it has on us and our loved ones shapes our consideration of the war and the draft. Our appraisal of birth control is made in terms of our own sentiments, our religious attitude, and the health factor. The specter of pollution is a threat to our very existence. We attend college to assure ourselves a better future; we "go steady" to insure a dependable date;

The Pirelli snow tire is made for tow trucks.

And cars that don't want to be towed.

To keep from being extremely embarrassed, a tow truck needs a snow tire that can go where ordinary snow tires are useless.

Fortunately for tow trucks, we made a snow tire that can. The Pirelli Cinturato Etna.

But unfortunately for tow trucks, we also make the Pirelli Etna for cars.

When you put it on a car, the Etna's radial ply construction flattens out and grips like the treads of a tank.

In fact, so fierce is its gripping power, drivers use it to get them up and down some pretty steep and snowy hills. Called the Alps.

But the Pirelli Etna doesn't out-grip ordinary snow tires only in deep snow. It also out-grips them on hard-packed snow and ice.

What's more, the Pirelli Etna out-handles ordinary snow tires. And it out-stops ordinary snow tires.

And if by some miracle we should

have a few nice days this winter, you'll be happy to know the Etna rides cool and quiet on dry roads.

The Pirelli Etna is available for American, European and Japanese cars. And it comes with a price tag you can afford.

Plus, for a few extra dollars, you can have the Etna with tungsten studs.

In case you're the kind of guy who does everything to extremes.

PIRELLI

Pirelli Tire Corporation Sixty East Forty Second St., New York, N.Y. 10017

Reprinted with permission of Pirelli Tire Corporation.

208

we buy insurance to provide for health care or income protection. In this world of violence and uncertainty, no generation of Americans has been as security-minded as this one. Countless ads like this one emphasize security as their major appeal.

Approval   Some of you are probably attending college now because you want to maintain the approval of your parents, friends, or employer. You might even dress in a style which is not particularly becoming to you because it is the in thing to do. Any store that promises the latest styles is selling approval along with its product. The drive for approval is particularly forceful. A person might spend months building a recreation room or weaving a fancy tapestry for the reward of being able to say, "I made this myself." The young hoodlum might risk a prison sentence to impress his fellow gang members with a particular daring crime. Approval is achieved by living up to or exceeding the expectations of others. It can be gained for a desirable personality trait or for some skill or ability. Most people admire such character traits as honesty, dignity, integrity, courage, and morality, and those who demonstrate these traits to others generally win their approval.

Popularity   Close to our desire for approval is the drive for popularity. If approval means to be "liked," popularity means to be "well-liked." It is strongest among young people, where being in the right group, learning the latest dance step, having a lot of dates, getting many yearbook signatures, and being well-liked are major goals.

The success of dance studios, charm courses, and books on personality development attest to the large number of older people who also have this need. This motive is closely linked to the sex motive. The American public is assured popularity if they buy the right deodorant, go to the right school, drive the right auto, and wear the right undergarments.

Success   The desire for success can be called the great American dream. The man who starts out on a shoestring and amasses a fortune, the beauty who becomes a star overnight, and the local rock group that wins national acclaim with a hit record are all forms of this dream.

For some, the drive for success can be so strong that it overshadows all others. Men have lied, cheated, stolen, and even killed for the sake of personal ambition. Some have endured years of hard work and deprivation in an attempt to develop an artistic or musical talent. Others have sought success by keeping up with the Joneses or living in the right neighborhood. Advertisers use the success appeal to sell products ranging from razor blades to real estate. Ads promising sartorial splendor, palatial elegance, and prestigious luxury appeal to this motive.

One major toothpaste commercial shows a young boy, Tommy, who repeatedly finishes second best to his friend George. Tommy sits on the bench while George quarterbacks the team to victory. George's ninth inning homer wins the ballgame after Tommy's error permitted the opposition to tie the game in the eighth. George presses his lips to those of the campus queen in the back seat of the car while Tommy presses his nose to the windshield, straining to see out into the storm.

But finally the tables are turned. George, a member of the control group in an experiment conducted by _____toothpaste, has a mouthful of cavities. Tommy, our new hero, is a member of the experimental group that has conquered tooth decay. Moral: Buy the right toothpaste and be a success.

ETHICS IN PERSUASION

Unfortunately, there are those in our society who operate with the attitude of getting away with whatever they can. Too many persuaders justify their intentional trickery with the slogan, "caveat emptor," let the buyer beware. With the vast influence wielded by professional persuaders in shaping opinion in our country, it is critical that we become more conscious of what is ethical in persuasion.

The question of ethics is complicated. What some might feel is an appeal to undesirable motives might be perfectly acceptable to others. What might appear to be a subjective use of information to some, might be defended by others as necessary to obtain the desired response. For this reason, we offer one principle: Persuasion is unethical when it is used intentionally to mislead an audience.

EXERCISES

DIRECTIONS:

I. Arrange the following words in some reasonable order and defend that order (two-three pages, preferably typewritten).

Fame
Integrity
Charity
Courage
Intelligence
Ability
Honesty
Affluence
Wisdom

II. Write an appeal similar to the one on page 204 to seek a response to the plight of the child below.

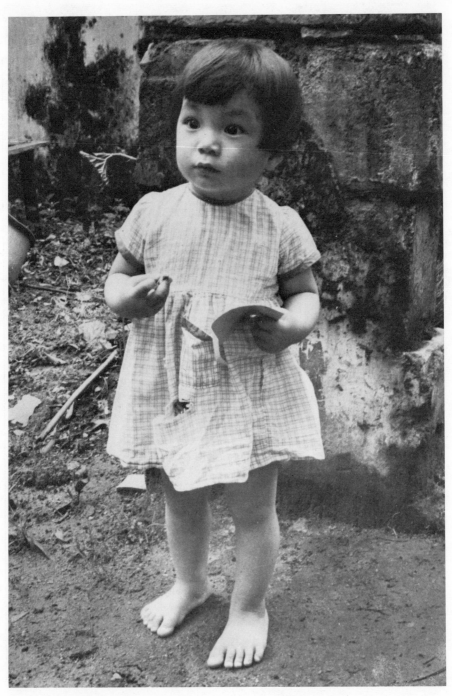

Reprinted by permission of the Christian Children's Fund, Inc.

III. Indicate the physical and social motives to which this ad appeals.

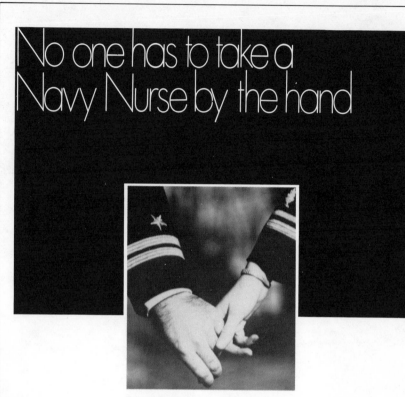

No one has to take a Navy Nurse by the hand

But some people do.

As an officer in the Navy Nurse Corps you're not only looked up to— you're looked at. It's a nice feminine kind of feeling.

And since most females get their way, so will you. Go where you want (here and abroad). Live like you want. And do what you want—in fields that range from coronary care nursing to operating-room management; from pediatrics to research and anesthesia.

Learn, advance, and have the time of your life doing life-giving work.

Mail the coupon below—you'll be in good hands.

The Navy If you're going to be something, why not be something special?

If you need a spare hand in the Navy Nurse Corps, I'm interested. Please tell me more.

Name_____Date of Birth_____

Address_____

City_____State_____Zip_____

____I am a registered professional nurse.

____I am enrolled in an accredited school of nursing and would be interested in your Candidate Program.

4.9-0014N

MAIL TO: Bureau of Medicine and Surgery Code 321, Navy Department, Washington, D.C. 20390

Reprinted by permission of the United States Navy Department.

PERSUASION TO REINFORCE

DIRECTIONS: Deliver a three-four minute speech or write a 300–500 word essay to reinforce. Persuasion to reinforce seeks to increase an audience's concern with a problem or course of action. The persuader should rely chiefly on psychological proof. He will appeal to the audience's emotions, motives, attitudes, and sentiments. The persuader must determine which appeals he can use to gain the desired response from his audience, so careful audience analysis is a necessity.

DELIVERY: This speech should be delivered extemporaneously. The speech to reinforce attempts to arouse the enthusiasm of the audience. The listener must feel that the speaker is sincere. Spontaneity and directness are fundamental qualities of such a speech.

SAMPLE TOPICS

1. Seatbelts save lives.
2. Be honest with yourself.
3. Be proud of your school.
4. We are our brother's keeper.

14

group
communication

Hardly a day goes by without your participating in a number of small group discussions. Most of them are informal talks with others about matters of mutual interest. Others occur more formally in organized committees and action groups.

Discussions have also been a vital part of your formal education. Most of us got our first taste of class discussion in kindergarten or the first grade. Probably a majority of the courses you are now taking are lecture-discussion courses. Yet, in spite of your considerable experience with group communication, many of the discussions that you engage in fail to produce fruitful results.

There are a number of reasons why discussions fail. Sometimes the participants do not have the necessary information and the discussion becomes a "pooling of ignorance." At other times the discussion lacks a spirit of cooperation and ends in aimless argument. Lack of communication, lack of understanding, and a tendency to stray from the subject may also lessen the possibility of agreement or understanding. How many discussions between parents and children have ended with the participants stalking off because of any or all of the above obstacles?

The advantage of becoming a more effective discussion member are obvious. A study of the forms and principles of group discussion, together with guided practice, will help you to become more effective in both formal and informal discussion situations.

TYPES OF DISCUSSION

The three basic types of discussion are the panel, the symposium, and the round table.

The Panel

A panel discussion usually involves from three to eight members, including a moderator. They sit in front of an audience in a circle or semicircle so that they can see and react to each other. Ideally, the members of a panel have varied backgrounds and viewpoints which make for an active exchange of ideas and experiences. The language of panel discussion is usually informal, with each member expressing his opinion in a normal, conversational way.

Many panels are followed by an open forum, an audience participation period. After the moderator has summarized the discussion, he invites the audience to ask questions of or make statements to individual members or the panel as a whole. It is the moderator's job to field the questions, repeating or rephrasing them when necessary.

The Symposium

While the panel discussion is essentially informal, give and take conversation, the symposium consists of a series of prepared speeches. The subject or problem is divided into parts, and each speaker develops the part assigned to him. The available speaking time is divided equally among the speakers, who talk directly to the audience rather than to each other. A moderator opens the discussion and introduces each speaker and his topic. After each speaker has come to the lectern and addressed the audience, either the moderator or the speakers themselves summarize the discussion. Following the summary, the moderator may turn the symposium into a panel or move to a forum period.

The Round Table

As its name implies, this form of discussion generally takes place around a round table or in a circle. The reason for the round table is to provide those involved members with a feeling of equality. The circle has traditionally been a symbol of unity; when seated in a circle, everyone is in a position equal to that of his neighbor. Like the panel, the round table discussion is a kind of magnified conversation, since the participants look at each other. The difference is that in this form of discussion everyone is in-

"Do you suppose, Bancroft, that for the duration of your term as a director of International Consolidated you could possibly forgo tilting?"

Drawing by Stevenson; © 1961 The New Yorker Magazine, Inc.

volved; there is no audience. Committee meetings and conferences are usually conducted as round table discussions. This form is especially appropriate for classroom discussion, where a stimulating topic handled well can result in a lively give and take among all members of the class.

THE FUNCTIONS OF DISCUSSION

In general, discussion has two functions: educative (information seeking) and problem-solving.

Educative Discussion

Many of the discussions in which you participate do not seek argument or action. Some are strictly social gatherings whose purpose is recreation or enjoyment. And yet, many times you get more than enjoyment from these discussions. They benefit you by adding to your background and experience. Their function is to make you better informed about the topic discussed. You often talk with others about dating, drugs, politics, or any matter of genuine interest in an attempt to increase your understanding. If you are lucky, and the information you get is accurate, you might become better equipped to make up your own mind on the question. Discussions of this type are called informative or educative discussions. Perhaps the most familiar example is classroom discussion, one of the important purposes of which is to stimulate thinking. This makes it especially appropriate for a course in communication skills. A lively classroom discussion of a controversial speech or essay can stimulate a speaker's or writer's thinking and motivate him to communicate to what has now become a more "real" audience. The informal exchange of ideas about a book or movie can often provide feedback as to the views of other members of the class. An all-class discussion during the first few weeks of the course can clear up many students' misconceptions about a communications course and indicate which attitudes need to be developed during the coming semester.

Problem-Solving Discussion

Life is a succession of personal problems and decision-making. Questions arise which require answers. Should I experiment with drugs? What kind of car should I buy? What should I major in? How far should I go with sex? What should we name the baby? Although these problems can be solved by the individual himself, chances are that a group solution will be more soundly conceived. Properly guided, group thinking offers a number of advantages over independent problem-solving.

First, the more people working on a problem, the more information is available to solve it. One individual's background and experience can seldom match those of a group. In order to be effective, there should be enough members in the discussion to provide for adequate contributions. Too few members limit the flow of ideas; too many create confusion. The preferred number of participants in a problem-solving discussion should range from three to eight, although a good classroom discussion of a provocative problem can be held with as many as 25.

Second, group thinking provides greater opportunities for problemsolving. The more people you have looking at a problem, the more likely you are to solve it correctly. In a group, an error by one individual is likely to be spotted by someone else.

A Pattern for
Problem-Solving Discussion

The process of group thinking can be organized into a series of steps roughly paralleling John Dewey's steps to reflective thinking. The sequence of steps can be used as an outline or pattern for discussion. The discussion usually begins with identification of the problem and proceeds step by step to implementation of the solution. The steps in the process are as follows.

Identifying the Problem Many discussions fail to get off the ground because the problem is not clearly understood by the participants. The first step in discussion, therefore, is to have the members pinpoint the discussion problem. Good teamwork in thinking can only begin when each member has a clear understanding of the problem at hand. Problems for discussion should always be stated as questions.

If the group is careful in phrasing the question as clearly as possible, they will avoid confusion later. For example, the question, "How can we halt pollution?" is unclear. Whom do we mean by "we"? Do we mean the group, the government, the people of the world? What type of pollution are we talking about? Do we mean air pollution, water pollution, noise pollution, or every type of pollution there is? The question, "What steps should the U.S. government take to curb industrial pollution of air and water?" avoids needless quibbling over definition of terms.

Analyzing the Problem Once the members have demonstrated a common understanding and agreement as to the issues, the causes and nature of the problem should be explored. There are times when a solution become obvious after the causes of a difficulty are identified. Once the causes are listed and agreed upon, an exploration of the problem can begin. The group should consider such questions as these: "Who is affected by the problem?" "How serious is it?" "Under what conditions must it be solved?"

A thorough investigation of the present situation will give members of the discussion a clear picture of the conditions that need correcting.

Finding the Best Solution   This step involves proposing possible solutions and then measuring them by the guidelines established above. It is usually a good idea to list all of the solutions before evaluating them. Such questions as these are asked: "How long will it take to carry out the solution?" "How much will it cost?" "Is the solution practical?" An important part of this step is for the group to determine that the solution will not cause some new problem.

Actuating the Solution   Whenever you deal with people, it is wise to consider just how a solution is going to be fulfilled. It might be useful to have members of the group role-play the parts of those people involved in carrying out the solution. When considering how people may react to a course of action, the group may discover that they cannot put their solution into operation.

The following example illustrates how a group of junior college students handle a problem, using the pattern discussed above.

Identifying the Problem   Consider the following situation:

> Your job is production foreman in an automotive parts fabricating plant. Company policy is to reward the first person who turns in a useful suggestion in written form. John has developed an idea concerning a manufacturing problem, but George, a second employee, learns of the idea and submits it as his own. These facts are known to you.
>   What should you do?

Adapted with permission of the author from William E. Utterback, Group Thinking and
Conference Leadership *(New York: Holt, Rinehart and Winston, Inc., 1964).*

Analyzing the Problem   In dealing with this situation, the group agreed that the foreman was faced with a dilemma; he should reward one of the employees, but which one? To reward John would violate company policy, which states that an idea must be submitted in written form. To reward George for stealing John's idea brought up the question of ethics. Either alternative was bound to cause repercussions. In order to determine the best way to handle the situation, the group began a search for the causes of the problem.

Their search revealed three contributing causes:

1. Although John developed the idea, he did not submit it in written form.
2. John revealed his idea to others before submitting it.
3. George submitted the idea as his own.

It can be assumed that both George and John have friends among their fellow workers who will have some reaction to whatever decision is reached.

Finding the Best Solution　The group next began to consider guidelines for selecting a solution to the problem. In the light of the factors discussed above, they arrived at the following guidelines:

1. The solution should be acceptable to the other workers.
2. The solution should be implemented as soon as possible.
3. The solution should be acceptable to John.

In establishing guidelines, the group concluded that plant harmony was an important consideration: The solution should be acceptable to the other workers and implemented as soon as possible. They further reasoned that whatever would be acceptable to both John and George would also be acceptable to the other workers. Therefore, they agreed on the following solution:

As soon as possible, have John and George work out an agreement among themselves as to a division of the money.

Actuating the Solution　After evaluating possible ways that the foreman could handle the situation, the group came up with the following suggestions:

Step 1. The foreman should call George and John into the office and explain to them that he is aware of the facts in the case, and that, in the interest of plant harmony, the two of them should settle the matter themselves.

Step 2. If George and John cannot reach an agreement, the foreman should call George into the office and in a very candid and forceful manner indicate his attitude toward the importance of honesty. If George still refuses to cooperate, as a final resort the foreman should tell him that he will do whatever he can to help prove it was John's idea.

Step 3. Have the foreman submit a recommendation to his superior that John be rewarded instead of George.

It should be pointed out that a group need not always think through a problem or arrive at a decision in the order we have indicated. Some of the steps may be eliminated because they are obvious. For example, an understanding of the problem might be perfectly apparent to the group, and they can start with the second step. At times the order may be varied. While establishing guidelines, for example, it might be necessary to consider how a solution is going to be carried out. Nevertheless, discussion groups will be more effective in problem-solving when they think their way through to a decision in the manner described above.

PARTICIPATING IN DISCUSSION

There are those who take part in discussion but contribute little or nothing to the outcome. Some think they have all the answers and reject any view contrary to their own. Others are so poorly prepared that they have nothing to offer in solving the problem. Still others lack an understanding of the nature of discussion. They would be glad to participate, but just don't know the rules of the game. The quality of participation may mean the difference between success and failure of the discussion. The duties of the discussant may be characterized as follows.

Be Prepared

There is a tendency among participants to let someone else do it when preparing for a group discussion. If the topic for discussion can be investigated ahead of time, do so. When you locate evidence important to the discussion, put it down on note cards, being sure to document it carefully. In a symposium, have your speech well enough prepared for an effective extemporaneous delivery with good eye contact.

Be Cooperative

Effective group thinking can only take place when members of the discussion put the common good of the group above personal interests. The purpose of the problem-solving discussion is to arrive at a solution acceptable to the entire group. This means that the members must be willing to compromise their viewpoints in order to resolve the conflict.

Be Friendly

Effective discussion is only possible when an attitude of goodwill prevails. When you find yourself disagreeing with others in the group, be sure to do so in a pleasant, friendly way. Remember, group thinking depends on teamwork. Personality clashes or any form of hostility in discussion inhibits participation. The free expression of ideas occurs only in an open, friendly atmosphere. To promote friendliness, discussion members should be encouraged to call each other by their first names.

From Parade Publication, Inc. Cartoon by Boltinoff. Reprinted with permission.

Keep An Open Mind

To be an effective participant in a discussion, you should learn to appreciate the views of others. When you listen to another's opinion, try to put yourself in his place, remembering that no two people see things alike. That doesn't mean that you should accept everything he says, but rather that your mind should be open to new avenues of thought. While it is important to value your own opinion, you must be willing to admit that other opinions may also be reasonable. Be aware that your opinion might be wrong and be willing to alter it. Only a fool never changes his mind.

Share the Spotlight

While you should take a full and active part in attempting to solve the problem, don't monopolize the discussion to the extent that others cannot be heard. In fact, when you notice that one of the discussants is not contributing, try to draw him out; find out how he is reacting to the ideas being presented. Group thinking is, necessarily, thinking out loud. Unless every person in the group makes his thoughts known to others, the full value of their knowledge and experience will not be brought to bear upon the problem.

Listen Carefully

Listening critically is indispensable to effective group thinking. Pay careful attention in an attempt to understand fully what the other fellow means.

Too many discussion members comment on what they "thought" someone meant without first making sure their understanding was correct. If you are in doubt, ask. Furthermore, it is each member's responsibility to test the thinking of others as it is expressed in the discussion. If you think someone is unclear in his thinking or on the wrong track, say so before the discussion continues.

Participate Freely and Enthusiastically

Each member of the group has a responsibility to participate. If you have a comment that you think is appropriate, make it. Avoid long speeches. Submit your contribution in one or two short sentences, or perhaps in the form of a question. The right question may prove to be just what the group needs to move forward in settling a problem. Furthermore, a question has a tendency to promote cooperation, whereas a critical comment might evoke hostility. Use your own background and experience to appraise and evaluate the contributions of others.

Stick to the Point

If you are like most discussion members, you probably have opinions or ideas that you would like to present to the group at the outset. You will greatly aid the progress of the discussion if you will withhold these remarks until they are pertinent. When you speak, speak to the point. This is especially important while evaluating and analyzing the problem. Follow the suggested pattern of the discussion and deal with the issues at hand. If you can deal with each aspect of the problem completely, you will avoid delay caused by backtracking to an issue that should have already been resolved.

MODERATING THE DISCUSSION

Although each member of the group must share the responsibilities of leadership, it is often wise to choose a moderator to guide the discussion. The specific duties of the moderator are to:

1. Open by briefly introducing the topic and the group members to the audience.
2. Guide the discussion, using a flexible outline.
3. Resolve tension by using tact and humor.
4. Stimulate all members to participate.
5. Provide transitions and summaries to help members see what has been accomplished and what remains to be done.

6. Be aware of the time to insure that all points are discussed.
7. Encourage informal, spontaneous participation.
8. Summarize the progress made at the close of the discussion and indicate the differences that remain unresolved.
9. Take charge of the forum period.

USING CASE PROBLEMS

Ability in group discussion is best developed through guided practice. The writers have found that the use of case problems as discussion questions is an effective way of stimulating this practice. Students respond to the challenge of coping with real issues geared to their level of interest and understanding.

Another advantage to dealing with problems in human relations is that they aid in developing those characteristics which contribute to the development of effective citizens—an understanding of and flexible attitude toward the beliefs and opinions of others, the recognition of a variety of points of view, a realization of the effectiveness of group problem-solving, and a greater belief in the worth of one's own opinion.

These case problems are brief scenes from everyday life and show only the incident, not its outcome. They are the kind of situations that the stu-

PEANUTS ®   **By Charles M. Schulz**

© 1956 United Features Syndicate, Inc.

dent has encountered or is likely to encounter at home, at work, or at school. They are designed to encourage the student to think carefully, analytically, and understandingly about the situations they describe.

There is no "right" or "wrong" answer to these case problems. The solution chosen will be a reflection of the attitudes and sentiments of the group. The group members should make every effort to reach agreement on a solution for each problem. If they cannot come to unanimous agreement, the solution should be chosen by majority opinion. A suggested format is the following:

1. Moderator introduces panelists.
2. Moderator identifies the problem.
3. Panelists, under the moderator's direction, analyze the problem, suggesting possible solutions.
4. Moderator opens the discussion to the entire group. Questions and comments may be addressed to the group or to individual panelists.
5. Moderator summarizes the conclusion of the panel.

CASE PROBLEMS

1. Mary F., who works at a sewing factory, ran a sewing machine needle through her finger. As superintendent of the factory you sent her to the company doctor. He declared it was a clean wound and sent her back to work without giving her a tetanus shot as a precaution against lockjaw. The company is responsible for payment of all expenses incurred by a worker in connection with a job-connected injury.
   What should you do?

2. Mr. Smith and Mr. Jones both worked at the same plant and have been good friends for several years. Smith, being more aggressive, was promoted and is now Jones's boss. Smith is getting along very well with all of his men except Jones, who has been causing a lot of trouble because he is jealous of Smith.
   What should Smith do about the situation?

3. Jack and Donna are very much in love. Although not married, they have been living together for several months. Donna's parents have insisted that they get married or break up. If this is not done, the parents threaten to call the police.
   What should Jack and Donna do?

4. Fred and John, close personal friends, work together part-time stocking shelves at a local super market. Fred has been working to buy himself a new car while John has taken the second job to help support his widowed mother and nine brothers and sisters. One night after closing time, Fred notices John carrying a case of powdered milk out to his car.
   What should Fred do?

5. You have two close friends, Bob and Jim. Jim has just been arrested for possession of heroin. The police found the heroin in Jim's car but Jim claims that he doesn't know how it got there. You know that Bob hid it there for safekeeping. Bob refuses to reveal this.
   What should you do?

6. John, a white student at a small out-of-state technical college, has fallen in love with Cindy, a black student at the same school. He plans to take her home for Christmas, but he doesn't plan to tell his parents beforehand that she is black. He argues that his parents have always insisted that they are unprejudiced, and now he will be able to judge by their reaction if they are honest. Cindy does not agree.

How should the situation be handled?

7. Joan and Donna have been friends since childhood. Both are eighteen. Lately, Donna has been seeing a lot of an older married man. Joan advises Donna to break this off, but Donna is convinced that the man plans to get a divorce and marry her. Donna has told her parents that she will be visiting Joan for the weekend so that she and the man can go off together.

What should Joan do?

8. Upon your college roommate's return from summer vacation, he tells you that he is engaged. When he shows you his fiancée's picture, you recognize her as a former classmate who has a reputation for being promiscuous. You like your roommate very much.

What should you do?

9. You have been assigned a term paper by your history instructor which will count for one third of your total final grade. After you have worked it out carefully, you find out from a reliable source, that over one half of those in class have bought term papers from an underground operation near your campus.

What should you do?

10. Paul found what he believed were LSD tablets in his sister's room. When he questioned her about it, she insisted they were antibiotics for a cold. He has noticed that she has seemed unusually withdrawn lately. He has revealed all this to his parents who have told him not to let his imagination run away with him.

What should he do?

11. Don and Alice are required by law to take a blood test before marriage. During the examination it is discovered that Don has had a venereal disease. When questioned about it he refuses to answer.

What should Alice do?

12. Ann has just found out from her family doctor that she has a venereal disease. The doctor asks her to reveal the name of the boy involved so that he can be treated. Ann has had intercourse with two boys, one of whom she plans to marry. She has no idea who gave her the disease.

What should she do?

13. When visiting his friend Ralph for the weekend, Carl sees him take $10 from his mother's purse. On the following day Carl is present as the mother accuses Ralph's brother Tim of stealing the money. She punishes Tim by taking away his use of the car for one month.

What should Carl do?

14. While you are riding home with Ed, a good friend, he backs into a parked car, causing considerable damage. Although he has liability insurance, he declines to leave his name, explaining that he has already had two accidents

this year, and that another will result in his insurance policy being canceled. Ed drives you to and from work every day.

What should you do?

15. Harry and Tom are hometown neighbors and dormitory roommates in college. Tom is concerned because Harry has been experimenting with hard drugs which have seriously affected his school work and his personality. Tom feels that something must be done before Harry becomes hopelessly addicted.

What should Tom do?

16. Paul writes very poorly in class. His essays indicate a lack of understanding of the simplest rules of grammar. The term paper that he hands in at the end of the semester is very well written and without error. The instructor suspects outside help but cannot prove it.

What should the instructor do?

17. Julia is engaged to be married to Fred. The wedding is less than two months away and Fred suggests that they begin their sexual relationship so that they will be sure that there are no physical or psychological barriers to a happy marriage. Julia believes very strongly that she should remain chaste before the marriage. Fred insists.

What should Julia do?

18. Your wife's brother is a senior at a major university. He confides to you that he is a member of a group that plans to blow up an R.O.T.C. building to dramatize the students' hatred of the war in Asia. Two weeks later the building is blown up and a passerby is killed by the explosion.

What should you do?

19. Harry Wisher, a 20 year old senior at a New York State University, is a quadroon (one-fourth Negro). He is very popular among both the white and the black students, none of whom are aware of his ancestry. In the past two years, Harry has become increasingly active in black student activities on campus. During this time he has developed a great pride in his African heritage and is strongly motivated to reveal his Negro origin. Harry has hesitated to do this because he fears that both his black friends and his white friends will resent his deception, and, perhaps, reject him. Recently, he has become infatuated with a black coed who refuses to date him because he is white.

What should Harry do?

20. In 1950 John Graff was sentenced to life imprisonment for the murder of his business partner, Harry Fosdick. During his trial and imprisonment, John had protested his innocence. After being released in April, 1970, having served the full twenty years at Joliet Prison in Illinois, where the crime was committed, he returned to Chicago, his hometown. Two days later he ran across Harry Fosdick, the man he had been convicted of murdering. At this meeting, Fosdick, in the presence of witnesses, admitted that he had intentionally framed Graff. The following day Fosdick was found murdered. When arrested for the murder, Graff admitted his guilt but claimed immunity since he had already served twenty years for the murder. The state insisted that although he had been falsely imprisoned for twenty years, the rule of "double jeopardy" did not apply since the original trial had been based upon a crime which had never taken place. While you cannot be tried twice for the same crime, the

crime for which he had been convicted had never occurred. The only crime committed occurred in 1970. The supreme penalty in Illinois for premeditated first degree murder is the death penalty.

What penalty should Graff get?

DISCUSSION FLOW CHART

The purpose of a flow-chart is to record the number and direction of contributions made by each participant. When a group member contributes, an arrow is drawn from his name to the name of the person to whom he is

DISCUSSION RATING FORM

Scale / 1 / 2 / 3 / 4 /

superior above ave. average poor

Names (John M.) (Mary S.) (Robert R.) (George S.)

PARTICIPATION—Listened carefully; was prepared; was spontaneous; used pertinent information; tested the thinking of others.

ATTITUDE—Was friendly; tactful; cooperative; flexible; objective.

THOUGHT PROGRESSION—Spoke to the point; stayed on the subject; used time wisely.

COMMUNICATIVE SKILLS—Used adequate volume; was clear, was conversational; observed the rules of grammar.

OVERALL RATING FOR GROUP _____

COMMENTS:

Problems 1 and 2 are taken with permission of the author from William E. Utterback, Group Thinking and Conference Leadership (New York: Holt, Rinehart and Winston, Inc., 1964).

speaking. If the remark is made to the entire group, the arrow is drawn with broken lines and stops in the center of the circle.

EXERCISES

1. Prepare a list of topics suitable for class discussion.
2. Write an original case problem that would be suitable for class discussion.
3. a. The instructor will divide the class into groups of four to six each. Each group will have a planning meeting to elect a chairman and choose a discussion topic.
   b. The group should decide upon an outline listing points in the order in which they will be discussed. A time limit should be established for the discussion.
   c. After the planning session, each member should research the topic in order to support his opinion with factual evidence and testimony.

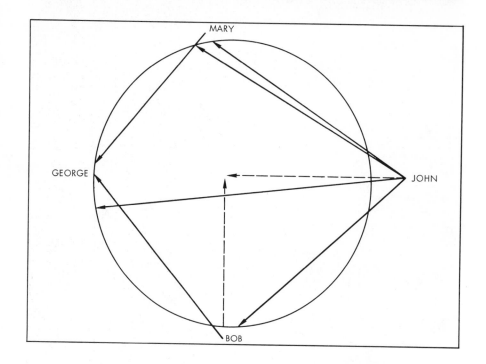

15

controversy:
food for thought

Chapters 11, 12, and 13 have dealt with the proofs of persuasion: personal, logical, and psychological. This chapter will enable you to apply your knowledge of persuasion to differing points of view about controversial issues relevant to our society: My Lai, the Space Shuttle Program, Pollution, Bangladesh, and the American System.

Each of these writers or speakers attempts to convince his audience of the reasonableness of his argument. Read the material thoughtfully, carefully analyzing the statements. Be prepared to show agreement or disagreement with the author's ideas. In evaluating this material, you should be able to recognize examples of personal, logical, and psychological proof, and identify fallacious reasoning when it appears. We live in a complex world. In order to operate in it effectively, we must be able to examine the important issues, to sift and winnow through them, culling out the good from the bad, the reasonable from the unreasonable, until we arrive at the truth. That is the cornerstone of democracy and the goal of education.

MY LAI

The tragedy at My Lai and the subsequent trial and conviction of Lieutenant William L. Calley, Jr., has provoked considerable disagreement from the American public. The controversy will continue for years to come. Your job as a critical reader is to concern yourself with the various proofs used by writers and to present their views. This section begins with a brief account of the charge and conviction. These are followed by four speeches delivered by congressmen on the floor of the House of Representatives, an editorial from a small town newspaper, an open letter to the President published in *The New York Times*, and a nationally syndicated editorial. Read them carefully. Then respond as your instructor directs.

The Charge

On November 24, 1969, the United States Army announced that it would court-martial First Lieutenant William L. Calley on charges of the premeditated murder of at least 102 Vietnamese men, women, and children in mid-March, 1968 in My Lai, South Vietnam.

Included in the four counts against Calley is the charge of having shot and killed a small child. The Army indicated that the case would be tried as a capital offense which means that, if convicted, Calley will face a penalty of death or life imprisonment.

The Verdict

On March 31, 1970, 19 days after his trial began, First Lieutenant William L. Calley Jr. was found guilty on three counts of premeditated murder in the slaying of no less than 22 unresisting civilians and on one count of assault with intent to commit the murder of a small child at My Lai. Besides being confined to prison for life, Calley was stripped of all pay and allowances and dismissed dishonorably from the service.

The Response

LAW IS AN UNEQUAL DISTRIBUTION OF JUSTICE

(Mr. Andrews of Alabama asked and was given permission to address the House for 1 minute.)

Mr. Andrews of Alabama. Mr. Speaker, a law student was in the class about half drunk, and the professor asked him What is law? The student said, "Law is an unequal distribution of justice."

Last night I was sickened and sad when I heard about that poor little fellow who went down to Fort Benning to enter OCS. He had barely graduated from high school. He had offered his life for his country. He was sent to Vietnam, and he wound up back at Fort Benning where he was indicted and convicted for murder in the first degree for carrying out orders.

I also thought about another young man about his age, one Cassius Clay, alias Muhammad Ali who several years ago defied the U.S. Government, thumbed his nose at the flag, and is still walking the streets making millions of dollars fighting for pay, not for his country.

So I think that half-drunk was right when he said that law is an unequal distribution of justice.

Where on earth is the Justice Department in this country? Why on earth is not that man Cassius Clay in the penitentiary where he should be?

Congressional Record, March 30, 1971, p. H2112.

LIEUTENANT CALLEY—POW

(Mr. Rarick asked and was given permission to address the House for 1 minute, to revise and extend his remarks and include extraneous matter.)

Mr. Rarick. Mr. Speaker, yesterday our people were shocked by one of the most morbid events in our Nation's history. Lieutenant Calley, a young Army officer, was convicted of premeditated murder of unnamed and unidentified people while serving our country in combat.

If there are any Americans who are not saddened by this tragic occurrence, it can only be that they do not understand the significance of the conviction.

In my district, public indignation at this affront to our fightingmen is hostile. Mothers and fathers are calling my offices stating that they will never allow their sons to serve in the military forces of a country which abandons its fightingmen. Veterans, highly enraged, are calling to say that if they were in Vietnam they would lay down their guns and come home.

The Commander in Chief and our top military brass may be proud of their accomplishment in giving world public opinion a sacrificial lamb. The members of the court-martial, like Lieutenant Calley, did their duty. Could it be that they did not realize that they more than Lieutenant Calley were destroying the U.S. military forces?

Now we Americans have two classes of POW's—those in Communist prisons and Lieutenant Calley in a U.S. POW camp.

Congressional Record, March 30, 1971, p. H2112.

THE CALLEY TRIAL

(Mr. Flynt asked and was given permission to address the House for 1 minute and to revise and extend his remarks.)

Mr. Flynt. Mr. Speaker, the Calley court-martial trial and the verdict in that trial constitute a very dangerous step toward the destruction of morale in the Army and the destruction of the Army as an effective instrument of U.S. foreign policy. The result of this verdict could be that in the future, no officer or noncommissioned officer can give any order with reasonable assurance that such order will be obeyed.

Lieutenant Calley was carrying out an assigned search-and-destroy mission which was the official policy of the Army at that time from the Pentagon on down. It is asinine to assess criminal responsibility on a lieutenant for carrying out an order, even if misunderstood, which originated at the very top of the chain of command. The search-and-destroy policy may have been changed since then but it was in effect on March 16, 1968.

In my opinion, the conviction of this young man destroys any possibility for an all-volunteer army. It makes the extension of the Selective Service Act more unpopular among Members of Congress and among the general public who have heretofore wholeheartedly supported it.

Congressional Record, March 30, 1971, p. H2113.

THE VERDICT OF THE CALLEY CASE

(Mr. Blackburn asked and was given permission to address the House for 1 minute, to revise and extend his remarks.

Mr. Blackburn. Mr. Speaker, the verdict in the case involving Lt. William Calley finds me with a bewildering mixture of emotions and views.

First, I find myself deeply concerned for Lieutenant Calley whose service to this country has brought him to this tragic point in his life.

Second, I find myself baffled that this matter proceeded through the ordeal of a public trial which has only brought comfort to those persons, both foreign and domestic, who have opposed our involvement in Vietnam. While giving comfort to the enemies of American policy, the trial has created great distress among all Americans from all walks of life. No benefit to this country has so far appeared as the result of this trial.

Finally, I am deeply disturbed at the long-term implications that this trial and conviction hold for the morale of our men serving in Vietnam and for the future morale and discipline of any citizen who may find him-self serving in the Armed Forces of our country.

The killing of fellow humans is a deplorable affair, whether such humans be civilian or military. A nation which sets about pursuing a policy involving the destruction of human beings cannot expect to apply the rules of conduct which govern our affairs in times of peace. Our Nation has never fought under circumstances as difficult and frustrating as those which have constantly faced our men in Vietnam. It was the decision of this Nation to set about to destroy those Vietnamese who opposed our policies in that country. If unconscionable acts have occurred in carrying out that policy, the blot is upon the Nation's record, and no one man should be singled out for special punishment.

Questions of legitimacy can now be raised as to the actions of our aviators during World War II whose bombs destroyed whole cities. Any-one who has served in time of combat and has observed the destruction from his weapons must now reassure himself, when thinking of Lieutenant Calley's plight, with the thought, "There, but for the grace of God, go I." The leaders of North Vietnam, since the beginning of our involvement in that struggle, have maintained that the American servicemen whom they hold as captives, under the most inhumane conditions, are actually war criminals and thus not entitled to the treatment normally accorded prison-ers of war. To what extent have we confirmed their charges?

The trial and the conviction of Lieutenant Calley have created far more questions than have been laid to rest.

Congressional Record, *March 30, 1971, pp. H-2113–2114.*

IF LIEUTENANT CALLEY IS GUILTY— THEN ARE WE ALL NOT GUILTY?

In this day of "Draft Dodgers," "Muhammad Ali's" and various other products of our culture, it seems incredible to me, that our society can convict a young man, that "we instructed to kill," for doing his job!

I am a World War II veteran. After weeks of training we were sent to do battle in New Guinea, in the South Pacific, a place that I'd never heard of, and I did not want to go! But, go, I did, with all my fears and doubts bottled-up inside me!

On our first invasion with the First Marine Division (of Guadalcanal) we were briefed by a Marine Major and at the end of his briefing he said "Boys look around you, some of you are not coming out of this invasion alive"—I kept my head down and looked out of the corners of my eyes and noticed everyone was doing the same thing, heads down, they would not look at each other. Not one of us wanted to believe that a friend would be killed. As luck would have it, none of us were, except for the Major, he was bayoneted to death the first night.

This was my first taste of combat and I soon learned to "shoot first and ask questions afterwards" if you wanted to see home again—and I sure did!

I personally know of one officer who is as guilty as Lt. Calley and a patrol that is guilty of carrying out the officer's order. But I don't believe the officer to be guilty nor do I believe the members of the patrol to be guilty!

Fighting a war is "One hell-of-a-lot different" than sitting at home watching it on television!

It makes a difference if you have a "Son" or "Husband" over there— ask any "Mother" or "Wife" if this is not true!

If you want "your young men" to protect and preserve this country— you'd better tell them "just who in the hell" is the "enemy." The "Gooks" or a bunch of desk soldiers that never saw a man killed! Nor ever saw a handsome young boy, who cried when he got a "Dear John" letter from his girl, shot in the stomach and "die a slow death" because there are no emergency rooms on the front line!

People—you had better think about this. Because none of the men out there, protecting you at home, is any "Braver" or more "Courageous" than you are! Most of your "Heroes" happen by accident! They do things they would not ordinarily do!

Just as a Marine Private did on my first invasion. He had the tri-pod shot off of his "water-cooled" 50 caliber machine gun and picked it up and cradled it in his arm and retook 3 positions on our front line! When I asked him why? He simply said, "They pissed-me off!"

Now! How many more men do you think you'll find to fight for you like this? When, as the gamblers say is, "The Best You Can Do is Lose!" If you don't lose your life over there we'll take "it" away from you when you get back!

I personally don't like these odds; nor would any gambler.

I know a lot of church goers and other groups are going to write me about the language I have used in this editorial . . . but this is the language I learned in War and the only way I know of to make you "Sit-up" and take notice of what is happening here!

Now, in comparison, I offer you the remarks of Lt. Calley at his sentence hearing . . . I believe he does a magnificent job and is a gentleman!

The text of Lt. William L. Calley Jr.'s plea Tuesday to the military jury deciding his sentence for premeditated murder at My Lai.

"Let me know if you can't hear me, sir.

Your honor, court members, I asked Judge Latimer and my other attorneys not to go on and into mitigation of this case. There are a lot of things really not appropriate and I don't think it matters what type of individual I am. And I'm not going to stand here and plead for my life and my freedom.

I would ask you to consider the thousand more lives that are going to be lost in Southeast Asia. The thousands more, that is, to be imprisoned not only here in the United States but also in North Vietnam and in hospitals all over the World as amputees.

I have never known a soldier nor did I ever myself ever wantonly kill human beings in my entire life. If I have committed a crime the only crime that I have committed is in judgment of my values. Apparently I value my troops' lives more than I did that of the enemy.

When my troops were getting massacred and mauled by an enemy I couldn't see, I couldn't feel and I couldn't touch; that nobody in the military system ever described as other than Communism—they didn't give it a race, they didn't give it a sex, they didn't give it an age. And they never let me believe it was just a philosophy in a man's mind. That was my enemy out there.

And when it became between me and that enemy I had to value the lives of my troops. And I feel that is the only crime I have committed. Yesterday you stripped me of all my honor. Please, by your actions that you take here today, don't strip future soldiers of their honor, I beg of you."

Editor's Note: I personally take my hat off to this man. A man that's asked no mercy for himself . . . but mercy for those who are "bound" to follow him!

Sincerely thank you,
Bill Robinson,
Editor

Clay County Free Press, *March 31, 1971. Reprinted with permission.*

TEXT OF CALLEY PROSECUTOR'S LETTER TO THE PRESIDENT

WASHINGTON, April 6—Following is the text of the letter sent to the President by Capt. Aubrey M. Daniels 3d., the prosecutor in the Calley case:

Sir:

It is very difficult for me to know where to begin this letter as I am not accustomed to writing letters of protest. I only hope that I can find the words to convey to you my feelings as a United States citizen, and as an attorney, who believes that respect for law is one of the fundamental bases upon which this nation is founded.

On Nov. 26, 1969, you issued the following statement through your press secretary, Mr. Ronald Ziegler, in referring to the Mylai incident:

"An incident such as that alleged in this case is in direct violation not only of United States military policy, but is also abhorrent to the conscience of all the American people.

"The Secretary of the Army is continuing his investigation. Appropriate action is and will be taken to assure that illegal and immoral conduct as alleged be dealt with in accordance with the strict rules of military justice.

"This incident should not be allowed to reflect on the some million and a quarter young Americans who have now returned to the United States after having served in Vietnam with great courage and distinction."

At the time you issued this statement, a general court-martial had been directed for a resolution of the charges which have been brought against Lieut. William L. Calley Jr. for his involvement at Mylai.

On Dec. 8, 1970, you were personally asked to comment on the

Mylai incident at a press conference. At that time you made the following statement:

"What appears was certainly a massacre, and under no circumstances was it justified.

"One of the goals we are fighting for in Vietnam is to keep the people from South Vietnam from having imposed upon them a government which has atrocity against civilians as one of its policies.

"We cannot ever condone or use atrocities against civilians in order to accomplish that goal."

These expressions of what I believe to be your sentiment were truly reflective of my own feelings when I was given the assignment of prosecuting the charges which had been preferred against Lieutenant Calley.

My feelings were generated not by emotionalism or self-indignation but by my knowledge of the evidence in the case, the laws of this nation in which I strongly believe, and my own conscience. I knew that I had been given a great responsibility and I only hoped that I would be able to discharge my duties and represent the United States in a manner which would be a credit to the legal profession and our system of justice.

I undertook the prosecution of the case without any ulterior motives for personal gain, either financial or political. My only desire was to fulfill my duty as a prosecutor and see that justice was done in accordance with the laws of this nation. I dedicated myself totally to this end from November of 1969 until the trial was concluded.

Throughout the proceedings there was criticism of the prosecution but I lived with the abiding conviction that once the facts and the law had been presented there would be no doubt in the mind of any reasonable person about the necessity for the prosecution of this case and the ultimate verdict. I was mistaken.

The trial of Lieutenant Calley was conducted in the finest tradition of our legal system. It was in every respect a fair trial in which every legal right of Lieutenant Calley was fully protected. It clearly demonstrated that the military justice system which has previously been the subject of much criticism was a fair system.

Throughout the trial, the entire system was under the constant scrutiny of the mass media and the public, and the trial of Lieutenant Calley was also in a very real sense the trial of the military judicial system. However there was never an attack lodged by any member of the media concerning the fairness of the trial. There could be no such allegation justifiably made.

I do not believe that there has ever been a trial in which the accused's rights were more fully protected, the conduct of the defense given greater latitude, and the prosecution held to stricter standards. The burden of proof which the Government had to meet in this case was not beyond a reasonable doubt, but beyond possibility. The very fact that Lieutenant Calley was an American officer being tried for the deaths of Vietnamese during a combat operation by fellow officers compels this conclusion.

The jury selection, in which customary procedures were altered by providing both the defense and the prosecution with three peremptory challenges instead of the usual one, was carefully conducted to insure the impartiality of those men who were selected. Six officers, all combat veterans, five having served in Vietnam, were selected. These six men who had served their country well, were called upon again to serve their nation as jurors and to sit in judgment of Lieutenant Calley as prescribed by law.

From the time they took their oaths until they rendered their decision, they performed their duties in the very finest tradition of the American legal system. If ever a jury followed the letter of the law in applying it to the evidence presented, they did. They are indeed a credit to our system of justice and to the officer corps of the United States Army.

When the verdict was rendered, I was totally shocked and dismayed at the reaction of many people across the nation. Much of the adverse public reaction I can attribute to people who have acted emotionally and without being aware of the evidence that was presented and perhaps even the laws of this nation regulating the conduct of war.

These people have undoubtedly viewed Lieutenant Calley's conviction simply as the conviction of an American officer for killing the enemy. Others, no doubt out of a sense of frustration, have seized upon the conviction as a means of protesting the war in Vietnam.

I would prefer to believe that most of the public criticism has come from people who are not aware of the evidence, either because they have not followed the evidence as it was presented, or having followed it they have chosen not to believe it.

Certainly, no one wanted to believe what occurred at Mylai, including the officers who sat in judgment of Lieutenant Calley. To believe, however, that any large percentage of the population could believe the evidence which was presented and approve of the conduct of Lieutenant Calley would be as shocking to my conscience as the conduct itself, since I believe that we are still a civilized nation.

If such be the case, then the war in Vietnam has brutalized us more than I care to believe, and it must cease. How shocking it is if so many people across this nation have failed to see the moral issue which was involved in the trial of Lieutenant Calley—that it is unlawful for an American soldier to summarily execute unarmed and unresisting men, women, children and babies.

But how much more appalling it is to see so many of the political leaders of the nation who have failed to see the moral issue or, having seen it, compromise it for political motive in the face of apparent public displeasure with the verdict.

I would have hoped that all leaders of this nation, which is supposed to be the leader within the international community for the protection of the weak and the oppressed regardless of nationality, would have either accepted and supported the enforcement of the laws of this country as reflected by the verdict of the court or not make any statement concerning the verdict until they had had the same opportunity to evaluate the evidence that the members of the jury had.

In view of your previous statements concerning this matter, I have been particularly shocked and dismayed at your decision to intervene in these proceedings in the midst of the public clamor. Your decision can only have been prompted by the response of a vocal segment of our population, who while no doubt acting in good faith, cannot be aware of the evidence which resulted in Lieutenant Calley's conviction.

Your intervention has, in my opinion, damaged the military judicial system and lessened any respect it may have gained as a result of the proceedings.

You have subjected a judicial system of this country to the criticism that it is subject to political influence, when it is a fundamental precept of our judicial system that the legal processes of this country must be kept free from any outside influences. What will be the impact of your decision upon the future trials, particularly those within the military?

Not only has respect for the legal process been weakened and the critics of the military judicial system been given support for their claims of command influence, the image of Lieutenant Calley, a man convicted of the premeditated murder of at least 21 unarmed and unresisting people, as a national hero has been enhanced, while at the same time support has been given to those persons who have so unjustly criticized the six loyal and honorable officers who have done this country a great service by fulfilling their duties as jurors so admirably.

Have you considered those men in making your decisions? The men who since rendering their verdict have found themselves and their families the subject of vicious attacks upon their honor, integrity and loyalty to this nation.

It would seem to me to be more appropriate for you as the President to have said something in their behalf and to remind the nation of the purpose of our legal system and the respect it should command.

I would expect that the President of the United States, a man whom I believed should and would provide the moral leadership for this nation, would stand fully behind the law of this land on a moral issue which is so clear and about which there can be no compromise.

For this nation to condone the acts of Lieutenant Calley is to make us no better than our enemies and make any pleas by this nation for the humane treatment of our own prisoners meaningless.

I truly regret having to have written this letter and wish that no innocent person had died at Mylai on March 16, 1968. But innocent people were killed under circumstances that will always remain abhorrent to my conscience.

While in some respects what took place at Mylai has to be considered to be a tragic day in the history of our nation, how much more tragic would it have been for this country to have taken no action against those who were responsible?

That action was taken, but the greatest tragedy of all will be if political expediency dictates the compromise of such a fundamental moral principle as the inherent unlawfulness of the murder of innocent persons, making the action and the courage of six honorable men who served their country so well meaningless.

MY LAI—AMERICA'S LIDICE

Popular support for Lt. William Calley fills this commentator with misgiving for the American people. For Calley committed murder, and encouraged other soldiers to commit atrocities. He was justly convicted, on overwhelming evidence. What sort of people are we, if we ignore crimes so long as they are committed by men in American uniforms?

Some liberals have spoken up courageously to affirm the justice of the sentence imposed upon Calley. But everyone concerned for the honor of the American Army and the American nation ought to approve the punishment of Calley. When are some eminent conservative politicians going to declare that justice must be done upon military malefactors, as upon all convicted malefactors?

Among liberal political leaders, Sen. Jacob Javits of New York and Gov. Patrick Lucey of Wisconsin have made very sensible declarations about the justice of the Calley court-martial.

Sen. Brown says "No, Thanks"

Michigan's Senate, like several other legislative bodies, passed a resolution asking for clemency for Calley. But one Michigan senator, Basil Brown, uttered the truth. "One child at My Lai was supposedly shot with a tracer bullet and lay there yelling and screaming while it burned through his body," Sen. Brown said. "And you want to pat this man (Calley) on the back? No, thank you, gentlemen."

What Charlie Company did at My Lai was as evil as what SS troops did at Lidice, in Czechoslovakia, during World War II—on the same pretext of saving soldiers' lives by a massacre of civilians, even down to the tiniest children of the village. Have we Americans come around to excusing—or even applauding—in our own troops, what we rightly have denounced in the military operations of Nazis and Communists?

What about Seale and Davis?

"When a democracy decides to make a confessed murderer of women and old men a national hero, we are in grave trouble," says James Michener. Those who have read Michener's "Tales of the South Pacific" will remember that he understands how war can warp character; he is not lacking in pity for an incompetent officer like Calley. But he knows that justice must be done—for the sake of the Army itself, indeed. The officers of the jury that convicted Calley knew this.

Let it be granted that Calley was fighting for a cause he believed to be good, as I believe it to be good: resistance against Communist terrorism. Even so, he disgraced that cause. Mere belief that one's cause is good cannot justify atrocious acts against the defenseless.

Bobby Seale believes that his cause is good; so does Angela Davis. If those two are found guilty, will the people now supporting Calley demand that Seale and Davis be pardoned, because whatever they did was merely a means to their grand object? Scarcely. I can't imagine Gov. Wallace and former Gov. Maddox leading "Save Bobby and Angela" rallies. Yet murder is murder, and the law should be no respecter of persons.

It may be that some of Calley's superiors and some of his subordinates are equally guilty. If so, let them be indicted and tried—as, indeed, some have been and will be. But let us refrain from beating our breasts and muttering nonsense about collective national guilt.

Some American soldiers committed atrocities in World War II, but that did not prove that President Roosevelt should have been hanged.

If, in the name of Americanism, the American people can embrace a child butcher like Calley—why, then we might as well let the Communists take the world. For we will have forfeited our claim to be defenders of order and justice and freedom against "the streamlined men who think in slogans and talk in bullets."

Russell Kirk

ANDREWS

1. Comment on whether the story of the half-drunk law student makes a valid point.
2. Was Calley convicted for carrying out orders? Explain.
3. Is the contrast between Calley and Clay valid? Does it add to the speaker's case? Explain.
4. Are there any fallacies in the argument by Andrews? If so, identify them.
5. Identify the motives to which Andrews appeals. Identify the attitudes.

RARICK

1. Was the conviction of Calley one of the most morbid events in this nation's history? Explain.
2. Was Calley convicted of murdering unidentified people in combat? Explain.
3. Do you agree with Rarick that the conviction of Calley is an indication that the U.S. military has abandoned its fighting men? Explain.
4. In what way are the members of the court-martial guilty of destroying the U.S. military forces?
5. Are there any fallacies in the argument by Rarick? If so, identify them.
6. Identify the motives to which Rarick appeals. Identify the attitudes.

FLYNT

1. Explain how the trial of Calley and its verdict are dangerous steps to the destruction of morale and effectiveness of the army.

2. Is Mr. Flynt's comment about officers' orders no longer being obeyed accurate? Explain.
3. Was Calley the victim of carrying out an official search-and-destroy policy? Explain.
4. How does the conviction of Calley destroy the possibility of an all-volunteer army?
5. If there are any fallacies in the argument by Flynt, identify them.
6. Identify the motives to which Flynt appeals. Identify the attitudes.

BLACKBURN

1. Is it correct to say that Lt. Calley's service to this country has brought him to this tragic point in his life? Explain.
2. Has no benefit to this country resulted from the trial and conviction of Calley? Explain.
3. Comment as to whether the comparison between aviators in World War II and Calley is accurate.
4. How has the conviction of Calley confirmed the charge that POWs are war criminals?
5. If there are any fallacies in the argument of Blackburn, identify them.
6. Identify the motives to which Blackburn appeals. Identify the attitudes.

EDITORIAL—CLAY COUNTY FREE PRESS

1. Was the search and destroy mission by Calley a question of "shooting first and asking questions afterward?" Explain.
2. How does the fact that an officer and patrol did the same thing in World War II support Calley?
3. Identify the "bunch of desk soldiers that never saw a man killed" that the writer refers to.
4. How does the statement about heroes happening by accident—doing things that they wouldn't ordinarily do—relate to Calley?
5. Is the statement, "If you don't lose your life over there we'll take 'it' away from you when you get back!" accurate? Explain.
6. Does Calley's statement at the trial enhance his image? Explain.
7. What do you think Calley meant by the statement, "... nor did I ever myself ever wantonly kill human beings in my entire life"?
8. Are there any fallacies in this editorial? If so, identify them.
9. How does Robinson use personal proof?
10. Comment on Robinson's usage and style.

AUBREY DANIELS—LETTER TO THE PRESIDENT

1. What is the function of the first paragraph of Capt. Daniels' letter?
2. Why does Capt. Daniels quote President Nixon in a letter he is sending to him?
3. Why did Capt. Daniels release this letter to The New York Times?
4. Is Capt. Daniels accurate in saying that most of the criticism came from those who are not aware of the evidence? Explain.
5. Does Capt. Daniels accurately state the moral issue in the trial? Explain.
6. Do you think Capt. Daniels' charge that politicians and the President intervened for political reasons is accurate? Explain.

7. How, according to Capt. Daniels, has the legal process been weakened by the President's intervention?
8. How has Lt. Calley's image been enhanced?
9. Is Capt. Daniels' comment about the meaninglessness of asking for humane treatment of prisoners accurate? Explain.
10. How does the fact that no one from the media criticized the trial attest to its fairness?
11. How does the fact that the jurors were all combat veterans support the fairness of the trial?
12. If there are any fallacies in the argument by Daniels, identify them.
13. How does Daniels attempt to establish his personal proof.

RUSSEL KIRK

1. Kirk says that many ignore crimes if they are committed by men in American uniforms. Do you agree? Explain.
2. Is the comparison between My Lai and Lidice accurate? Explain.
3. Does Kirk offer any evidence which indicates that Calley was an incompetent officer?
4. Is the comparison among Calley, Seale, and Davis accurate? Explain.
5. Are there any fallacies in this editorial? If so, explain them.
6. Identify the motives to which Kirk appeals. Identify the attitudes.

EXERCISES

1. Choose one of the selections with which you disagree and prepare a rebuttal in either written or speech form.
2. Write a 300–500 word essay or deliver a three-four minute speech expressing your feelings about the My Lai incident and the trial and conviction of Lt. Calley.
3. Conduct a survey among class members to determine their attitude toward the trial and conviction of Lt. Calley. Divide the class into three groups on the basis of this survey: (1) those favorable to the verdict, (2) those unfavorable to the verdict, (3) those who are neutral.
   Form two-member debate teams to argue the affirmative and negative side of the Calley conviction.
   a. Each speaker will have a five minute introductory speech and a three minute rebuttal speech. The first affirmative speaker will speak first in the introductory speeches. The first negative speaker will speak first in rebuttal.
   b. Have the class vote at the conclusion of the debate to see which side did the most effective debating.
   c. Resurvey the class to see whether any attitudes have changed.
4. Conduct an all-class debate of the Calley issue. Elect a chairman, who remains neutral, to handle the discussion according to parliamentary procedure. Divide the class into sections according to the survey. Seat those favorable to the verdict (the affirmative) on the right and those unfavorable (the negative) on the left. The neutral group shall be seated in the middle.
   a. A timekeeper shall be appointed from the neutral group.
   b. The chairman will recognize a member from the affirmative group, who will speak to uphold the verdict for four minutes. Next, the chairman will

recognize a member of the negative group, who is also allowed four minutes. Thereafter, the speakers will be alternated until ten minutes remain of the class period. At this time the timekeeper will call for the question and the class will vote. After the class vote, the neutral group will vote to see which side did the most effective debating.

5. Write a one to three page paper in which you compare or contrast what Charlie Company did at My Lai to what the Nazi SS troops did at Lidice during World War II.

SPACE SHUTTLE

Below is a newspaper editorial supporting the space shuttle program proposed by President Richard Nixon. It is followed by a rebuttal by Senator William Proxmire. Read both selections, then perform the exercises which follow.

SPACE SHUTTLE NEXT

President Nixon has given the go-ahead for development of the space shuttle, the necessary next step if space exploration is to become economical and full benefits are to be derived at a reasonable cost.

With the Apollo moon program ending, the US space effort is at a crossroads. The kind of costly space race that stimulated Apollo is no longer politically acceptable. Nor should it be. There are too many earthbound problems that have greater priority for the kind of concentration of human and material resources that went into our moon effort. But space should not be abandoned. This would be a terrible waste of the enormous investment made so far. The program is on the verge of payoffs that can help improve life on earth. Space is a frontier that man is bound to explore.

If man is to continue to invade space physically with any amount of frequency, some way must be found to cut the large costs of getting there. The reusable shuttle will do this. As *Fortune Magazine* has stated: "Ultimately, perhaps the economic justification of the shuttle rests upon the plain proposition that if the US is to have a progressive space program at all, it cannot continue to throw away multi-million-dollar vehicles on every trip."

The shuttle, designed for up to 100 trips, will pare expenses dramatically. We now throw away almost $300 million in equipment on an Apollo flight. Unmanned launches cost from $20 million to $35 million. Fortune points out that a shuttle launch would cost about $5 million. The shuttle probably would return in savings its development costs by 1990.

The shuttle offers the opportunity to make space flight fairly routine, of taking large numbers of people and supplies in and out of space, of manning earth resource space stations continuously, of monitoring and repairing communications and resource satellites. It is a worthwhile program.

Milwaukee Journal, January 7, 1972. Used with permission.

IN MY OPINION: Space Shuttle a Costly Boondoggle;
Money Badly Needed Elsewhere

I must take issue with your editorial of Jan. 7, 1972, entitled "Space Shuttle Next."

One of the principal arguments advanced for the space shuttle is that it will save costs. But save costs from what? Anyone can devise a very expensive space program, requiring scores of booster rockets, and then conclude that the shuttle would be cheaper than the expendable booster if enough trips were made.

The key question is: How many flights must be made—how much payload do we have to put into orbit—before the shuttle begins to pay for itself? The US Air Force commissioned a study to look into that very question. The study was completed in October, 1970.

Its conclusion: that the shuttle would not be cost effective unless the US planned to put at least $141 billion worth of equipment and manpower into orbit during the shuttle's 13 year lifetime. If we're not planning to spend at least that amount, then the shuttle's cost would not be justified, and it would be cheaper to continue using expendable boosters.

That $141 billion comes out to $2,800 for every American family. That's a pretty substantial price to have to pay in order to justify a decision to proceed with the shuttle.

When one considers what this money could do to alleviate poverty, improve education, control pollution, construct housing or meet other vital needs—needs that must continue to go unmet if we fund the shuttle—it becomes the height of folly to proceed with this new space extravaganza now.

This is especially so in light of the fact that we can achieve almost as much with unmanned exploration as we can with manned flight. Unmanned exploration, of course, would be much less expensive and involve no risk to life. Unfortunately, NASA continues to opt for the more glamorous and more costly manned programs, despite the fact that the benefits are approximately the same.

It's also a complete mystery to me what tangible benefits the shuttle is going to provide. Last year, I wrote to the NASA administrator asking him to specify for me what specific benefits we could expect from the shuttle. This is what he responded:

"The basic premise leading to the conclusion that this nation should proceed with the development of a space shuttle is that the US should and will continue to have an active space program from now on."

There was no mention whatsoever of tangible benefits. There was no indication at all how the shuttle would improve life on earth. The only rationale, in fact, seems to be that the shuttle will keep our space program going (until something better comes along, perhaps?). It will keep the NASA technicians occupied. And it will keep the aerospace industry happy.

If this is the only justification NASA can come up with, we have no business spending a single dime on the space shuttle. Congress can, and must, insist on much more than this before it approves money for this program. If nothing more is forthcoming, I will do all I can to persuade my colleagues in the Congress to deny all funding for this space age boondoggle.

From The Milwaukee Journal, January 24, 1972.
Used with permission of the writer, Senator William Proxmire.

EXERCISES

1. List the main points of the editorial.
2. Identify the types of supporting material used in the editorial.
3. List the main points of Senator Proxmire's rebuttal.
4. Identify the types of supporting material Proxmire uses.
5. List the fallacies that Proxmire identifies in the editorial. Indicate whether he is correct.
6. Check the major sources from which each article draws its statistics. Indicate which sources are the most reputable.
7. Write a 300–500 word opinion in which you defend either view. Back up your viewpoint with evidence you collect through your own research.
8. Deliver a three-four minute speech to convince the audience of one of the two views. Support your ideas with material from your own research.

POLLUTION

The following speech and article both recognize the problem of pollution, but react to it differently. Read both carefully, then perform the exercises which follow.

THE COST OF ECOLOGY

Mr. Passman. Mr. Speaker, for many months we have heard more about ecology and environment than almost any other subject. In fact, these words have almost become the daily passwords, and the Congress has gone so far in legislating and proposing additional legislation that we have frightened industry to the extent that in many instances they are actually reluctant to make capital investments so as to create jobs and support our economy.

I have supported several of the laws on the statute books, and I shall continue to support a well-planned program to clean our streams and air and control pollution. But we must not go too far with too many programs until we have devised a positive plan by which industry and the Government can live.

It has been estimated in many places that legislation presently on the statute books, if carried to conclusion, would cost the American taxpayers who, in reality, are American industry and the workingman, as much as $450 billion. Others have estimated that the cost could reach one-half trillion dollars. This would exceed our entire public debt.

In addition to the legislation presently on the statute books, it would appear that sooner or later S. 2770 will be considered by the House, and if this legislation should be enacted into law, it could conceivably have as bad an affect on the American economy as a mild depression because there is a limit to which industry could and should go. If we would only give industry time to absorb some of the present laws, in all probability, they would come up with a much better solution to some of our pollution problems than some of us who spend time thinking up ways to spend money that the other fellow earns.

Congressional Record. *Speech given by Hon. Otto E. Passman of Louisiana in the House of Representatives, December 7, 1971.*

RADICAL ECONOMIC CHANGE CALLED ONLY CURE FOR POLLUTION

WASHINGTON—Trying to save the environment may pose a bigger challenge to the U.S. economy than the depression of the 1930's or the inflation of the 1970's.

In fact, if Washington University ecologist Barry Commoner is right, meeting that challenge will give the United States the biggest economic shock in its history.

In Dr. Commoner's analysis, the driving force of environmental decay is the technological transformation that has made the American economy prosperous since World War II. Only radical dislocation and reordering of the technology will save the environment, Dr. Commoner says.

He adds that you can say as much for every other industrialized economy on earth, be it labeled socialist, capitalist, or mixed.

Dr. Commoner gave his analysis at the second session of the "international conference on ocean pollution" held by the sub-committee on oceans and atmosphere of the U.S. Senate Committee on Commerce. So he keyed his remarks to the sea.

To him, the ocean is the link that integrates environmental problems. All pollution, whether of air, land, or fresh water, ends up eventually in the sea, Dr. Commoner observed. The ocean is the sink for all the poisons man produces. Hence pollution of the sea is synonymous with general environmental decay.

Also, mankind's ultimate dependence on the sea, whose plant life produces much of the world's oxygen, makes the ocean a critical element of earth's life-support system. If the sea dies, mankind perishes, Dr. Commoner explained, picking up a point many experts have been making.

Archaeologist Thor Heyerdahl made this same point in reporting extensive marine pollution he had observed during his two drifting voyages across the mid-Atlantic in the papyrus vessels Ra 1 and Ra 2.

He said men must change their viewpoint on the ocean. They must stop thinking of "the vast sea." They must recognize that it is merely the largest landlocked water body. And like lakes that have already succumbed to pollution, it has a finite capacity to absorb man's wastes.

That capacity could well be exceeded and ocean life effectively killed within the next three to four decades if present trends continue, Mr. Heyerdahl warned.

However, in underscoring that warning, Dr. Commoner focused on what he considers the root cause of the environmental challenge on land as well as at sea.

It is not population growth as such, he said. It is not a few "guilty" industries, such as pesticidemakers and users. It is the total economic system that has grown up largely over the past 25 years that threatens us today.

As examples, he cited the fourfold to fivefold increase in the use of nitrate fertilizers in farming. This has brought a rise in per-capita food production of only about 11 percent, he said. The vastly increased fertilizer use largely contributes to pollution that ultimately goes into the sea.

Or consider nylon and other wonder fabrics. It takes chlorine to produce them. So American chlorine production has leaped ahead fifteenfold. Mercury plays a role in chlorine production. And this, Dr. Commoner said, is the major source of coastal mercury pollution.

Many of the new technologies are power hungry. This helps bring on the much publicized energy crisis. It stimulates air pollution and heat pollution of water bodies by demanding more power plants. It takes three times as much energy to produce the aluminum tops for flip-top beverage cans than to make the old steel tops, to take just one example.

These new technologies are more efficient and more profitable than the technologies they displace, Dr. Commoner explained. There's more money in nylon than cotton or wool. Soapmakers earn far more selling detergents than the old-fashioned, nonpolluting soaps.

It has been economically sensible to switch to the new technologies. But it is also ecological folly, Dr. Commoner said, for all these technologies bear down hard on the environment.

No economic system that ruins the environment will survive, because men themselves can't live in that case. But, Dr. Commoner warned, to bring the present economic system in line with ecological needs means major dislocations. We can't switch from synthetic fibers back to wool and cotton or go back to using soap without severe economic hardship, he said.

The need today, he added, is to realize the magnitude of this challenge. The need is to begin now to plan for the kind of major economic overhaul required so as to minimize the hardships it could entail.

Robert C. Cowen
Reprinted by permission from the Christian Science Monitor,
© *1971 The Christian Publishing Society. All rights reserved.*

EXERCISES

1. List the main points of "The Cost of Ecology."
2. Identify the types of supporting material Congressman Passman uses.

3. List the main points of the article by Robert Cowen.
4. Identify the types of supporting material Cowen uses.
5. Write a 300–500 word opinion in which you defend either viewpoint. Back up your argument with evidence you collect through your own research.
6. Deliver a three-five minute speech to persuade the audience to support one of the two views. Support your ideas with material from your own research.
7. Identify the fallacies you see in either argument.
8. Identify the motives and attitudes to which each communicator appeals.

BANGLADESH

Below is a background briefing on the India-Pakistanwar by Presidential Advisor Henry A. Kissinger. It is followed by a letter from Bangladesh by Father E. Goedert, a Holy Cross Catholic Missionary. Read both carefully; then perform the exercises which follow.

INDIA-PAKISTAN (Background briefing with Henry A. Kissinger)

Dr. Kissinger. I thought I would talk to you about how we have approached the problem in South Asia: what we have done and what has led to the number of pronouncements that have been made by official spokesmen at the U.N. in recent days.

I do not have any organized notes, so I am going to speak to you extemporaneously, and I may refer to an occasional paper just for accuracy in the question period.

First of all, let us get a number of things straight. There have been some comments that the Administration is anti-Indian. This is totally inaccurate. India is a great country. It is the most populous free country. It is governed by democratic procedures.

Americans through all Administrations in the postwar period have felt a commitment to the progress and development of India, and the American people have contributed to this to the extent of $10 billion. Last year, in this Administration, India received from all sources $1.2 billion for development assistance, economic assistance, of which $700 million came from the United States in various forms. Therefore, we have a commitment to the progress and to the future of India, and we have always recognized that the success of India, and the Indian democratic experiment, would be of profound significance to many of the countries in the underdeveloped world.

Therefore, when we have differed with India, as we have in recent weeks, we do so with great sadness and with great disappointment. . . .

The issue today is not opposition to India but opposition to the use of armed forces across borders to change the political structure of a neighboring state.

There is no question that the events in East Pakistan since March 25 require a political solution. The position of the United States has been that any solution must be worked out between the people of East and West Pakistan. The United States has not supported the particular solution that was attempted in March. The United States has also recognized that events there—principally the influx of refugees into India—imposed a substantial burden on India. We have recognized that it imposed a strain on the already scarce economic resources of that developing country and created the danger of communal strife there.

What has been the Administration's strategy? United States has attempted two efforts simultaneously:

On the one hand, the Administration has made a major humanitarian effort (a) to ease the suffering of those refugees who had already fled to their homes and (b) to avert the possibility of famine in East Pakistan which could have created more refugees.

On the other hand, we have attempted to bring about a political resolution of the conflict which caused the refugees to leave their homes in the first place.

In summary, the Administration:

Through humanitarian efforts sought to achieve a framework which would allow sufficient time for a political solution;

Supplemented the political process already going on within Pakistan by seeking to facilitate a serious negotiation between the government of Pakistan and Bangla Desh leaders outside;

Painstakingly, though unsuccessfully, sought India's cooperation in making the necessary political process succeed;

Put forward numerous proposals to reduce military tension which threatened to disrupt the political process—proposals which were by and large accepted by Pakistan and ignored by India.

In short, the Administration made energetic efforts towards the achievement of a peaceful solution. Throughout the process, India refused to contribute in a constructive way and instead chose to resort to armed force to achieve its objectives. It is the U.S. view that India's recourse to military action was unjustified. Under these circumstances, the American people cannot but question the use to which extensive U.S. economic assistance to India will be put. If the U.S. were to accept the principle that "might makes right" and that a nation, by greater numbers and power, can impose political solutions on its neighbors, then anarchy must ensue.

Congressional Record, December 9, 1971, pp. S21012–16.

Dt. Dacca, Bangladesh

Dear Nancy and Charlie: All I got for Christmas was my life—a gift from Mrs. Gandhi. We endured eight months of terror while the nations of the world did nothing. Finally India came to our aid. You may question her motives but this war has saved millions of lives; and one of them was mine. For eight months the West Pakistan Army carried out a program of extermination, with orders to loot and burn and rape and kill until they had destroyed forever the courage of the Bengali people. This savagery was not against a rebel army, but against the unarmed men, women and children of Bengal. I was in the middle of it. I saw them die, women and children deliberately shot by the most savage and cowardly army in modern times. I saw their homes put to the torch. I saw thousands fleeing in terror. In our instant hospital for bullet wounds only, I watched a five year old boy take a month to die, in pain and in fear. Every time a gun went off, he whimpered, "Mummy, will they shoot me again?" And this is the brutality that, incredibly, the U.S. Government supported. Father Bill Evans was brutally murdered by the Pak Army. We hoped the U.S. Government would protest strongly; but he was just one more of a million human sacrifices offered on the pagan altar of State Department policy.

I'm still a Republican, but my party loyalty stops at murder. Nixon is a national Disgrace. He put America on the side of savagery. Yahya Khan terrorized and murdered millions; yet Nixon supported him, and even allowed the shipment of military supplies to help in the slaughter. The question is not whether Nixon should be re-elected in 1972, but whether he should be tried for complicity in mass murder in 1971. Through malice or through stupidity, this man's hands are bloody. He used the prestige of his office to help a murderer, degrading the presidency as no man before him has done. When India intervened to stop the slaughter, he tried to block her, in the U.N. The U.N. resolution demanding a cease fire without doing anything to stop the massacre of Bengali civilians by the Pak Army, was reversion to barbarism. In effect it gave tacit approval to the slaughter of a million people, and told India to withdraw and let the slaughter go on. Had India listened, the Pak Army would have been freed to continue the extermination of the Bengali people. And I would be dead along with my people.

What a mockery Vietnam is now. American boys died to save Vietnam from the Communist camp. Now, with incredible stupidity, Nixon has forced 75 million Bengalis into the same camp; he has pushed 500 million Indians into the Russian camp. And he has even put West Pakistan more firmly on China's side. Alger Hiss was labeled a traitor. I doubt that Hiss did near as much harm to the U.S. as did the diplomania of Nixon and his advisors.

Our agony isn't over yet. If the past is unbelievable, the present is unbearable and the future uncertain. Our people's homes are destroyed; they are hungry; they are mourning their dead. They need massive help. But at least we no longer live in terror of the Pak Army. And the kids will be fleeing and screaming and dying, only in their sleep.

Father Ed Goedert,
Holy Cross Missionary

Congressional Record, March 6, 1972, p. E2025.

EXERCISES

1. List the main points of the explanation by Kissinger.
2. Identify the types of supporting material he uses.
3. List the main points in the letter by Father Goedert.

4. Identify the types of supporting material Father Goedert uses.
5. Write a 300–500 word opinion in which you defend either view. Back up your viewpoint with evidence you collect through your own research.
6. Deliver a three-four minute speech to convince the audience of either of the two views. Support your ideas with material from your own research.
7. Identify any fallacies you see in either argument.
8. Identify the motives and attitudes to which each communicator appeals.

THE AMERICAN SYSTEM

The section which follows deals with America. It includes selections highly critical of our system of government, those which recognize both the good and the bad, and those which say, in effect, "America, love it or leave it." Read the selections carefully. Choose one which you feel is particularly provocative, and respond as your instructor directs.

THE NEW GENERATION GAP

As I watched the marines' magnificent sunset parade last Thursday I thought of the report I had received earlier in the day of the commencement speeches at Yokohama High School. The young speakers had eloquently vented their disgust with the establishment and the awful state of the world. Pollution, the war in Indo China, racial discrimination, poverty—all were attributed to the middle-aged and their callous failure to make things bright, clean, safe and untroubled. Nothing could be as bad as conditions in 1970.

I thought back to the days when the present establishment was entering the world of reality. Things were not very good then either. The smoke from the crematoriums of Dachau and Buchenwald was slowly extinguishing the lights in Europe. Poison gas was being used in Africa to control the Negroes of Ethiopia. There was real poverty in the United States as a result of the economic collapse of the early 30's. Arrogant young intellectuals wanted a communist/socialist type political framework in America which was supposed to bring an era of peace, equality, and goodwill to the country and to the world. There was also a very marked generation gap.

Today there is another gap between many in the current generation and the old folks who are their parents. The young protestors demand peace now, racial equality now, and freedom now. The parents remember that the young have the freedom to protest and they have that freedom because the middle-aged preserved it for them at places like Anzio and Guadalcanal.

As a demonstration-weary member of the establishment I welcome these brave young people into the struggle. I hope they have new solutions to the grim problems which beset mankind. I'm afraid, though, that they will have to find a way to prevent human beings from behaving like human beings.

I don't know the ultimate answer to peace, security, and progress but as long as four-fifths of the world adheres to the principle that power flows from the barrel of a gun I hope these fine young people keep their powder dry because if they destroy the shining sword of America as symbolized by our superb marines, a long darkness will soon settle over the free world.

Congressional Record, July 9, 1970, p. H23689.
With permission of the writer, Capt. Paul N. Gray, USN (ret).

RICH AND POOR

Mr. Hart. Mr. President, for those who question the priorities and logic of our system, last week was most instructive.

The administration was urging Congress to approve a bill which would permit the Federal Government to guarantee a $250 million loan to bail out the Lockheed Corp. from financial difficulties.

On Thursday, an administration spokesman told the Senate Nutrition Committee that the Department of Agriculture would not spend at this time an additional $20 million which Congress had provided for feeding programs for hungry adults and children.

It is fair to state, I believe, that one of the principal reasons given to justify that decision was that here are inefficiencies in the systems used to distribute food to the hungry.

In other words, at the same time the administration asks Congress to bail out Lockheed from a predicament at least in important part of its own making, the administration is telling a Senate committee that it will not spend money for food to help people in predicaments not of their own making.

The administration is willing to take a $250 million gamble on saving a big business from its own inefficiencies, but the administration is not willing to spend $20 million to feed hungry adults and children because of reported inefficiencies in the distribution system.

Certainly the Federal Government should always press for more efficient administration of its programs, but is it right to ask a hungry person to wait a little longer for food while bureaucrats tinker with the distribution system?

In short, while Lockheed is to be "rewarded" for its failings, the poor are asked to wait because of someone else's inefficiencies. I suspect that if those interests pressing for approval of the Lockheed bill and if those persons administering our food programs were hungry, we would find some way of getting the food distributed. In all probability, rather than refusing to spend the funds, the administration probably would be asking Congress to provide even more money.

Approval of the emergency loan guarantee bill then would not only be another step toward establishing a national policy of socialism for the big and powerful and free enterprise for the small and less powerful, but approval would also be further proof that our system appears to demand less of its wealthy that it does of its poor.

Regardless of how Senators may vote on the guarantee bill, I would hope all would join in urging the administration to release the additional $20 million Congress provided for food programs.

To do otherwise would be, at a minimum, to ignore the fact that the Senate has taken the unusual step of approving two amendments supporting expenditure of the same $20 million.

In Public Law 92–32, Congress authorized the transfer of $20 million from section 32 funds of the act of August 24, 1935, to supplemental food programs. The wording of that amendment made it quite clear that these funds were to be in addition to any money made available elsewhere for such feeding programs.

In approving the agriculture appropriations bill, which provided $16.4 million for these programs, the Senate passed a second amendment emphasizing that the $20 million was to be in addition to money provided in that appropriations bill.

Let us at least keep faith with commitment.

Congressional Record. *Speech given by Hon. Philip A. Hart of Michigan in the U.S. Senate, July 26, 1971.*

TYRANNY'S TIMETABLE

Mr. Schmitz. "Mr. Speaker, on November 28, the lead editorial in the largest newspaper in my district, the Santa Ana, Calif., *Register*, entitled "Tyranny's Timetable," made a chilling prediction for the next 12 years in America—from now until 1984, the future year already made famous in George Orwell's well known novel.

I am not sure the predictions in "Tyranny's Timetable" are accurate. Certainly I hope they are not. But in view of what has already happened this past year, in view of this House's action December 10 in extending the President's power to control our Nation's trillion-dollar economy with just 33 votes cast against it, I believe this editorial deserves the most serious and thoughtful consideration. If every Member of this House read it carefully and thought long and hard about what it says, there would be a much better chance that its predictions will not come true."

In the interest of history, we suggest parents clip this editorial and preserve it for their children.

We are persuaded now that a timetable for the complete replacement of American freedom by a dictatorship can be diagrammed with reasonable accuracy. We do not mean a camouflaged dictatorship, but an open, brazen establishment of rule by supreme edict.

When the Nixon years are reviewed by future historians, he will be characterized as the architect of the "New America." He will not actually establish the new order completely, but his trail-blazing actions will mark the path for his successor who may be the last duly elected President of the U.S.A.

Mr. Nixon has already fearlessly shown that the American President may disregard the traditions of his party and his country. He may repudiate his promises, and by executive order replace the freedom by control boards whose members received not a single vote from American tax payers.

And he has proven it can be done with scarcely a whimper from the people.

The major obstacle remaining is the powerful labor union bosses who see their own demise in the new scheme of things. But minor concessions will be made to this power base until Mr. Nixon is secure in his second term.

The myth of "success" which will be ballyhooed effectively during the second Nixon term, will bring other "phases" and it will be effectively shown that labor unions, as such, will be obsolete.

With the complete reorganization of the Federal government, a new kind of Presidential cabinet will provide a bureaucracy to establish not only wage and price limits, but job placements with Federal work cards directing who shall work at what job and when and where ... after all, why should there be two people seeking the same job?

Individual determination will be "proven" wasteful and not in the national interest. This program will start among the unemployed, move into the common labor pool and progress eventually to the professions including doctors and lawyers. Lawyers will be the last to go.

Industry, already feeling tighter government controls, will quietly fall into line. Initial steps will be Presidential orders eliminating "costly competition."

Newspapers, of course, will have to be brought into the age of enlightenment, and this transition can be smoothly engineered through government control of the manpower. Critical newspapers will be permitted to survive for a few years as effective barometers to test the mood of the people.

Americans, already moving to such countries as Australia, Canada and Israel will begin to move in larger numbers until "in the interest of national security," a Presidential order will prohibit such departures.

Meanwhile, as Nixon's current economic phase anesthesizes the public, a group of U.S. senators is currently at work to set aside the two-term limit for Presidents. It will be effectively "proven" that by limiting a President to only two terms, he becomes a "lame duck" in the second term and therefore loses effective influence.

This will be such a great idea that Representatives and Senators will become "lifetime public servants" just as are Federal judges.

The people who demand elections are reactionaries. It's a waste of money and energy to stage these charades every two years. After all, when you have a "good man" in office, why try to change?

With those little technicalities out of the way, Mr. Nixon will bow out of office and with tears and appreciation of a grateful nation, he will call for continuing efforts to move America ahead along the enlightened pathway he has courageously established.

The election of the new President will be a vigorous drama in which failure to vote will bring criminal indictment. The new President will call for renewed sacrifices to keep America aggressively active in the rebuilding of the world community, hand in hand with our gallant allies in the Soviet Union and the People's Republic of China.

By the end of his second term, it will be effectively "proven" that the madness of periodical elections is costly and unnecessary. After all, congressmen and judges serve for life, do they not?

The taxes which pay for major party campaigning can be eliminated simply by accepting the idea that the President should continue in office so long as he wishes to so sacrifice his personal life.

And there you have it.

The elapsed time in this schedule is approximately 12 years.

Does that seem too soon?

The date will be 1984.

Congressional Record. *Speech made by Hon. John C. Schmitz of California in the House of Representatives, December 14, 1971. Editorial. With permission of the Register, Santa Ana, California.*

BARGAIN FOR SKIERS ON DOLE STIRS DISPUTE— WELFARE DISCOUNT OFFERED

SACRAMENTO—A flurry of controversy is developing in the High Sierra over whether to give welfare recipients a lift.

Squaw Valley ski resort says yes. But other resorts catering to super skiers say no.

Even county welfare departments are at odds.

Skiers returning to Santa Clara County after a fun-filled weekend at Squaw Valley reported that resort is offering welfare recipients a $3 discount on $9 ski lift tickets every Friday.

Employees at the former Winter Olympics Games site confirmed the reports. "But we really don't have that many (recipients) come up here," a sweet young voice said over the telephone.

So presumably, once the welfare recipients rented or purchased skis, bindings, poles, boots and ski clothes, drove to the high country and carried extra change for meals he could take advantage of the $3 bargain.

How does one prove he's on welfare? "Oh, there's no set way, really," the voice said. "I guess you show your food stamps or something."

Squaw Valley's public relations man Hans Vonnolte said the program for welfare recipients started about a month ago and "not more than 25" welfare recipients take advantage of it each Friday.

"We have various group programs," Vonnolte said. "We have programs for local areas, for military personnel and on Thursday we have discounts for doctors, veterinarians and professional people. For Friday we thought we'd make it a day for welfare recipients."

He explained, "I'm not talking about the food stamp receivers, but about persons laid off in the Sunnyvale area, for example, who have been hurt by cutbacks in federal spending."

Word of the welfare discount caught other resort operators by surprise. "Really?" a girl at another resort asked.

A woman working at Heavenly Valley Ski Resort who asked not to be named told the News, "I just heard about it at the hair dresser this morning. As a taxpayer, I would object to it myself."

Milton Lewis of Sugar Bowl resort added, "It seems to me skiing is something you do over and above other bills you have if you're on food stamps or AFDC (Aid to Families with Dependent Children)."

Bear Valley, Incline Village and Boreal Ridge said they, too, offered no special discount to welfare recipients.

But Bob Dunbacher at Bear Valley said, "We've never heard of it before but there is a possibility it might be arranged. The boss always tries to bend over backwards to accommodate such requests," he said. Bear Valley, as do all resorts, offers special discount packages for groups, especially on weekdays.

Welfare department employees differ on the subject.

Helmuth Stobbe, assistant director of income maintenance for the Santa Clara County Social Welfare Department, said he thought the department would inform its clients of the service if it knew about it.

But Larry Coleman, deputy director of the Sacramento County Welfare Department, said his department would not.

Both agreed welfare recipients, unless they lived in Truckee, could ill afford a ski trip, especially when the recreation allowance in their monthly welfare check ranges from $1 to $3.

"Usually a family couldn't even begin to go," said Stobbe.

Coleman said Sacramento County would not inform its recipients of the $3 discount. "We would make a judgment that a client couldn't use it because he couldn't afford the trip," said Coleman.

The average mother with three children and no husband in the house receives about $280 a month, Coleman said. Of that about $3 is ear-marked for recreation.

However, there is little to stop a recipient from spending more of his welfare check on recreation than $3. Coleman explained that the federal government has insisted upon a "flat grant" approach under which recipients are given a prescribed total each month. It is left up to them how to spend it.

In cases where there has been obvious abuse, the welfare department can issue restrictive payments and, for example, pay the recipient's landlord directly.

But, otherwise, it is possible—although a mother on welfare interested in her children would probably not consider it—to spend a fun filled weekend in the snow.

Larry Stammer
With permission of Larry Stammer and the San Jose, California News.

EXERCISES

1. Choose a selection which typifies "American life" for you. Write what you feel is a main idea statement of the selection. Then defend the statement with evidence from research or your own experience.
2. Find a selection with which you disagree. Write what you feel is the main idea statement. Then indicate what you feel are the fallacies in the argument.

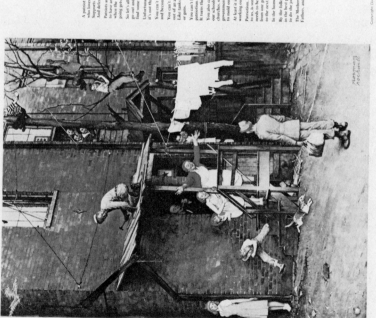

Reproduced with permission from Norman Rockwell and The Saturday Evening Post. ©1946

Copyright Davi-Callihan, Inc. 1972. Reprinted by permission.

3. List the stereotypes implied in any of the selections. Indicate whether these stereotypes are correct or incorrect. Support your views with evidence.

4. Formulate a debate statement suggested by one of the selections. Form two-member teams to debate the issue. Follow the procedure outlined.

5. Write a 200–400 word essay or deliver a two-four minute speech from personal experience which refutes any of the selections above.

6. Find newspaper articles which either refute or defend the point of view expressed in one of the selections. Show how these articles support the point of view you espouse.